THE SPIRIT OF

Liberty

THE SPIRIT OF
Liberty

PAPERS AND ADDRESSES OF

LEARNED HAND

COLLECTED,

AND WITH AN INTRODUCTION AND NOTES, BY

IRVING DILLIARD

SECOND EDITION, ENLARGED

NEW YORK   Alfred A. Knopf

1953

L. C. CATALOG NUMBER: 51-13215

THIS IS A BORZOI BOOK,
PUBLISHED BY ALFRED A. KNOPF, INC.

PUBLISHED MAY 5, 1952
REPRINTED THREE TIMES
SECOND EDITION ENLARGED, JANUARY 1953

INTRODUCTION

LEARNED HAND

A PERSONAL APPRECIATION
by IRVING DILLIARD

I

JUSTICE Oliver Wendell Holmes was the speaker of the day when the Harvard Class of 1861 met for the fiftieth anniversary of its graduation, June 28, 1911. Remembering with proper pride, as he so often did, his Civil War service in the Twentieth Massachusetts Volunteers, that noble warrior of life and the law told his "brethren of the alumni":

> I learned in the regiment and in the class the conclusion, at least, of what I think the best service that we can do for our country and for ourselves: To see so far as one may and to feel the great forces that are behind every detail . . . to hammer out as compact and solid a piece of work as one can, to try to make it first rate, and to leave it unadvertised.

It would be hard to find an approach to life which more accurately describes the purpose and practice of Learned Hand than these words of the late judge and friend whom the younger man, himself now just past fourscore, has so deeply admired.

For Learned Hand has sought to see as far as he could. He has tried to feel the great forces that are behind the details. He has hammered out a compact and solid piece of work. He has made it first rate. And he has left it un-advertised.

Learned Hand has left his work so unadvertised that though he has no superior in the jurisprudence of the English-speaking world, at the time this is written not a single book-title card in the vast catalogue of the Library of Congress bears his name. This is hard to believe; still it is true. And yet there are few men who have spoken or written with Learned Hand's mastery of the language, with his understanding of the limitations as well as the capacities of democratic institutions, with his learning in the law and his wisdom in life.

It is a strange circumstance that a society that pub-lishes so profligately on such an infinite variety of things has not until now got around to gathering together these eloquent and inspiriting papers and addresses. Even now the pleasant task of assembling them falls to one outside the law, as he has been pointedly reminded at times by certain lawyers and judges. The task goes to an outsider, however, only by default of those many members of the bench and bar, professors of law, professional teachers of philosophy, and others, any one of whom might long ago have so appropriately collected the writings and addresses of Learned Hand for the wide reading they richly deserve. But no one of them has done it, and the harvest must no longer go ungathered for want of a pro-fessional hand in the field.

Perhaps it is just as well that a layman rather than a member of the legal craft assumes the duty. After all, Learned Hand does not belong to the lawyers alone. He is of them, but not solely so. To read his brief classic, "The Spirit of Liberty," delivered on I-Am-an-American

Day 1944 in Central Park, New York, to a great throng, including many new citizens, is to realize that he belongs to us all.

Truly Learned Hand is a part of the American heritage. Through him a large share of the American dream is fulfilled.

II

The sketch of Learned Hand in *Who's Who in America* is a characteristically modest one of only seventeen lines. He was born in Albany, New York, January 27, 1872, to Samuel and Lydia Coit Hand, their only son and the second of their two children. He chose his paternal grandfather as carefully as he did his father. But, then, the entire Hand line was selected with discrimination. The first Hand in America was John Hand, who emigrated from Kent, England, some time between 1629 and 1644, when his name first appears in this country in Southampton, Long Island. He soon moved to Easthampton, where he became one of the nine original settlers. His estate, it is said, consisted of a Bible, a Psalm Book, a sword, and a pistol.

After a century and a half in New York, the Hands moved up to Shoreham, Vermont, on Lake Champlain. It was there that Learned Hand's grandfather Augustus Cincinnatus Hand was born in 1803. Augustus Hand— there is some doubt in the family about the authenticity of the name Cincinnatus, though it appears in the *Biographical Directory of the American Congress*—studied in the pioneer law school founded by Tapping Reeve in Litchfield, Connecticut. He was admitted to the bar in 1828 and began the practice of law at Crown Point, New York. In 1831 he moved to the primitive Adirondack village of Elizabethtown, north of Albany, thereafter his home.

For eight years Augustus Hand was Surrogate of Essex County, and then in 1838 he was elected as a Democrat to the national House of Representatives for the term 1839–41. After this brief interval in Washington, he returned to the Adirondack area, and in 1844 was elected to the state Senate at Albany. From 1847 to 1855 he was Associate Justice of the New York Supreme Court and in 1868 he was a delegate to the Democratic National Convention that nominated Horatio Seymour to oppose Grant for the Presidency. After these years on the bench and in political life, he resumed law practice in Elizabethtown, and there he died in 1878. His grandson, Learned Hand, was then six years old.

Augustus Hand's son Samuel, the father of Learned Hand, was born in 1833 in Elizabethtown, which was then still a frontier hamlet. Samuel Hand, following his father in the law, moved to Albany, with its larger opportunity. There he distinguished himself at the bar. He received in 1878, at the instance of Samuel J. Tilden, a gubernatorial appointment to the New York Court of Appeals at Albany—New York's highest state court. His judicial tenure was cut short, however, by a split in the Democratic Party followed by a Republican victory that swept Democrats generally out of office. Learned Hand describes his father as "a devoted and consistent Democrat" who "lived through the years when Northern Democrats were regarded almost as traitors."

Samuel Hand died in 1886 when Learned was only fourteen years old. But although the boy's life overlapped that of his father not much more than it touched the span of the grandfather's, still the impress of the two judges before him was made and left on Learned Hand to grow into full flower in the third generation. The sequence is worth the attention of sociologists and students of biographical factors.

III

Learned Hand attended Albany Academy, an old private school. There he studied hard and played football—"in a very feeble way," as he describes it. He was also hunting and trapping editor of the *Albany Cue*, the school paper, and fancied himself as Deerslayer Hand, though he confesses that he gathered much of his woods lore from reading the outdoor magazines. But he did have his camping trips in the Adirondacks, and on these his companion was his cousin Augustus Noble Hand. This cousin was the closest friend of his boyhood, as he has been throughout Learned Hand's life. Augustus Noble Hand was named for their paternal grandfather. His lawyer father, Richard Lockhart Hand, remained in Elizabethtown, and it was there that Augustus Noble was born in 1869. For summer vacations Learned, the Albany city boy, went up to little Elizabethtown to visit his country cousin. These holidays in the Adirondacks consisted in no more than an overnight stay somewhere in woods around Elizabethtown, an adventure for which the boys did no end of planning. Augustus was just two and a half years older than Learned, who looked up to his older cousin, as he subsequently did through a quarter century of joint service on the same great bench, and still does now that each is in his ninth decade of active, vigorous life.

Throughout his boyhood Learned Hand used his first name, Billings. But as a young man he decided it was "vastly formidable" and "pompous" and so discarded it it in favor of his middle name, Learned, a family name on his mother's side.

After juvenile discussions of free will and predestination, the cousins went to Harvard College, Augustus Noble in 1886 and Learned in 1889. At Harvard, where Learned wore a drooping mustache and a pointed black beard, he majored in philosophy under a great faculty, which included William James, Josiah Royce, and George Santayana. The brilliant native of Ávila, Santayana became a young instructor the year Learned entered as a freshman. It was a golden age in Cambridge, and the eager young New Yorker lived it to the full. New currents were astir, and he was one of those they touched. His literary interests won him the editorship of the *Harvard Advocate*, his scholarship brought him the golden key of Phi Beta Kappa, and his skill as a youthful speaker led to his choice as orator for the class of 1893, with which he was graduated *summa cum laude*.

IV

A Harvard commencement was merely the beginning of the education of Learned Hand. He returned to Cambridge and received his master-of-arts degree in 1894. Then, following in the footsteps of so many Hands before him, he turned to the law. In the eighties and nineties the Harvard law faculty, no less than the philosophy department, had its great teachers, among them Christopher Columbus Langdell, James Barr Ames, James Bradley Thayer, and John Chipman Gray. About halfway through Learned Hand's law-school years the pioneering Langdell stepped down from the deanship and was succeeded by Ames, under whom the school progressed rapidly. Faculty and students were at work on a new publication called the *Harvard Law Review*, and in due course Learned Hand was called to editorial work. Graduation with honors came in 1896, and the next year he was admitted to the bar of New York.

For two years, 1897–9, he was a clerk in the Albany law office of Marcus T. Hun, after which he became a member of the firm of Hun, Johnston & Hand. This connection ended in 1902 when he moved to New York City and became managing clerk for the firm of Zabriskie, Burrill & Murray. In 1904 he joined Gould & Wilkie as a member of that firm. He says he was not very successful as a young lawyer and never was too happy at the bar. He found foreclosures, mortgages, and estates dull and petty and formal. Nobody was seeking for the forces behind the detail.

Fortunately for the speculative young lawyer and the country, President William Howard Taft had made up his mind to improve the federal judiciary. Taft's Attorney General, George W. Wickersham, knew Learned Hand and liked him. One of the new Attorney General's first acts was to recommend the young lawyer to fill a vacancy on the bench of the Federal District Court for Southern New York. This recommendation was supported by Charles C. Burlingham, of the New York bar. The appointment was made in April 1909, when Taft had been in office scarcely more than one month. Learned Hand was then only thirty-seven years old, and the New York *World* noted that he was "one of the youngest men ever appointed a United States Judge in this federal district."

Taft did not know how irregular his youthful choice could be or he never would have considered him, to say nothing of giving him a lifetime seat on the federal bench. In less than three years this son of an upstate New York Democrat, appointed by a standpat Republican President, was supporting Bull Moose candidate Theodore Roosevelt for President. That was bad enough, but to make things much worse, in 1913 the young judge himself ran unsuccessfully on the Progressive ticket for the post of Chief Judge of the New York Court of Appeals at Albany against the eminently regular Willard Bartlett. This was Learned Hand's first and last foray into politics. He did no campaigning and stood for the elective judicial post because "it was necessary for someone to be knocked down." By putting his name to the Progressive Party he showed his opposition to the control of the country by vested economic interests—"the Hanna thing," to use his own expression. It was a stand that the Republican Old Guard would remember for a long while to come.

V

By the time he was forty Judge Hand had become skilled in presiding over a courtroom and in conducting jury trials. Though he had had no previous experience in admiralty or patent law, he soon found himself confronted with many difficult issues in these highly specialized fields, and so he steeped himself in their problems and precedents.

Learned Hand served for fifteen years on the Federal District Court in New York, and in all that time nothing in his own court pleased him so much as to have his cousin Augustus Noble Hand, who also had gone into law, confirmed for the same federal district bench in New York, on the nomination of Woodrow Wilson in 1914. So the old companions were together again, until just a decade later, when they were separated by Calvin Coolidge's raising Learned to the Federal Court of Appeals for New York, Connecticut, and Vermont; but the separation was a short one. Acting on excellent advice, Coolidge joined them once more by elevating Augustus Noble to the Federal Court of Appeals in 1927.

With Learned Hand as its senior judge and in time its Chief Judge by Act of Congress, the Court of Appeals for the Second Circuit—the "C.A.2"—grew to be the most esteemed bench in the country. Coolidge also appointed to it Thomas Walter Swan, from the deanship of the Yale Law School, and Harrie Brigham Chase, of Vermont. Franklin D. Roosevelt adhered to the same standards in the three appointments made by him: Robert P. Patterson, from the Federal District Court, Charles Edward Clark, also dean of the Yale Law School, and Jerome N. Frank, former chairman of the Securities and Exchange Commission.

It would be difficult to overstate the importance of the work of this court in the years that Learned Hand sat on it. To a very large extent it is a court of last resort. For although the Supreme Court in Washington may have the final say on appeal, the Supreme Court has its say in only a few cases a year, which it accepts for review from all the circuits and from the state supreme courts. Because so much litigation concerning corporation and commercial enterprise originates in New York, the C.A.2

is in practice the court that decides to a large degree the business law of the country. Over a ten-year span its six judges have handled an average total of close to four hundred cases annually, ranging in issues all the way from bankruptcy to civil rights. In recent years the nine justices of the United States Supreme Court have written decisions in about one hundred cases annually.

A notable example of the C.A.2's important business cases is the federal government's celebrated antitrust suit against the Aluminum Company of America. Because the Supreme Court in Washington had so many members previously associated with the issue that it could not produce a quorum, Congress referred the appeal to the Supreme Court back to the court of the Hands. The task of writing the decision went to Learned Hand, who was confronted with a trial record of forty thousand pages covering four years of testimony. By practice a man of relatively few words, Chief Judge Hand summarized the facts and his views of them in a twenty-eight-page opinion. Answering the company's contention that if it had a monopoly of the aluminum business, it had not taken advantage of this to extract more than a "fair" profit, he said:

Many people believe that possession of unchallenged economic power deadens initiative, discourages thrift and depresses energy; that immunity from competition is a narcotic, and rivalry a stimulant, to industrial progress; that the spur of constant stress is necessary to counteract an inevitable disposition to let well enough alone. Congress did not condone "good trusts" and condemn "bad" ones; it forbade all.

VI

In his more than forty years on the federal bench Learned Hand has written many opinions that have applied Justice Holmes's great principle of "freedom for the thought that we hate" or otherwise bulwarked the liberties of the individual citizen which are declared in the Bill of Rights. In 1950 there came to him on appeal the case of the eleven American Communist leaders, convicted in Federal District Court in New York City for violation of the Smith Anti-Subversives Act of 1940. The essence of the charge was that Eugene Dennis and his associates had "wilfully and knowingly" conspired to organize the Communist Party of the United States as a group to "teach and advocate the overthrow and destruction" of the government "by force and violence." They were also charged with conspiring to advocate and teach "the duty and necessity" of violent overthrow.

Chief Judge Hand, supported by Judge Swan, and with Judge Chase concurring, upheld the convictions. Concluding an opinion over which he must have worked as hard as on any decision in his judicial career he said:

Once the question is answered whether the Smith Act is valid, and whether there was evidence before the jury from which they might hold it violated, we can find no privilege and no right denied them which had substance. We know of no country where they would have been allowed any approach to the license here accorded them; and none, except Great Britain, where they would have had so fair a hearing. Their only plausible complaint is that freedom of speech, which they would be the first to destroy, has been denied them. We acknowledge that that freedom is not always easy to protect; and that there is no sharp line which marks its scope. We have tried to show that what these men taught and advocated is outside the zone; our Brother Chase believes that we have enlarged it too much, and he argues his view with great persuasiveness. But we all agree that they have not brought themselves within its protection, and it is not a matter of great moment how far outside they are. Conviction affirmed.

Even here the skeptic in Learned Hand was at work, for just before reaching the above conclusion he had said:

The record discloses a trial fought with a persistence, an ingenuity and—we must add—with a perversity, such as we have rarely, if ever, encountered. It is of course possible that the defendants are inspired with the fanatical conviction that they are in possession of the only gospel which will redeem this sad Planet and bring on a Golden Age. If so, we need not consider how far that would justify the endless stratagems to which they resorted; and it is not for us to say whether such a prosecution makes against the movement or, on the contrary, only creates more disciples; ours is only to apply the law as we find it.

For so applying the law Learned Hand was widely applauded and also respectfully but firmly criticized. Many said he had recognized the realities of the world. Others found that he had transformed Justice Holmes's test of a "clear and present danger" into a "probable danger at an indefinite time." Some felt that he had not applied Justice Holmes's Golden Rule for freedom of thought: "not free thought for those who agree with us but freedom for the thought that we hate." Among those who believed that Judge Hand had unfortunately parted company from Holmes at this very important point was the admiring collector of the addresses and papers that make this book.

Ten months later his decision became the basis of the Supreme Court opinion by Chief Justice Vinson in which Justices Reed, Burton, and Minton joined. Justice Frankfurter concurred in affirmance of the judgment announced by Chief Justice Vinson. Justice Jackson also concurred. Justices Black and Douglas dissented strongly. Justice Clark did not participate, as he was Attorney General when the indictments were issued.

The influence of Learned Hand's opinion is made plain by frequent references to it in the Supreme Court case. At one point Chief Justice Vinson wrote:

Chief Judge Learned Hand, writing for the majority below, interpreted the phrase [clear and present danger] as follows: "In each case [courts] must ask whether the gravity of the 'evil,' discounted by its improbability, justifies such invasion of free speech as is necessary to avoid the danger." We adopt this statement of the rule. As articulated by Chief Judge Hand, it is as succinct and inclusive as any other we might devise at this time. It takes into consideration those factors which we deem relevant, and relates their significances. More we cannot expect from words.

A short while after sustaining the conviction of the Communist leaders, Judge Hand's court reversed the conviction of Judith Coplon on charges of espionage. He wrote that her guilt was plain, but that the government failed to obtain a warrant for her arrest and that the prosecution had offered inadequate proof that illegal wiretapping had not been a factor in obtaining evidence on which the case in large part rested. And so "the conviction cannot stand."

VII

This, however, is not the place to review Learned Hand's work on the bench. He has written—and rewritten almost in his own life's blood—close to two thousand opinions on nearly every conceivable subject from maritime liens to income taxes, from banks and banking to naturalization and citizenship, from labor to trademarks. They are to be found in more than three hundred volumes of the *Federal Reports*. The Harvard Law Review Association compiled a list by topics for the years 1909–46 in connection with its observance of Judge Hand's seventy-fifth birthday in 1947. This mimeographed list of only the titles of his opinions required eighty pages, and since then many more have been added.

The qualities of style and organization which mark the addresses and papers there collected distinguish his opinions. Epigram and stately utterance appear again and again and again. In *United States* v. *Kirschenblatt* (1926), he pointed to the Fourth Amendment's guarantee against unreasonable searches and seizures and said:

Such constitutional limitations arise from grievances, real or fancied, which their makers have suffered, and should go pari passu *with the supposed evil. They with-*

stand the winds of logic by the depth and toughness of their roots in the past. Nor should we forget that what seems fair enough against a squalid huckster of bad liquor may take on a very different face, if used by a government determined to suppress political opposition under the guise of sedition.

In the copyright infringement case of *Sheldon v. Metro-Goldwyn-Mayer* (1936), he cleared a technical point in this way:

It is plain beyond peradventure that anticipation as such cannot invalidate a copyright. Borrowed the work must indeed not be, for a plagiarist is not himself pro tanto an "author"; but if by some magic a man who had never known it were to compose a new Keats's Ode on a Grecian Urn, he would be an "author," and, if he copyrighted it, others might not copy that poem, though they might of course copy Keats's.

On the wise self-restraint of judges he wrote in his opinion in *Spector Motor Service, Inc. v. Walsh* (1944):

Nor is it desirable for a lower court to embrace the exhilarating opportunity of anticipating a doctrine which may be in the womb of time, but whose birth is distant.

When he spoke at the seventy-fifth anniversary dinner of the Legal Aid Society of New York on February 16, 1951, Judge Hand left this epigrammatic commandment for his fellow members of the bar: "Thou shalt not ration Justice." It was his way of emphasizing the vital importance of making sure that accused persons do not lack for counsel needed by them to assure a fair trial.

As Felix Frankfurter has said of Justice Holmes, so may it be written of Learned Hand: to quote from his opinions is to string pearls. Surely a harvest of his work on the bench will now be gathered to stand by this collection of his speeches and papers.

VIII

Learned Hand looks as his name sounds. Stockily put together, he is as solid as a granite boulder. His squarish face might have been hewn by a sculptor. Bushy eyebrows accent rugged features. For years he often walked each morning, except in the worst of weather, the four miles from his three-story, book-lined brownstone house at 142 East Sixty-fifth Street, on Manhattan's upper East Side, to the United States Courthouse at Foley Square. He has been an indefatigable hiker all his life. When at his summer home, Low Court, near Cornish, New Hampshire, he has until recently tramped the woods as he did when a boy back in the Adirondacks.

His close companion and careful protector through life is the former Frances Amelia Fincke, a Bryn Mawr graduate, of Utica, New York. They were married on December 6, 1902, and to them were born three girls, Mary Deshon, Frances Lydia, and Constance. All the daughters are married, and there are grandchildren for whom the robust grandfather has played Indian and worn a wastebasket for a headdress and whooped war cries that reached to the highest ceiling.

Already Learned Hand is a kind of legend. Stories are told of his fondness for sea chanteys and for Gilbert and Sullivan; of his dislike for barking dogs and the ring of the telephone and gum-chewing; of his thrift in the use of electric light in his office; of his extensive repertoire as a mimic, including an "address" by William Jennings Bryan in the campaign of 1900; of his singing hymns at noon in the courthouse to accompany the chimes of a church; of his rectitude in declaring for customs a pair of old shoes he had had half-soled in Rotterdam; of his attachment to his law clerks from Harvard, each of whom he calls "Judge" and promotes to "Mr. Justice" when one of them goes to Washington to be law clerk to a Supreme Court member; of the wide range of his friendships from the world of learning and highest achievement to Italian-speaking M. Speciale, who used to address him as "Illustrious Sir" and sign himself "your humble shoemaker." Intermingled fact and lore could be long extended.

IX

What the bench and the bar of the country had known for many years, the public generally began to find out after the phenomenal reception of Learned Hand's address on "The Spirit of Liberty." Magazine and newspaper writers began to seek out the "Tenth Justice of the Supreme Court" and tell about him in feature articles to readers all over the country.

In anticipation of his seventy-fifth birthday, *Life* (November 4, 1946) presented an extended illustrated article, "The Great Judge," by Philip Hamburger, who called Learned Hand "the spiritual heir of Marshall, Holmes, Brandeis and Cardozo." When the birthday itself came, the *New York Times* (January 28, 1947) said editorially "that he is a judge with a passionate concern for truth in detail and in the large and an instinct for justice in a changing society." In connection with the occasion Irwin Edman recalled in a letter to the *Times* (February 5, 1947) that Learned Hand once went as a visitor to a meeting of the New York Philosophy Club addressed by John Dewey. After comments by the professional teachers of philosophy and their guests, Dewey said: "It took a layman really to understand the philosophical point of my paper."

Then came the issue of the *Harvard Law Review* (February 1947) dedicated to Learned Hand because his "wisdom and eloquence have made his seventy-fifth birthday an occasion to be celebrated by all who serve the law." Justice Frankfurter described him as "one at whose feet I sat almost from the time that I came to the bar and at whose feet I still sit." Charles C. Burlingham, who had recommended the District Court appointment back in 1909, now called him "unquestionably first among American judges." George Wharton Pepper said his literary style was "English at its best." Judge Herbert F. Goodrich of Philadelphia, writing of Judge Hand's long association with the American Law Institute, recalled that " his comment upon any legal question carried such great weight that an expressed doubt by him was a source of danger to the acceptance of any proposition, no matter how plausibly urged."

Three of the many Hand law clerks wrote for the issue. Federal District Judge Charles E. Wyzanski, Jr., of Boston, dealing with his former chief's contributions to public law, said: "For the role of prophet, innovator and statesman Learned Hand has never billed himself. To him the judge who took the central role would have betrayed his trust. He was commissioned for a different part—a leader of the Greek chorus interpreting and appraising the drama. The artistry, the forbearance in judgment, and the faithfulness with which Learned Hand has performed that part are his principal contribution to the public law."

Archibald Cox, professor of law at Harvard, discussing Judge Hand and the interpretation of statutes, wrote: "The opinions of Judge Hand have had significant influence both in breaking down the restrictions imposed by the dry literalism of conservative tradition and in showing how to use with sympathetic understanding the information afforded by the legislative and administrative processes. More important, if we can read them right, we shall find in them a philosophy which, if not the last solution—and he would not offer one—nevertheless can help to mark both the extent and limits of the judge's function and so supply a basis for his administration of statutory law."

Concluding a summary of "Hand and Patents and Copyrights," Stephen H. Philbin, of the New York bar, said: "A master of his craft, with impressive and genuine dignity, he conducts smoothly and surely the business which comes before him. Wise in applying the reason and spirit of the law, serving only truth and right, his court is an inspiration. The faith and confidence in the judicial process which Judge Hand has created and strengthened are of inestimable value. A great judge."

Orrin G. Judd, of the New York bar, dealt with the criminal-law phase. Summarizing it he wrote: "Judge Hand is neither a 'hanging judge' nor a 'defendant's judge.' He has provided, not a one-sided approach to the criminal law, but a wise and impartial judgment which

balances the public interest in prompt and efficient prosecution with the individual interest (which is not without its social importance) of each defendant in a fair
trial. During the important period in federal criminal law
which has marked his service on the bench, he has made
a major contribution toward making that law an effective
instrument of justice."

X

The legal profession had begun to yield Learned Hand
to the country at large. John P. Frank, of the Yale Law
School, wrote a careful and detailed appraisal of the work
of the court of the Hands and their fellow judges for
Fortune (January 1951). Professor Frank called it "The
Top U. S. Commercial Court," but he showed how much
other important work it handled and emphasized the
need for careful replacements when time would force
changes. Popular monthly magazines assigned writers to
tell their readers about the man who delivered "The
Spirit of Liberty." [1] So did the newspapers, including the
St. Louis Post-Dispatch (July 15, 1951), which through
the years had repeatedly urged the appointment of
Learned Hand to the United States Supreme Court. To
Spencer R. McCulloch, *Post-Dispatch* special writer,
Judge Hand quoted, as the key to his over-all philosophy,
Oliver Cromwell's plea just before the Battle of Dunbar:
"I beseech ye in the bowels of Christ, think that ye may
be mistaken." These words Judge Hand said he would

---

[1] Bill Davidson: "Judge Learned Hand: Titan of the Law," *Coro-
net*, September 1949; Irwin Ross: "The Legend of Learned Hand,"
Reader's Digest, July 1951.

like to have written "over the portals of every church, every courthouse and at every crossroads in the nation." For, he added, "it seems to me that if we are to be saved it must be through skepticism."

When word of Learned Hand's retirement came, the *New York Herald Tribune* (May 18, 1951) expressed a regret that reached into far corners. Reassured in the knowledge that he would be on call for assignments, the *Herald Tribune* said: "The law, said Burke, sharpens the mind by narrowing it; but in a few of our great judges law has lifted the mind to a level of comprehension and has kindled a degree of humane ardor unsurpassed in any other profession. Judge Learned Hand has been among these few, and has preserved his gayety and grace of spirit undimmed to the threshold of the ninth decade."

For on May 15, Learned Hand had written to President Truman:

Having attained the age of more than seventy years, and having served as United States Circuit Judge for the Second Circuit for more than ten years continuously, I wish to avail myself, and do hereby avail myself, of the privilege granted me by § 371 of Title 28 of the United States Code "to retain" my "office but retire from regular active service." My retirement will take effect on June first, 1951.

With the highest regards I have the honor to be,

Respectfully yours,
LEARNED HAND.

And on May 23 the President had sent this letter from the White House:

Dear Judge Hand:

Your impending retirement fills me with regret, which I know is shared by the American people. It is hard to accept the fact that, after forty-two years of most distinguished service to our Nation, your activities are now to be narrowed.

It is always difficult for me to express a sentiment of deep regret; what makes my present task so overwhelming is the compulsion I feel to attempt, on behalf of the American people, to give in words some inkling of the place you have held and will always hold in the life and spirit of our country.

Your profession has long since recognized the magnitude of your contribution to the law. There has never been any question about your pre-eminent place among American jurists—indeed among the nations of the world. In your writings, in your day to day work for almost half a century, you have added purpose and hope to man's quest for justice through the process of law.

As judge and philosopher, you have expressed the spirit of America and the highest in civilization which man has achieved. America, and the American people, are the richer because of the vigor and fullness of your contribution to our way of life.

We are compensated in part by the fact that you are casting off only a part of the burdens which you have borne for us these many years, and by our knowledge that you will continue actively to influence our life and society for years to come. May you enjoy many happy years of retirement, secure in the knowledge that no man, whatever his walk of life, has ever been more deserving of the admiration and gratitude of his country, and, indeed, of the entire free world.

XI

It is a privilege to have a part in presenting to his many old friends and to introduce to even more friends-to-be the addresses and papers of Learned Hand. In these words of this great and good man lives the spirit of our liberty.

Collinsville, Illinois
Lincoln's Birthday, 1952

CONTENTS

1   Class-Day Oration [1893]   3

2   The Speech of Justice [1916]   13

3   Christians and Jews [1922]   20

4   Mr. Justice Holmes at Eighty-five [1926]   24

5   The Preservation of Personality [1927]   30

6   Is There a Common Will? [1929]   47

7   Mr. Justice Holmes [1930]   57

8   Sources of Tolerance [1930]   66

9   To Yale Law Graduates [1931]   84

10 Democracy: Its Presumptions and Realities

                                              [1932]   90

11 How Far Is a Judge Free

                    in Rendering a Decision? [1935] 103

12 To the Harvard Alumni Association [1936]   111

13 At the Harvard Tercentenary Observance

                                              [1936] 115

14 Foreword to the Harvard Law Review

                           Volume L [1936] 123

15 In Memory of Charles Neave [1938]   127

16 Mr. Justice Cardozo [1939]   129

17 On Receiving an Honorary Degree [1939]   134

18 Foreword to Williston's Life and Law [1940]   140

19 Liberty [1941]   144

20 The Contribution of an Independent Judiciary
                          to Civilization [1942]   155

21 Mr. Justice Brandeis [1942]   166

22 At the Fiftieth Anniversary Commencement
                                        [1943]   175

23 Philip Littell [1944]   180

24 Philhellene Editorial [1944]   183

25 The Debt of the World to Greece [1944]   186

26 The Spirit of Liberty [1944]   189

27 A Pledge of Allegiance [1945]   192

28 Simon Flexner [1946]   195

29 Chief Justice Stone's Concept
                  of the Judicial Function [1946]   201

30 Thomas Walter Swan [1947]   209

31 Charles Evans Hughes [1949]   220

32 The One Condition [1951]   223

33 Morals in Public Life [1951]   225

34 At Fourscore [1952]   253

35 Robert P. Patterson [1952]   263

36 A Plea for the Open Mind
                  and Free Discussion [1952]   274 .

THE SPIRIT OF
Liberty

1

CLASS–DAY ORATION
[1893]

THE class-day oration for the Harvard class of 1893 was delivered on commencement day, June 23, by Billings Learned Hand, who was on that occasion graduated summa cum laude. Only with the first address in this collection does the name of Billings Learned Hand appear. Soon thereafter the name of Billings was dropped by its owner and the simpler form of Learned Hand used.

Classmates: We have come at last to the time when we must put away childish things and think as men. Our general education is completed, our days of irresponsibility are over, our work is about to begin. Our position, therefore, so obviously offers itself to retrospection that, despite its familiarity, it is always interesting, and particularly so to us who are feeling it for ourselves. We cannot tell now what our University has really meant to us; no one can tell it until we have gone among other men and proved ourselves well or ill. But we can tell what we think it has meant to us, and however imperfectly we may have understood it, our comment will be of some value to others, as that of the statue might be upon the sculptor's art. Into our stony comprehension little of the truth may have come, but to those who are responsible for that comprehension, that at least is some light. We have been shaped after a new ideal in education, a distinctly American ideal, which our University has accepted more radically than any of her sisters; they regard us as

3

an experiment, and to us and to our fellows they are looking for results. What has our University meant to us?

Let us suppose a young man whom we should accept
as a kind of class type—not one which any of us actually
attains, but rather an ideal to which we might approximate. Suppose, for example, a boy thrown upon his own
choice, fresh from the limitations of a schoolroom, to
believe that science is an epitome of human desires.
There is so much to fire his imagination and lend eager-
ness to his pursuit, that it is no wonder if he thinks it.
Men of today are so astounded with the advance of em-
pirical observation beyond what their fathers had accomplished, they have results that would so have exceeded
even their predecessors' fancy, that they go mad in the
search for scientific truth, and shall not the rasher judgment of a boy be likewise moved? The mere ideals strain
his imagination and extend his view into the eternities,
backward or forward. His power is absolute, he is the
only real prophet, the prophet who after his baptism of
patience and of faith finds the whole world at his feet, if
only he has the determination and the courage to make
it his. The contempt with which the prophet may regard
the loose and inaccurate babblings of other men who
have less scope and make less splendid promises, is after
all excusable when his prophecies are found so often true
and his results so useful.

Yet with all the attraction that it has, our youth cannot
long remain without feeling the narrowness of simply a
classification of the world. Life is not a thing of knowing
only—nay, mere knowledge has properly no place at all
save as it becomes the handmaiden of feeling and emotion. His life of mere acquisition is a poor, unsatisfying

4

thing beside the richer and fuller interests of those of his companions who devote themselves to the arts. And so he deserts his old pursuits, and loves the Muses. Doubtless it is an arduous courtship, and he must be content with few favours, but if they are only few, they are still dear and worth the labour. Yet even though his awkward fingers cannot paint or carve or play; and even though his sluggish brain can tell no new stories of the world or of the soul, or set them in beautiful forms, can he not wonder at and admire what better men have done? Reverence is the real recognition of the soul by itself in a comparison with its possibilities; and shall he not reverence the masters of the arts; knowing how hard their task has been from his own efforts? And if he will contemplate and appreciate, rather than try to create, he will learn that none of the great works in its isolation is complete; that only as the outcome of a gradual development can it be understood and sympathized with. A man's works imply all the influences which have shaped his character, and these are far-reaching beyond his time and race.

Our youth is, in short, led to history; first to history of art and of literature, whence his path leads off indefinitely into the history of national character, of laws and customs, of wars and governments, and of great leaders. The ancients, if they have not already attracted his attention, will not now fail to seize hold upon him, for aside from the masterpieces which they have themselves executed, they are so intimately connected with his own and all modern times as to be absolutely necessary to an understanding of them. Nor can he stop with them, but he must go back beyond civilization, beyond even language, till he at last becomes again only a classifier of physical facts, and the fields which seemed separated as heaven and earth have become one.

Perhaps this is enough of our youth's adventures! In truth, he will not be contented to stop here, but will seek a unification for his world, a complete point of view which shall be final. In his search for the real constitution of things he will pass through what the best have said, and in his career of sage weigh the ultimate questions with their aid. Whatever his results, the experience will be a valuable one, for at least he has not feared to probe as far as his talents will allow, and has faced with courage what the world has to offer. He need hereafter no more fear its hidden skeletons, however grim they may be preached.

And when he has finished it all and is graduated; and when he goes out among men who have long abandoned his attempt at universality and those who have never made it, in what, if at all, does he surpass them? In neither more nor less than sympathy—sympathy with all the activities of the world, a stretching out of his life beyond the narrow limits of his own occupation, whatever it may be, so that his interest and his real life is the life of all men. He knows the relations of things, the value of all the parts, and hereafter his own activity will have the mellowness of subordination to his larger self, the flavour of humanity. He has found the whole pattern of which he is to work a part, the harmonies of the whole will be in his mind, and he can never choose so crudely as before.

This rather grotesque person is far enough removed from any one of us to seem very unreal, nor did I intend to picture the development of any individual collegiate life, because it is not as a rule a very comprehensive affair. Yet I believe that it is the ideal to which each one of us in some degree approaches. It is the policy of our University, however, quite the reverse of my picture, that each one, if he finds any interest paramount, shall follow it as far as he can. So with most of us who have been in earnest at our work, there has been from the first, or there has soon developed, one predominant bent in accordance with which we have tended to specialize our work in the hopes of gaining some approximate mastery of the subject. The more we have done this, however, the more we have felt not only our own limitations, but those of the best progress which has been made at all. As we have advanced, the goal has flown on; as we have mounted, the horizon has receded and the outlook broadened, till we are at a loss for the end. And so we should have gained the negative element of knowledge, a modesty of the value of the little that has already been accomplished. Far be it from me to suggest that we have this admirable quality; I do not think it; but I do believe that we realize better than we could otherwise have done the real limitations of human attainment in all fields. Yet had we only this, we should be in the position of the professional schools, where, if anywhere, modesty of acquirement ought to be gained. And had we really mastered this, we should be in no wise well started to be men. It is no accurate knowledge of any detached field of inquiry—it makes no difference how important it may in itself be—that gives the development to which as men of education we should have the opportunity. Without the sense of the adjustment of human needs we can never attain that. Civilization implies specialization,

7

specialization is forgetfulness of total values and the establishment of false ones, that is Philistinism. A savage can never fall into this condition; his values are all real, he supplies his own wants and finds them proceeding from himself, not from an estimate of those of others. We must in practice be specialists; the division of labour ordains us to know something of one subject and little of others; it forces Philistinism down our throats whether we like it or not. Because a man is an artist is no reason why he is no Philistine, if he is only an artist and has no sympathy with unartistic activity.

How then are we to avoid the dread country, Philistia? By mutual contact. In a body of men so large as this, all interests are represented; and in an intercourse so close as this, breadth of view is fostered. It is on this that the hope for the completeness of the ideal rests. Unless one becomes a hermit and shuts himself off from communication with his fellows altogether, he cannot remain interested in his specialty—if he have one—alone. If he will be heard himself, he must listen to others; if he hopes to gain the consideration or respect for his work that he himself feels for it, he must in a measure abrogate its claims to predominance and value the work of others. We are in a very seething caldron of opinion, where herbs of all flavours distill their essences into one another, and the final elixir contains them all. So there grows up a sort of solidarity of learning, a professorship of things in general—exactly that, for, in spite of the smile the term may cause, it is "professors of things in general," like Teufelsdröckh, that all men in heart must be.

The difference between this new ideal and the old one which it is superseding will now, I think, be evident. The

8

scope was there attempted by a set form of work through which all the students passed. There was not the play for individuality that there now is, nor the passionate devotion to a single line of study that there sometimes now is, though there was a certain degree of uniformity upon which you could rely. It would not be in place here, as indeed it would be impossible, to give a comparative judgment of the two ideals, yet we who have experienced the one cannot help looking upon the more rigid and formal training as rather an accomplishment, as somewhat a *sine qua non* of respectable gentility, something a little apart from the serious concerns of life. We like rather to dream of a body of young men as a live thing, as a tree where all the branches are nourished by a single sap, and where each part is meaningless and incomplete except in connection with its fellows. You may lop away the dead branches, you may bend the trunk, you may dig about it and water it; but leave it to assume its own form, do not constrain the peculiar shoots, or you will have a crippled, gnarled monster, and no tree.

It is upon us and our immediate successors that the realization of such a dream will rest, for only by the general conviction that the ideal has proved good, will it be perfected. There are dangers to avoid, dangers that one would not expect. The mid-day sun is too much for most eyes; one is dazzled even with its reflection. Be careful that too broad and high an aim does not paralyze your effort and clog your springs of action. Surround a man with too many beauties and he has no more than a sense of bewilderment; his principle of choice is gone; he is merely contemplative and loses the power of even the smallest degree of realization. He is like one in a garden of

9

beautiful flowers, where tulips or wonderful orchids distract his eyes and the languorous odours of others overcome his senses, who is not able to choose when he must be content with one, but rather cries, "Give me them all, let me keep all the beauty." Believe me, there is something real in this! When they talk of indifference and lack of enthusiasm, they mean this danger. To be pulled in many opposite ways at once results negatively, but it is not the same thing as to feel no impulse at all. An ass between two bales of hay is said to have died of starvation, but not from indifference. What shall we say, then—are we to be equipped carefully and to fail in the end? Our professorship of things in general must not be forgotten, but it must not be a professorship of nothing in particular. That is our danger. We have the pattern; can we make it real? No, never can we do it all. We have the pattern; will we make it real? Yes, in what we can, yes; by our manhood, by the centuries of pain and death that have gone before us, by our ideal and for our ideal we must. Let us beware, friends, professors of things in general; we have business to transact; it will avail us nothing that the heavens are glorious above us, if we cannot look up to them in pain, when the world shall have no charm and the work shall seem too long What shall my ideal be to me, if never, "Tired with all these, for restful death I cry"; if it shall not send me down the warm hope of better things, when my heart is sick and my courage faint. Else it is a poor, cold thing that mocks me, "like the sun from a wintry sky." Aye, verily, what shall it profit a man, if he gain the whole world in fancy and lose his own soul from reality?

Some work then, some good work for ourselves and

for others, for there is work to do and no place for
drones! Those who went before we must be worthy of.
Their part of the pattern was red, and they wove it with
their blood and with their lives. Our part is not that, but
the woof needs life and sacrifice yet. Forty years hence
it will have been decided. If we meet then, when the
ranks are not full, when the ardour for the fight is not so
fierce and the courage calmer, can we look back to some
work done that will need no undoing? If we cannot then,
God help us!

There is a poem of Goethe's that Carlyle has translated. It is the last word I would say to you.

> *The Future hides in it*
> *Gladness and Sorrow;*
> *We press on the thorow,*
> *Nought that abides in it*
> *Daunting us—onward.*
>
> *And solemn before us*
> *Veiled, the dark Portal,*
> *Goal of all mortal;*
> *Stars silent rest o'er us,*
> *Graves under us silent.*
>
> *While earnest thou gazest,*
> *Comes boding of terror,*
> *Comes phantasm and error,*
> *Perplexes the bravest,*
> *With doubt and misgiving.*
>
> *But heard are the Voices,*
> *Heard are the Sages,*

The Worlds and the Ages:
"Choose well, your choice is
Brief and yet endless;

"Here eyes do regard you,
In eternity's stillness;
Here is all fullness,
Ye brave, to reward you;
Work and despair not."

2

THE SPEECH OF JUSTICE
[1916]

EARLY *in his career as a lawyer Learned Hand began to
write for the Harvard Law Review, by whose permission
"The Speech of Justice" is reprinted from the issue for
April 1916 (Vol. XXIX, pp. 617–21). Previously he had
written four articles for the Harvard Law Review. They
were: "Restitution or Unjust Enrichment," November
1897 (Vol. XI, pp. 249–57); "Historical and Practical
Considerations Regarding Expert Testimony," May 1901
(Vol. XV, pp. 40–58); "Due Process of Law and the
Eight-Hour Day," May 1908 (Vol. XXI, pp. 495–509);
and "The Commodities Clause and the Fifth Amendment," February 1909 (Vol. XXII, pp. 250–65).*

Conservative political opinion in America cleaves to the
tradition of the judge as passive interpreter, believing that
his absolute loyalty to authoritative law is the price of
his immunity from political pressure and of the security
of his tenure. Therefore, since he should have no aim but
to understand the law as he finds it, conservative opinion
finds it monstrous to require of him results which shall
suit the changing popular aspirations, which, being un-
formulated, must be vague, undifferentiated, and fragmentary. His is the role of a faithful administrator whose
success depends upon his interpretation of the written
word, not of the full heart. In its passionate adherence
to this tradition such opinion is not disinterested; it
would as eagerly encourage judicial initiative, if the laws

were framed by labor unions, as it insists upon rigid obedience in a system framed for the most part for the protection of property and for the prevention of thoroughgoing social regulation. Under such a system nothing seems to it more subversive of ordered liberty than to permit the judge to make a personal interpretation of the uncertain and distracted yearnings of a suppositious public opinion.

This attitude is in part right and in part wrong. Much of the law is indeed written in formal shape, the authoritative emanation of the state through agencies to which the judge is confessedly inferior. Beyond the limits of such ambiguity as the words may honestly carry the judge surely has no duty but to understand, and to bring to his understanding good faith and dutiful acquiescence. For the results he may not justly be held accountable; to hold him is to disregard the social will, which has imposed upon him that very quiescence that prevents the effectuation of his personal notions. There is a hierarchy of power in which the judge stands low; he has no right to divinations of public opinion which run counter to its last formal expressions. Nevertheless, the judge has, by custom, his own proper representative character as a complementary organ of the social will, and in so far as conservative sentiment, in the excess of caution that he shall be obedient, frustrates his free power by interpretation to manifest the half-framed purposes of his time, it misconceives the historical significance of his position and will in the end render him incompetent to perform the very duties upon which it lays so much emphasis. The profession of the law of which he is a part is charged with the articulation and final incidence of the successive efforts towards justice; it must feel the circulation of the communal blood or it will wither and drop off, a useless member.

When Plato tried to define justice, he found he could not stop short of building a commonwealth. No concept would answer which did not comprise the sum of the citizen's relations to the state at large. Yet we know that such a definition does not define until it be filled with purposes which the people feel and the state sets out to realize. Ulpian might take as the constitutive principle of justice the steady and eternal purpose to give each man his own, but no *a priori* concepts can determine in advance what each man's own shall be, and the form of justice will be without content till we fill it with the ardor of life. It can from time to time become realized in fragmentary compromises, the ingenious expedients of those who can penetrate and satisfy the cravings of the time, but it will submit to no eternal rationalistic, any more than any other manifestation of the human soul.

Two conditions are essential to the realization of justice according to law. The law must have an authority supreme over the will of the individual, and such an authority can arise only from a background of social acquiescence, which gives it the voice of indefinitely greater numbers than those of its expositors. Thus, the law surpasses the deliverances of even the most exalted of its prophets; the momentum of its composite will alone makes it effective to coerce the individual and reconciles him to his subserviency. The pious traditionalism of the law has its roots in a sound conviction of this necessity; it must be content to lag behind the best inspiration of its time until it feels behind it the weight of such general

acceptance as will give sanction to its pretension to un-
questioned dictation. Yet with this piety must go a
taste for courageous experiment, by which alone the law
has been built as we have it, an indubitable structure,
organic and living. It is in this aspect that the profession
of the law is in danger of failing in times like our own
when deep changes are taking place in the convictions of
men. It is not as the priest of a completed revelation that
the living successors of past lawmakers can most truly
show their reverence or continue the traditions which they
affect to regard. If they forget their pragmatic origin,
they omit the most pregnant element of the faith they
profess and of which they would henceforth become only
the spurious and egregious descendants. Only as an articulate organ of the half-understood aspirations of living
men, constantly recasting and adapting existing forms,
bringing to the high light of expression the dumb im-
pulses of the present, can they continue in the course of
the ancestors whom they revere.

Yet the conditions of the enterprise have changed.
Until within a very few decades the American bench and
bar could utter justice without misgiving or constraint.
Differences of course there were, but the self-conscious
elements of society were homogeneous and the diver-
gences not fundamentally distracting. At least, such genuine distraction as there was was latent, class grievances
were inaudible, justice might be vague but it was consistent. Lawyers got by a kind of natural right the authority to interpret justice, since they were in a broad sense
genuine representatives of all that could achieve repre-
sentation. Nor was it different in Great Britain. When
Lord Mansfield made the modern commercial law of

England, he had no need to force his native convictions; he spoke with authority because the resultant values in his mind substantially accorded with that of all other men who ever conceived that their scale of values could gain any effective recognition.

All this has changed; the profession is still drawn, and so far as we can see, will always be drawn, from the propertied class, but other classes have awakened to conscious control of their fate, their demands are vocal which before were dumb, and they will no longer be disregarded. If justice be a passable accommodation between the vital and self-conscious interests of society, it has taken on a meaning not known before. But the profession has not yet learned to adapt itself to the change; that most difficult of adjustments has not been made, an understanding of and sympathy with the purposes and ideals of those parts of the common society whose interests are discordant with its own. Yet nothing can be more certain than that its authority as interpreter of customary law must in the end depend upon its power to learn precisely that adaptation. As mediator it must grasp from within the meaning of each phase of social will; it must divine the form of what lies confused and unexpressed and must bring to light the substance of what is half surmised. To adjust and to compromise, to balance and to value, one must first of all learn to know, not from the outside, but as the will knows. This is the condition of the continued high position of the lawyer; without this he must degenerate to a mere rational automaton, expounding a barren scholasticism which his society will quickly learn to value at its true worth.

It may be said that this fate is in any event inevitable,

that the obvious purport of the present is towards an increasing body of minute formularies which leave no option and permit no latitude. Yet one must not be too hasty to confuse cause with effect. A large part of the tendency towards such meticulous prolixity rests in the very inability of the profession to show a more enlightened sympathy with the deeper aspirations of the time. Moreover, as we are coming now to learn, no human purpose possesses itself so completely in advance as to admit of final definition. Life overflows its moulds and the will outstrips its own universals. Men cannot know their own meaning till the variety of its manifestations is disclosed in its final impacts, and the full content of no design is grasped till it has got beyond its general formulation and become differentiated in its last incidence. It should be, and it may be, the function of the profession to manifest such purposes in their completeness if it can achieve the genuine loyalty which comes not from obedience, but from the according will, for interpretation is a mode of the will and understanding is a choice.

In so far as we have realized that definition must follow application, the movement has been to intrust broad powers to administrative commissions, which thus become charged with the execution of wide legislative purposes, and which establish upon them a customary law through the slow accretion of their own precedents. Such functions should more properly lie with courts, who by training and experience ought to be better fitted for their discharge. The movement reflects a suspicion of courts in the end resting upon that very scrupulousness to the written word which has been their undoing. Yet they stand in a dilemma, because, while no ritualistic piety can save them from the necessity of an active partisanship amid the contests of their time, their partiality must endure the final test of a genuine social ideal which shall be free from class prejudice. Like every public functionary, in the end they are charged with the responsibility of choosing but of choosing well. Courage and insight alone can in the end win confidence and power. Democracy must learn to value and to trust such qualities or democracy cannot disentangle its true purposes and realize its vaguely formed ideals; but democracy is quick to understand those who respond to its fundamental feelings, and is ruthless in casting aside those who seek cover behind the protection of the written word, for which it may, and even in the same breath, itself profess reverence.

The profession of the law has its fate in its own hands; it may continue to represent a larger, more varied social will by a broader, more comprehensive interpretation. The change must come from within; the profession must satisfy its community by becoming itself satisfied with the community. It must assimilate society before society will assimilate it; it must become organic to remain a living organ. No political mechanism designed to accomplish this by fear will succeed, if the inward disloyalty of purpose remain. The lawyer must either learn to live more capaciously or be content to find himself continuously less trusted, more circumscribed, till he becomes hardly more important than a minor administrator, confined to a monotonous round of record and routine, without dignity, inspiration, or respect. There can be no ambiguity in the answer of those who are worthy of the traditions and the power of a noble calling.

3

CHRISTIANS AND JEWS
[1922]

In the early 1920's President A. Lawrence Lowell had under consideration a proposal to introduce a quota system at Harvard, primarily for the purpose of limiting the proportion of undergraduate students from Jewish families. Learned Hand, as an influential alumnus of Harvard College and the Harvard Law School, volunteered a letter in opposition to the proposal to the chairman of the Committee of the Faculties, Professor Charles Hall Grandgent, for many years head of the Romance languages department at Harvard. Judge Hand's strong letter, dated November 14, 1922, may well have been a factor in the decision against establishing the clausus numerus at Harvard.

New York
November 14, 1922

Charles H. Grandgent, Esq.
Harvard College
Cambridge, Mass.
Dear Sir:

I have understood that your committee welcomes the opinion of alumni on the question of limiting the numbers of Jewish undergraduates. This is my excuse for writing you. The difficulties are no doubt real in a sense that a graduate of thirty years ago would find it hard to realize. I have been told that the college now contains large numbers of Jews, insensitive, aggressive and ill-conditioned, whose presence causes much hostility among the Christians. I shall assume this to be true, and that their increase, to say nothing of their present numbers, will be likely to drive away many students of the kind to which we have been accustomed.

Notwithstanding, I cannot agree that a limitation based upon race will in the end work out any good purpose. If the Jew does not mix well with the Christian, it is no answer to segregate him. Most of those qualities which the Christian dislikes in him are, I believe, the direct result of that very policy in the past. Both Christian and Jew are here; they must in some way learn to live on tolerable terms, and disabilities have never proved tolerable. It seems hardly necessary to argue that they intensify on both sides the very feelings which they are designed to relieve on one. If after acquaintance the two races are irretrievably alien, which I believe unproven, we are, it is true, in a bad case, but even so not as bad as if we separate them on race lines. Along that path lie only bitterness and distraction.

But the proposal is not segregation or exclusion but to limit the number of Jews. That, however, is if anything worse. Those who are in fact shut out are of course segregated; those who are let in are effectively marked as racially undesirable. Intercourse with them is with social inferiors; there can be no other conceivable explanation for the limitation. The results of that will be deplorable to both sides. The argument is put somewhat differently; that the effort is to prevent Jews from concentrating in too great numbers in any one college. They must be spread about in equal proportions. This does not escape the same vice, I think. They are spread involuntarily, which must mean that some are excluded and all are only tolerated wherever they eventually come to rest; the same objections remain.

If anyone could devise an honest test for character, perhaps it would serve well. I doubt its feasibility except to detect formal and obvious delinquencies. Short of it, it seems to me that students can only be chosen by tests of scholarship, unsatisfactory as those no doubt are. A raw, ill-bred and barbarous student will be offensive; he will in the end feel it, perhaps he will improve. At least one may hope for it. A sensitive, well-nurtured student will dislike him; if he has no humanity in him, it will rest there; if he has any, he will see something more. At least let him learn decent toleration, and if he will not, we should not fear to lose him. I cannot feel that college should be a retreat from what he must learn somehow to live with.

After all, the Jews who can qualify among the increasingly limited numbers that get in at all, must excel in scholarly tests. If there are better ways of testing scholarship, let us by all means have them, but whatever they are, success in them is success in the chief aim of a college, an interest in, and aptitude for, learning. The rest is secondary, and so far as there are any who will be turned away because they find themselves in too great a company of the uncouth, their prime purpose is not scholarship. Perhaps it is here that the real difference lies between those who would limit and those who would not. A college may gather together men of a common tradition, or it may put its faith in learning. If so, it will I suppose take its chance that in learning lies the best hope, and that a company of scholars will prove better than any other company. Our tests do not indeed go far to produce such a company but they are all we have.

Sincerely yours,
LEARNED HAND

MR. JUSTICE HOLMES AT EIGHTY–FIVE
[1926]

OLIVER WENDELL HOLMES, JR. (1841–1935) served as
Associate Justice of the Supreme Court of the United
States from 1902, when he was appointed by President
Theodore Roosevelt, until his retirement in 1932, at the
age of almost ninety-one. He and Learned Hand, despite
a difference of three decades, were close friends and
kindred spirits on the federal bench and in the literature
of the law. This tribute was written for Justice Holmes's
eighty-fifth birthday and appeared in the New York
World, March 8, 1926. It was reprinted in Mr. Justice
Holmes, edited by Felix Frankfurter and published by
Coward-McCann, Inc., in 1931.

Judges are usually taken from that part of the bar
which has distinguished itself in the field of action. They
are likely to be men of strong will, set beliefs and conventional ideals. They are almost inevitably drawn from
the propertied class and share its assumptions. Perhaps
it is on the whole better so; law is the precipitate of a
long past of active controversy and cannot be successfully administered by those to whom equilibrium has
no proper values of its own. Still, its virtues are also its
defects, for no formulas are final and the political re-
sultants of a past generation seldom very adequately
measure the opposing forces of the next. If we must not
change too quickly, at least we must not refuse to change
at all. Yet, to the pious, change is at best a hard necessity

and at worst a sacrilege, since truth is in its nature fixed and change inevitably infringes its validity.

And so perhaps a sceptical disposition is a hazardous equipment for a judge; the interpreter need not analyze, his mission primarily is to discover to the faithful such congenial dogmas as will come to them with warmth and intimacy as all along their own. Many a judge, not a few great judges, have succeeded largely through such divination of the deeper moods of their time; they justly live in fame, not because their intellects have been penetrating, but because by nature they are gregarious. Scepticism is not social, and as often results from recalcitrance as from diffidence within.

Probably Mr. Justice Holmes has never been wholly welcome among the company of the men of this world. About him has always lingered the aura of a universe of other discourse than what is soundly current; an unwelcome overtone that things which stout men feel to be eternal may after all be no better than transient compromises, this day inalterable dogmas, the next apparent makeshifts. His mind, his nature, his attainments, his contribution, have had their fullest recognition, and will always have it, among those to whom life is complex and universals slippery and perilous; to whom truth is a dangerous experiment and man a bungling investigator. To them he will indeed in his field be the premier knight of his time; his armor is the lightest, his sword is the deftest, his attack the most impetuous and the most relentless. But these are a fragile folk, who live at sufferance, whom the world will never adopt, though it can never quite abjure them. Had his fame rested alone on them he could scarcely be the large figure in his world that he is today.

He has established himself more widely and at the last has come into a general recognition which puts him among the highest figures in American law. That has been a curious phenomenon; it was not on the whole to be expected.

The law, being an inherited accumulation, imposes itself on each generation willy-nilly. Any society whose members enter and leave it severally must for very convenience, to say nothing of deeper reasons, proceed by tradition; the neophyte must adopt existing habits and ways of acting, if for no better reason, through inexperience and diffidence. Mere custom will do the rest as he proceeds. And so the rule is canonized, its origins, and therefore its meaning, are ignored. But genuine learning is quite different. When Maitland from an ancient charter restored a lost scene and gave it to us with the fresh colors of life, he appeared to use it as a window through which we looked directly into the past. So it is with all high scholarship; we are not aware of it, it translates at once the records into terms of the life of those who made them.

A sense of this has come upon us all in the work of Justice Holmes. By a line or two we see a doctrine as a sagacious solution of some lost conflict never meant to wear the aspect of eternity. We learn to use it and we are rid of it as an absolute from our rule book; it has entered into our living understanding as it drops from the literal mandates of the past. We have become aware of a background of learning which enlightens its subject and leaves itself unknown. To the mere mechanics of the profession, this alone would be a high achievement; such scholars are rare anywhere; they are nearly unknown upon the bench.

Men ask more than scholarship, however, of a judge, and in this they are right, for while scholarship may clear the thickets it can build little. In the end, and quite fairly, a judge will be estimated in terms of his outlook and his nature. He cannot evade responsibility for his beliefs, because these are at bottom the creatures of his choice. The temper of detachment and scrutiny is not beguiling; men find it more often a cool jet than a stimulus, and it is a little curious that they ever can be brought to rate it highly. Yet, in the end, it has so obvious a place in any rational world that its value is forced upon their notice and they look behind to the disposition which produces it. If they do, they find it anything but cold or neutral, for the last acquisition of civilized man is forbearance in judgment and to it is necessary one of the highest efforts of the will.

It is in his position on constitutional questions that this has been most apparent in Justice Holmes. However we may view it, these are nearly related to policy and preference. There are two schools, rather two tendencies; one is to impose upon the Constitution the fundamental political assumptions which for the time being are dominant; it views the general clauses of the amendments as protecting the individual from the vagaries and extravagancies of faction. The other does not depart from the first in theory but in application is more cautious. That caution in the end must rest upon a counsel of scepticism or at least upon a recognition that there is but one test for divergent popular convictions, experiment, and that almost any experiment is in the end less dangerous than its suppression. Of the second school, Justice Holmes was one of the earliest and has been one of the foremost members. His decisions are not to be read as indicating his own views on public matters, but they do indicate his settled belief that in such matters the judges cannot safely intervene, that the Constitution did not create a tri-cameral system, that a law which can get itself enacted is almost sure to have behind it a support which is not wholly unreasonable. His influence has indeed been indirect, as he has been more frequently than not in the minority, but it has been none the less real; it has gained a currency among the younger profession due very largely to his consistent presentation of it. Its deeper influence upon the political life of the country may reach far. In such matters the odium of disappointing large numbers of persons must rest somewhere, and perhaps the most important question involved is at whose doors that odium shall lie. Shall the courts bear it, and can they while they keep an official irresponsibility to public opinion? To withdraw them from such controversies may in the end be the surest protection of their powers.

Forty years ago, when Justice Holmes went upon the Supreme Court of Massachusetts, this doctrine was getting its foothold, that the court should be the bulwark against improvident, selfish, and uninformed legislation. That doctrine he did not assent to then and he has not since. Whatever it was, the capaciousness of his learning, the acumen of his mind or his freedom from convention, forbade him to interject the judge into heated controversies best settled by political impacts. This must in the end be to the laymen the most significant result of his service. To the profession he will remain the example of the accomplished judge—sagacity, insight and acuteness; courtesy, dignity and humor; wisdom, learning and uprightness, as his commission reads; all these he has given to his generation as no other man has given them, and his generation has had the penetration to recognize what it has received before it was too late for him to know it. The world does not generally deal so generously with its benefactors. What it does the judicious should applaud.

5

THE PRESERVATION OF PERSONALITY
[1927]

"THE PRESERVATION OF PERSONALITY" was presented as
a commencement address at Bryn Mawr College, Bryn
Mawr, Pennsylvania, June 2, 1927. It appeared in the
Bryn Mawr Alumnae Bulletin, October 1927 (Vol. VII,
No. 7, pp. 7–14), from which it is reprinted with per-
mission.

It is a pleasant naive custom which, as you are about
to break from your cloisters and stampede joyously to
the arms of an expectant world, calls upon some one of
indubitably mature years to whisper into your ears a
parting word of admonition. A generation ago it was already a vague concession to those ancestral gods, imps, or
spectres, whom the colleges still found it prudent to
placate, lest being deprived of their accustomed offerings,
they should return and send the plagues that the rituals
were intended to avert. Still the form remains, and
pseudo prophets annually come in their disguise, to
strike the rock with solemn pantomime; the phantom
waters gush forth; and the docile congregation of God's
chosen affect to slake an assumed thirst. So we pour our
libations to our traditions after they have ceased to
mean what once they did. Piety, as piety should, preserves
the symbol, in the hope that it may seem precious in
proportion as, its content disappearing, it provides those
ineffabilities which the heart demands.

So far as from a rather withdrawn nook I can look

about, it scarcely seems to me that that hope will any longer be fulfilled. Nothing is more hazardous, I know, than for one who has for thirty years marched in the file where chance fixed him, and has not, like a teacher, seen the new formations as they fell into line in the rear— nothing is more hazardous than for such a one to pass a judgment based upon the few stragglers that may have come across his way. Still, one cannot help conclusions, however one may disclaim their validity, and for myself the one thing which I should suppose your generation is not likely to have, is that temper which makes no demand for fresh inquiry, but fills its place with faith and wise saws. I would not flatter you with the assurance that in this you show your superiority; the sense of continuity by which the individual enlarges the span of his own experience, and accepts as valid conclusions of a simpler and perhaps less competent generation, has often enough been the condition of a rich and poignant life. Those ages which ruthlessly break the moulds their forebears laboriously made do not always find freedom in their indeterminism, or reality because their expression is untrammeled.

Yet we must accept each generation as it comes, knowing that it is formed by circumstances beyond our powers, and whatever your gifts or your defects, there can be no plausible doubt that you are sceptical and unsatisfied; that at the risk of finding neither treasure nor skeleton in any, you wish to open all the closet doors, so that nothing shall be left to hearsay. If it makes any difference, I do for myself approve that temper. Experience soon teaches the seeker, not so much that he can find the key to the universe, as the limits of his search and the paucity of his trove. Tolerance, scepticism and humility are the commoner end-products of a determination to see for oneself, than of docile and tractable acceptance of what has been revealed to the past. A generation which has determined to start at scratch, and to accept nothing that is told it, may indeed be in peril, and may not realize the impossibility of its presuppositions, but it is on a crusade and I care very little who is cast for the role of St. Bernard. They may not know where they are going, but the fact that they are on the way is charming. I can talk with them, feel with them, enjoy them, and, fatuously enough, allow myself the illusion that I am at one with them, better than with many of my coevals who so often seem to wear their defenses on the outside, like crabs and lobsters, long since outclassed for their timidity.

Yet like everything else in a world where harmony must be achieved, and can arrive spontaneously only when the adjustments are simple, the dangers are as obvious as the gains. For especially in youth, though men's powers of assimilation may be at their peak, the manifold of an environment which so multitudinously as ours assails our senses, our emotions and our powers, may overwhelm our capacity for selection and leave us prostrate before the very riches with which it endows us. A wise man once said, "Convention is like the shell to the chick, a protection till he is strong enough to break it through." One may welcome the viability of an age that can live without the proper biological equipment of its kind, but one must feel a concern for the outcome before the battle is won. I can welcome much nonsense with gusto where I can see a fair chance that the young prophet has in her the assurance of some ability to learn from herself, but there must always be a question how far she will harken to her own daemon within. On the whole I am disposed to believe that that benign sprite is not in very constant attendance upon those who in a decade or two will be in charge. Indeed, they seem to me to lack direction, and to be trying to make up for it by an omnivorous curiosity and a somewhat questionable self-confidence. Is that anything more than the inevitable judgment which age is doomed to pass upon itself under the delusion of acquired experience? Perhaps not; perhaps there is little change in fact, and we go on repeating our predestined roles as the tissues become less flexible, and the powers of adaptation less responsive. Yet I shall assume the opposite: Who shall be so bold as not to accept for absolute the limitations of his years, his experience and his age?

The supposed change has been laid to the war. We are told that a period of dissolution always follows such upheavals. During the eighties of the Eighteenth Century the colonies were also full of jeremiads; customs corrupted, political and moral authority gone, the younger generation dancing down the primrose path, already in plain proximity to the everlasting bonfire, no more Lares and Penates, the social cement washed out, and the stones patently slipping to mere ruin. No doubt it was all true, but still the cataclysm was avoided. One wonders whether it has not always been true, whether man does not live forever on a thin crust likely at any minute to break through. Break through indeed he does again and again, carrying down into the pit great conceptions, well-wrought institutions, illustrious achievements. We have no warrant of exemption. Civilization is in a fleet of small craft, of which now one, now another, founders, all of which have a precarious hold upon the stormy surface of life, and each of which in the end must perish. But I am not for the moment concerned with our eventual fate, but with the putative dangers from the high seas running after this storm. I venture to believe that like most waves, they look larger as they approach than when you ride their crests; that we must look for our hazards rather to the steady currents which may carry us to the Pole, or to the Trades which may throw us unawares on some treacherous reef.

Our dangers, as it seems to me, are not from the outrageous but from the conforming; not from those who rarely and under the lurid glare of obloquy upset our moral complaisance, or shock us with unaccustomed conduct, but from those, the mass of us, who take their virtues and their tastes, like their shirts and their furniture, from the limited patterns which the market offers. I fancy that it is a question less of numbers than of communication, for while our cities are of a size never known before, their populations are not pre-eminently easy to manipulate, nor are they more likely to be carried away by hysterias than the country. It is, for instance, very doubtful whether any city of a hundred thousand people could have been got into the mood of Dayton, Tennessee, in the summer of 1925. The moral momentum which carried the Eighteenth Amendment was chiefly rural. We are not to confuse the conservatism of the results with the radical quality of the agitation. In town and country modern invention has merely given a new technique to suggestion.

At the disposal of those who seek mass production of

ideas, tastes, morals and habits, are the press, the tabloid, the weekly, the radio, the moving picture; these are the great engines of our modern Levellers. Along with them are sales catalogues, advertisements, posters, fiction, popular preachers and, probably at the end, demagogues. Since our ancestors fully straightened their knees and rose upon their hind legs to become Homo Sapiens, there have never been one-tenth as many people in the world who felt alike, thought alike, ate alike, slept alike, hated alike —so far as they hate at all—loved alike, wore the same clothes, used the same furniture in the same houses, went to the same games, saw the same plays, approved the same sentiments, believed in the same God, and, most important of all, were all confidently assured that nothing was lacking to their complete realization of the Human Ideal. Over that chorus the small voice of the individual sounds not even the thinnest obbligato; it seems senseless and preposterous to sing at all. Why not accept the accredited chant and swell the din?

Man, one would think, must have been a gregarious animal for a very long time to be susceptible of such management, and I suppose that he was gregarious because that served his purpose. Without teeth or claws or speed, he must have made a pitiful go of it, and have managed to get through at all only because of his disposition to run when the rest ran, stand when they stood, and fight when there was nothing else left open. And so one can say much for a policy of letting well enough alone. There must in any event be a few who look below the surface, and know how the game is played. These can determine what the fashions shall be, and being, as it were, at the transmitting station, they can make them what they want. After all, most men are incapable of deciding for themselves, and have got to have a leader somewhere. If the new discoveries in mass suggestion enable us to make government easier, not only political, but moral and aesthetic, why not welcome them like other useful inventions? Why should science be limited to improvements in our control over nature, and exclude the most important part of our environment, our fellows? Get on the inside, join, as I used to be told, some party, and learn where the ropes come down within your reach. Adopt the high calling of Manipulator and save the State.

Such Machiavellis are not confined to Russia and Italy; one may find them all about even in this Land of the Free. Yet, though the role of Circe is full of personality, there has been a steady prejudice against her which appears to me to go behind prejudice and convention. I know how such childish obsessions will obtrude into later years, and balk the reason; possibly my scruples are merely an adolescent residue. Still there remains in me a strange misgiving about making use of one's fellows through an appeal to their weaknesses, even when all you do is to select their objects for them. In the elegant diction of Mr. Mencken, and in spite of the great weight of his authority, a government of the boobs, for the boobs and by the boobs to me still has its morbid charms.

Moreover, when I try to imagine a present day Machiavelli, the picture always keeps dissolving into Mr. Lothrop Stoddard, contemplating the inevitable superiority of the Nordic, as *Ding an sich*. The dice get loaded, in spite of what one may do; there seems to come out nothing much better or more unfamiliar than the kind of exploitation which we have known so long, and relished so much or so little, as we were its practitioners or its objects. Perhaps some of you will agree with me not to be content with an order in which even the enlightened We might be the wire-pullers, who make the mannikins dance, whilst they, falsely imputing to their prancing a meaning we supply, live and die in ignorance of what it has ever been all about. Such sentimental reluctances have a curious persistence.

Well, if we are not to be so content; if, on the contrary, we absurdly insist upon the underlying tenet of democracy that man has a fate which it is better for him to attempt himself to direct, whatever his blundering, what have we to say about the results and the possibilities? Our problem, as I see it, is how to give the mannikin, assailed on all hands with what we now so like to call propaganda, the chance of survival as a person at all, not merely as a leaf driven by the wind, a symbol in a formula. The normal answer, at least in America, is to tell him to excel, to charge him with ambition, to fire him with the craving for distinction. Competition and emergence will preserve him from the pangs of anonymity, and wealth and power will make him envied and respected, and therefore enviable and respectable.

Alexander Hamilton, at the age of twelve, wrote, "I contemn the grovelling condition of a clerk . . . and would willingly risk my life, though not my character, to exalt my station. . . . I mean to prepare the way for futurity." And indeed he did. That is the key in which the American bugle usually sounds to action; each soldier carries a marshal's baton in his knapsack; there is always room at the top; every American boy has the makings of a president. The mannikin learns that he will be more of

37

a man, and less of a mannikin, in proportion as other mannikins look to him as high mannikin. It is the last infirmity of noble minds that makes them noble.

This is not the place to consider the uses and disuses of emulation in human life. How far is ambition essential to whip a lazy being to action; how widely are the fruits of it spread among those who do not win the prizes; how inexorable is the dilemma which forces us to choose between whirling the wheels of our cages and lapsing into beachcombers? All I want to point out is that as a principle of universal application competition defeats itself; it can be justified at all only on the notion that the success of the winners, who are few, equals the disappointment of the losers, who are many. While, therefore, it may be true that by ordering a group competitively the result will be that you get by-products worth the cost, necessary perhaps to its very existence, competition *simpliciter* as a prime motive is negative; it leaves the group worse off than it would be without it, always assuming that disappointment is as bitter as triumph is sweet. In our calculus of these values, I think we are consciously partial; it has been for so long a part of our sportsman's morale to ignore the pains of defeat, and to exalt the pleasures of success, that we are not altogether willing to weigh without bias the profit and the loss.

Moreover, in competition there lies latent a fatal antimony. Men take their color from one another, catching a reflection from sources that themselves send out no light; they are chameleons surrounded by others of their species, mysteriously acquiring hue from a colorless environment. Such is the defeat which inevitably attends a community organized upon fame as a universal motive.

Surely this was the apple which Satan, that impotent but still ardent spirit, champion of confusion, whelp of the goddess Chaos, tendered our mother Eve, and she in turn put into the unsuspecting maw of her not too sportsmanlike mate. And we, their children, have munched the fruit, disguised with various condiments, since the first pithecanthropoi held their Olympic games, or strove in war for empire, glory and prestige.

Tired with all these, man has found unbearable the vision of his never-ending flux, the flame which flares and sputters, the formless, flickering accompaniment that seems, but only seems, to direct the predetermined tropisms of his nervous organization, and is no more than an irrelevant accompaniment to the fatal motifs of his animal constitution. In all ages individuals have tried to escape. On the barren wastes of Thibet at this very hour live hermits, walled in for years, in a ceaseless round of senseless ritual, seeking to evade the remorseless procession of sense and memory, aspiring to the self-sufficiency of the grim masses of rock and ice which form the ramparts of their world, and are perhaps the key to their renunciations. In the desert of Thebes, in the plains of India, in monasteries and in solitary cells, the East has for centuries sought to throw off the oppression of our kaleidoscopic existence, to lay hold on some ghostly rock of salvation, to attain the dignity of permanence and the quietude of Nirvana. Nor have we of the West altogether escaped the spell. Throughout our history men have seen the vision of a life which might avoid the oppression of mere experience, and which should give them some sense of actuality, the belief in a personality more real than the phosphorescences of their animal moods.

39

"Life, like a dome of many-coloured glass, stains the white radiance of eternity."

To those who, like the saints, can strip away the natural impediments of their earthly state, whose lungs can bear the thin air of the Empyrean, and find in the tenser glories of thought and contemplation a substitute for the warmer activities of this too-solid flesh, we make obeisance. It seems to me quite idle to urge that they do so only in default of less alien opportunities. Nature is as much herself when she compensates for the denials of her intended course, as when she succeeds. A bone that knits, a wound that heals, a spirit that mends itself before the blows of fate, is as true to its nature as though it had gone scatheless. I must own to some impatience with those facile doctors who exclude from human perfections the recoupments which indomitable souls can make from a naughty world, thought admirable only as it is moulded nearly to the heart's desire.

Yet to fewer is it given "to be beatified by anguish and by grievous penance done," than "to furnish forth the age's pride, and to be praised of men beneath the sun." And fewer still will choose, or can, "to stand perplexed aside from so much sorrow." When all is said, by hook or crook we are here, indubitable presences, facts in a universe, in which, however hostile, we have a part. The final upshot of our fluttering may leave no monument when the world goes cold except to cast "a slightly different shadow across the face of the moon," but that must be to us, and, therefore, absolutely, irrelevant. For in the universe of values we are supreme; we make them, and they have no meaning save as we insist. Those astronomers who, being yet sane, make their devotions to size and distance and time, are a confused folk. We justly claim the right to be as impenitent towards a star whose diameter will comprise the orbit of Neptune as towards an uneasy electron ceaselessly circling in its futile course about its mother centre. We, impertinent waifs of destiny, here now and gone tomorrow, it is we in whom all values inhere; we bow to whom we choose. We recognize no dignity in incandescent gas, or dead suns whirling inanely through a space, itself at last become equivocal. Ours is the universe of good and evil, be the world of matter about us ominous or benign.

But this, our everlasting yea, carries us but shortly ahead. Neither as saint, nor as chameleon, we may resolve to live, but how does it profit us to affirm an empty self, if we cannot fill it? Though we eschew the quietism of the sage, is it enough to plunge aimless into the stream of sensation, the spray thrown off the turbulent current of our animal life? Men have tried that often enough, not usually with success. Somewhere there lurks a craving to impress some form upon the stuff about us, a craving which that abdication suppresses, and now, you know, of all the devils, suppression is the least respectable. I must be friendly with the whole of this Me, in which I live and move and have my being, this formless thing, wayward, unaccountable, inconsequent and wanton. In its deep recesses it has the itch to leave upon an indifferent universe even the print of its hands upon the clay. If, in the words of a noble friend of mine, we would be a success as human beings, the only kind of success worth having, this disposition we may not gainsay. Out of it, rather, I think we may weave the surest fabric of a self.

When I was a little boy and went to the circus the

ladies who performed upon the trapeze their hair-raising tricks, at the end always used to come before the audience, pirouette a step or two, and give us a bow. Oh, the still amorous recollection of those bows! It was a graceful gesture, a kind of quieting chorus, a coda, to still the agonies which we had endured in their behalf. Now, you may, if you choose, interpret that as no more than a bid for applause. Perhaps so. But for myself I undertake to give it a deeper meaning. They had done their bit, and done it as they had planned it. You might enjoy it and understand it, or you might, like any other yokel, be left uncomprehending. That was a matter between you and yourself; they had something else in mind. They had exhibited in their conduct a pattern of their own making; they had done a job, and done it handsomely. If others knew it, so much the better; if not, for themselves it was there, the manifestation in action of a purpose, the realization of an imagined plan.

Some anthropologists have said that we do not still chatter in the trees, and caper in dubious antics with one another, only because our thumb is opposed to our other fingers. Be it so, though it is possible that the cause is here the effect. For aught I know the learned pig may have an acute sense of craftsmanship. But for one reason or another, which we must leave to the psychologists if they can ever find out, you and I know that children take joy in making mudpies and block houses, that men like to set out in a wholesail breeze, to put a horse over a troublesome jump, to play a good game of tennis, to do anything which calls for skill and self-control. These are only temporary and occasional performances; happily similar satisfactions do not stop there. May I borrow from my personal experience? A judge's life, like every other, has in it much of drudgery, senseless bickerings, stupid obstinacies, captious pettifogging, all disguising and obstructing the only sane purpose which can justify the whole endeavor. These take an inordinate part of his time; they harass and befog the unhappy wretch, and at times almost drive him from that bench where like any other workman he must do his work. If that were all, his life would be mere misery, and he a distracted arbiter between irreconcilable extremes. But there is something else that makes it—anyway to those curious creatures who persist in it—a delectable calling. For when the case is all in, and the turmoil stops, and after he is left alone, things begin to take form. From his pen or in his head, slowly or swiftly as his capacities admit, out of the murk the pattern emerges, his pattern, the expression of what he has seen and what he has therefor made, the impress of his self upon the not-self, upon the hitherto formless material of which he was once but a part and over which he has now become the master. That is a pleasure which nobody who has felt it will be likely to underrate. I know an old gentleman, deep in the eighties, who has lived that life for near upon half a century. His shoulders stoop a good deal, his hair is quite white and so are those dashing military moustaches—the kind we used to call "dragooners." But his mind is as alert as ever it was, and you must watch your guard if you cross swords with him. Not long since he said to a young man: "My son, life is all ahead of you; it is a splendid and a precious thing. I am an old man but it is still to me as it was. If the Great Panjandrum" (for he is not an altogether reverent old gentleman) "were to say to me, 'Oliver, in five minutes

43

you have got to jump,' I should still say, 'Lord, I'm sorry it isn't ten.' "

I speak but as I know, and yet I know beyond what I speak. For all of us are alike human creatures, and whether it be in building a house, or in planning a dinner, or in drawing a will, or in establishing a business, or in excavating an ancient city, or in rearing a family, or in writing a play, or in observing an epidemic, or in splitting up an atom, or in learning the nature of space, or even in divining the structure of this giddy universe, in all chosen jobs the craftsman must be at work, and the craftsman, as Stevenson says, gets his hire as he goes. Even this obdurate and recalcitrant world is perhaps in the end no more than a complicated series of formulae which we impose upon the flux. If so, we are throughout its builders, unconscious but always at work. In part at any rate, we consciously compose; and as we do, a happy fortuity gives us the sense of our own actuality, an escape from the effort to escape, a contentment that the mere stream of consciousness cannot bring, a direction, a solace, a power and a philosophy.

Observe, I suggest no sense of service. More cant, I fancy, is poured out to youthful ears in the name of serving mankind than would fill the tally of those papers on which Panurge passed his momentous judgment some three hundred years ago. I can remember for myself the droning on that score I had to listen to, when I was of your years, the hopeless sense that I ought to abandon all that made this iridescent world so brave a show, and become a drudge in some distasteful pursuit to assist a mankind, not visibly affected by similar endeavors. If it be selfishness to work on the job one likes, because one likes it and for no other end, let us accept the odium. I had rather live forever in a company of Don Quixotes, than among a set of wraiths professing to be solely moved to the betterment of one another. Don Quixote was, it must be confessed, not an adept in correcting from experience, yet the real nub of the matter to him was to exemplify knightly conduct for knightly conduct's sake. In that he was right and Sancho was wrong, and to that he was true and, in spite of all, in that he was happy, till by a stroke which I could never forgive, his creator insisted upon restoring his wits as a preliminary to his execution. But a community of creatures engaged primarily in serving one another, except for the joy of meddling in other people's business, appears, to me at least, so dreary and so empty, that I had as lief sing for eternity in the heavenly choirs as to have any part or parcel in their pallid enterprises. Let us then, if one insist on candour, do our jobs for ourselves; we are in no danger of disserving the State. For I venture to guess, if that be our scruple, that though six associations, groups, companies, combinations or societies for the melioration of mankind with their combined boards of directors, secretaries, stenographers and field agents, were to be put into some Aristophanic scale against six honest carpenters who liked their job, they would kick the beam as high as Euripides. For who knows, though you be as crazy as the poor knight, but you may serve as a beacon for all time, and men will love you, though they laugh at you. Be that as it may, you will have a chance to save yourself, and that is quite enough to ask in a time when the streets are so full of motor cars, and the radios bark at every other corner.

45

At any rate that is my sermon and people over fifty are almost sure to preach. If your president did not expect it she should have asked somebody younger for today. We all have our prayer-wheels which we set up on the steppes. The indifferent winds come and carry most of them away to gasp out their little lives in the desert, for few reach Heaven. Mine will have as small a chance as the rest, but I am not much concerned about that. The joy is in the game. As for their fate, like my other children they must shift for themselves. What does it matter though they may later seem to me thin and frustrate? Anatole France says somewhere that it was only in the ardor of composition that the Almighty Himself could have looked forth even upon His creation and seen that it was good.

6

IS THERE A COMMON WILL?

[1929]

THE question: *"Is there a common will?"* was asked and explored by Learned Hand in an address at a banquet of the American Law Institute, in the Mayflower Hotel, Washington, May 11, 1929. It appeared in the Michigan-Law Review, November 1929 (Vol. XXVIII, pp. 46–52) and the Commercial Law Journal, June 1929 (Vol. XXXIV, pp. 305–8) and is reprinted with permission.

In New York we have a new police commissioner. He is a gentleman of urbanity and elegant apparel. For years he has officially welcomed all distinguished guests to our city. We have come to regard him, like his chief, as the epitome of many of the brighter aspects of our life. But he conceives himself as far more than a bird of plumage. When he took office he determined to show the city that his administration should have results. There was to be vigorous enforcement of the law. And so he began by rounding up all those of the nether world who were on the black list of the police. These were gathered in large vans, following raids in those parts of the city which they were known to frequent, and they were taken through the streets, with every circumstance of publicity, to the magistrates, where, as there was generally no tenable charge against them, they were nearly all immediately released. This, coupled with the announcement of a determination to harry and drive all evildoers from the city was, so far as we could gather, the measure of the achievement.

The press treated these efforts on the whole with approval. It declared that they were a sign of genuine effort to rid the city of its undesirable element. There were one or two exceptions which somewhat mildly suggested that the whole thing had been without any warrant of law, and that after all it might be desirable to pay some attention to procedure provided for the protection of the individual against groundless accusation. Even this general dissent seemed to nettle the commissioner, who shortly afterwards, in a speech before a large dinner of responsible men, defended himself in the full consciousness of rectitude. The diners were of his own mind; passed resolutions of commendation, and assured him of their unanimous support in his battle for the preservation of law and order.

A few weeks later a judge was charging a grand jury and took it upon himself to suggest that in the prosecution of crimes it was necessary to be circumscribed by the evidence. Indeed, he went perhaps a little further, and at least by indirection he suggested that the methods pursued did not have his commendation. But the grand jury in turn went out of its way to declare that they were not in accord with the learned judge. They said in substance that they thought the occasion was one when something more was necessary than barren adherence to legal form; that as for them, they believed in direct action.

Now, I think that this action of the commissioner, the business men and the grand jurors, would command the overwhelming assent of the good citizens of New York.

As to such supposed offenders they would ignore any procedure designed to sift the truth, would call it a technicality, and think of it as an impediment to their protection from violence. Yet if you asked them whether they believed that any man should be punished at the will of an official or without some evidence of his guilt, they would resent the question. They are loyal to our institutions in the abstract, but they do not mean to take them too seriously in application. Their will is uncertain and self-contradictory; they have no definite will at all and wish to follow the emotion which is most imperative at the moment. I suppose all of us are in somewhat the same position. I know for myself, although all my traditions oppose it, that after a particularly bloodthirsty murder or robbery in the streets of New York, something explodes within me which demands summary and bloody vengeance; that is no time for a nice legalism.

Let me take two other examples: In 1917 and 1918 we were at war, with all of the common will and all of the common passion that war generally creates. That did not mean that there were no dissenters, and we passed laws to control their interference with our purpose. These men came before the courts in large numbers and demanded the usual procedure in their cases. I think if we could then have canvassed the country we should have found only a small minority that would have been willing in practice to grant that demand. The accused were out of sympathy with the war; their intent was plain; they had traitors' hearts, and they deserved a traitor's fate. It was intolerable that they should mince and confound the words of a statute, even though it might not be wholly clear.

49

Again in 1919 and 1920 when the Russian Revolution
had frightened us, we felt the same way about those
aliens whom we vaguely grouped as socialists, communists
and anarchists—ignoring vital distinctions and grouping
together the most deadly enemies, to their own conster-
nation and disgust, by the common bond of a rebellious
disposition towards the existing political and economic
order. I cannot go into the question here of how far
their deportations were lawful, nor is it necessary. My
point is that people were not disposed to stand upon
their propriety, and if they were deported unlawfully, no
tears were shed. Some of the things then done were
clearly unlawful; and would be generally so accepted today; for example, the expulsion of the Socialists from
the New York Legislature. Yet I should guess that at the
time it had the approval of a great majority of the
people.

We have been long accustomed to think of law as
having that approval; it is a part of our inherited formulas that only by the consent of the governed can there
be any valid law at all. Very good; then I submit that the
law which professes to give to men of all classes, when
accused of any offense whatever, an opportunity to challenge the evidence against them and to go free when it
does not give rational support to some definite charge
—that that was not law in 1917 and 1918 and is not law
in New York today. It is law for some but not for all;
as a universal rule it does not carry popular consent; what
stands upon the books to contradict it has been repealed
ad hoc. I do not quite expect any of you to accept that
statement as it reads; but I believe that it is not a serious

parody upon a good deal that has always been said, and that still is being said, in very reputable quarters.

The argument goes that there is a kind of prescription which may run against any law; that long desuetude may effect its repeal. Back of this lies the notion that law is an expression of a common will which immanently pervades and broods over a society, and is something higher and more authoritative than what can be found in any accredited sources. I am going to ask you to examine this doctrine with me for a few moments to see whether it has a tenable basis. To me it seems to ignore the facts. As to the great body of our common law which we have inherited from the past, I think it can be demonstrated that there is nothing of the kind, if by common will we mean the assent of a majority of men and women alive today. It was not made in that way originally; no general recension has been accepted by any generation.

Life in a great society, or for that matter in a small, is a web of tangled relations of all sorts, whose adjustment so that it may be endurable is an extraordinarily troublesome matter. Men have indeed in periods of revolution tried to start afresh and contrive a new scheme from the bottom up. The surprising thing about it is that when they finish they have accomplished no very startling changes. The French Revolution shifted the center of political power from one class to another, but the relations of the individual to the government did not very deeply change for long after, if they have ever changed at all. Habit was too strong for any fabric which could be woven from the brain of Jean Jacques Rousseau. So far as we can judge the same is very largely true of Russia, where some of the old institutions like the Cheka have been deliberately carried over and in general a new bureaucracy is governing in ways not very unlike the old. In ordinary times at any rate men have no time and no capacity to draw new patterns for their society; they must make their living and answer the other problems of their individual lives. Until something in the general frame of things is so irritating as to tease them into action, they go along with what is usual, not consciously accepting it, having no opinion and therefore no will about it. The fact that much of the law which governs their lives is the result of the compromises of conflicts long since dead, does not trouble them. They do not know or care that in many cases its real significance can be determined only after painstaking research by scholars and that even then it will remain debatable. To impute to them any actual assent is to create a fabulous entity.

For many ages, for thousands of years indeed, mankind lived along without being able to change at all the traditional codes which regulated the details of their lives. Custom had the sanction of the gods and being divine, men feared to meddle with it. In civilized times we have indeed acquired that power and it is upon it that we must rely if we are to say that we are governed by our common consent. In one way or another we set up officials who innovate, and when they do, we call it our common will at work. This we have made the cornerstone of our structure. Our common law is the stock instance of a combination of custom and its successive adaptations. The judges receive it and profess to treat it as authoritative, while they gently mould it the better to fit changed ideas. Indeed, the whole of it has been fabricated in this way like a coral reef, of the symmetry of whose eventual structure the artificers have no intimation as they labor. Sometimes for this reason we speak of the judges as representing a common will, and this was more nearly true before the advent of democracy, since they were of the class which alone had political power. It is a fiction to say so now, out of which indeed some of our present troubles proceed. Besides, even if it is not, the part they fashion is very small in each generation; they are not charged with power to decide the major conflicts, and quickly learn their limitations if they try.

We think of the legislature as the place for resolving these, and so indeed it is. But if we go further and insist that there at any rate we have an expression of a common will, it seems to me that for the most part we should be wrong again. I will not of course deny that there are statutes of which we can say that they carry something like the assent of a majority. But most legislation is not of that kind; it represents the insistence of a compact and formidable minority. Nor are we to complain of that, for while we may be right to say that the problem of democracy lies in its minorities, we are not to suppose that the bulk of government can go on on any other terms. Our experience in making all the people legislate all the time has not as yet encouraged us to look to that as the way out. So far as we can forecast the future, it is more likely to see an increase in minority rule. The truth appears to be that what we mean by a common will is no more than that there shall be an available peaceful means by which law may be changed when it becomes irksome to enough powerful people who can make their will effective. We may say if we like that meanwhile everybody has consented to what exists, but this is a fiction. They have not; they are merely too inert or too weak to do anything about it.

This may seem to you a little flat and trite, but it has I think a practical consequence to the doctrine I am talking about. If law does not usually carry along any common will or common opinion and if it is not essential to its sanction that it should, it makes no difference if in fact there be a common will opposed to it, supposing that it was ascertainable. That may have means of making itself effective in the way prescribed by the law itself, after which, if it succeeds, the law has changed. It may not, when it has no resort but violence which is not law, however much it may be justified. But there can be no intermediate hybrid which either creates or repeals law by recourse to a standard not fixed by some means itself the creation of law.

Nor is this a barren truism or an arbitrary fiat, but a practical necessity reaching into the heart of any ordered society whatever. Assuming it to exist at all, there is nothing more impalpable, nebulous and fugitive than common will, as any political doctor will agree. We do indeed create something of the sort by modern salesmanship and propaganda, but it has no fibre to withstand the tempests of a naughty world. We can only ascertain it by counting noses, and when we have counted we do not agree on the meaning of the result. To be sure, there were devices, popular a decade or more ago, for a more direct appraisal, but these have very largely fallen into disuse, and in any case they are formal and legal, not nebulous and irregular. But to substitute the right of

54

each one to make his own estimate is to invite chaos to preside. City and country, ward and parish, block and village, house and house will give different returns, till the speech of the men of Babel would seem unanimous. In this as in so much else we must be content to accept some convention and hope that it will not bear too heavily to provoke rigid analysis. It is beside the point to argue that in the past there have been laws which fell into the scrap basket. In large part this is no more than an index to the immaturity of the society in which they prevail, of its incapacity to adapt itself to civilized life. To raise it into a part of the theory of government indicates our own immaturity and our own incapacity to understand the conditions of social existence.

Mind, I am not speaking of how far an individual owes allegiance to every part of existing law. Tyranny is tyranny, no matter what its form; the free man will resist it if his courage serves. But let him beware that in his rebellion he lay hold of some fundamental affirmation of his spirit. There may be a heavy price for him and there will certainly be for the community in which he lives, if he succeeds in drawing along others with him. Of the contrivances which mankind has devised to lift itself from savagery there are few to compare with the habit of assent, not to a factitious common will, but to the law as it is. We need not go so far as Hobbes, though we should do well to remember the bitter experience which made him so docile. Yet we can say with him that the state of nature is "short, brutish and nasty," and that it chiefly differs from civilized society in that the will of each is by habit and training tuned to accept some public, fixed and ascertainable standard of reference by which conduct can be judged and to which in the main it will conform.

It is because we believe in the supreme importance of such a standard that we meet here again this year. We would make it more ascertainable; we believe that we are doing so. We realize its inevitable imperfections. Bone of our bone, flesh of our flesh, it shares our faults of which we would rid it if we could, as we would rid ourselves. Much might be gained in precision, for example, if we could use a technical terminology like that of science, whose conquests depend so largely upon its coined symbols, free from the emotional connotations of colloquial speech. This can not be. There is something monstrous in commands couched in invented and unfamiliar language; an alien master is the worst of all. The language of the law must not be foreign to the ears of those who are to obey it. Much again might be gained if it could be cast more nearly to accord with the aspirations of the best of our time. That, too, we can not undertake; it must fit more easily upon prevailing conventions and even prejudices; it must not be a divine code handed down from Sinai.

These defects do not lessen its paramount consequence to us and to our civilization. We welcome any changes, in proper season and in proper place we shall urge and demand them. But we will not forget that we have a duty perhaps even greater than that, a duty to preserve. While we know that we can do little to help these men in their amazing labors, we come to pledge our faith in it and in them. We set our eyes to the future but we plant our feet upon the foundation of the common law.

7

MR. JUSTICE HOLMES
[1930]

A PORTRAIT of Justice Oliver Wendell Holmes, Jr., by Charles Sydney Hopkinson was presented to the Harvard Law School, on March 20, 1930, just after the Supreme Court judge's eighty-ninth birthday. Learned Hand made the address of the occasion in Langdell Hall. His tribute to one whom he knew as philosopher of the law was printed in the Harvard Law Review, April 1930 (Vol. XLIII, pp. 857–62), from which it is reprinted with permission. This address was also printed in Mr. Justice Holmes, edited by Felix Frankfurter and published by Coward-McCann, Inc., in 1931 in honor of Justice Holmes's ninetieth birthday.

Carlyle says somewhere that he would give more for a single picture of a man, whatever it was, than for all the books that might be written of him. We are fortunate in having a painting which justifies that opinion; it will in part at least preserve the fleeting essence for others who have not had direct acquaintance with the racy speech, the light and shade, the simplicity, the reserve, the dignity, that must some day perish and leave so much the losers such of us as remain. Books and speeches cannot hold these, and we are much the debtors to Mr. Hopkinson that his brush has been cunning enough to catch so large a part. We piously commend his work to those who shall come after us, whom time will rob of the richness of our own possession.

I take it that it is not alone to receive this picture that we came here today, but also to testify why we have thought it well to have it made and to hang it—to the gratification of its subject—opposite the effigy of the great Chief Justice, before which it need not flinch. Certainly you have not asked me to appraise his place in the law, you who are well skilled to do so, and who cannot care for what I could say. His work has been so various and so prolific that it must be left for judgment to those expert in its different fields; I have neither the capacity nor the learning to deal with it. Nor again do I suppose that I am asked to discuss his views on public law, the distribution of political power in the United States, or his understanding of the meaning of law, so strictly Austinian, so out of step with much that we hear lightly bandied about in these present times. All this must be left to other hands and other occasions. I deem *The Common Law*—all the more when one considers the time of its appearance—an extraordinary work of historical scholarship; but then I am not competent to judge it. I find the general objective approach to legal transactions a method more simple and helpful than any other; but I am not a legal philosopher. I might speak of the judge's proper part in government, but I am a judge myself, and my tongue is tied, most of all on such matters.

It is rather in the outlook of the man towards life at large, in the deeper significance of his morals, so to say, that I have thought I could alone speak to you, for in that there are no specialists; not because all are equally competent, but rather because no one is competent at all. For these depend upon preferences, arbitrary and imperative—as he is himself so fond of saying—which dis-

58

cussion and controversy can at best do no more than lay
bare. If you like diamonds and I pearls, we may with
good will reduce our differences till this appears; thereafter nothing is left for us but battle, compromise, or a
jeweler who has both.

He has been called a Liberal, a champion of Freedom,
and surely it is true, if those words are to have any meaning. Yet as their etymology shows, the terms are only
negative; they are the battle cries of convictions usually
undisclosed to the warriors themselves, presupposing ineffabilities which when reduced to speech generally prove
mixed, empty, and futile. Least of all do they suit him,
who so unsparingly searches implications. Freedom will
do well enough as a catch-word for those who are conscious of constraint, but once set free, their lives may
prove more inane than when they were hemmed about.
It is a gift only to those high spirits to whom Life itself
is a gift to spend it as they will; whose souls are harmonious enough to fall in with the course of nature and
each other. These are the godchildren of the angels, incorruptible because consistent, unruffled by the remorses
of mutability. To most of us, who, like the defendant in
Trial by Jury, love this young lady today, and love that
young lady tomorrow, freedom is a curse; we slink back
into our cages however narrow, and our disciplines however archaic. They are the defenses against the intolerable agony of facing ourselves. We prate of freedom; we
are in deadly fear of life, as much of our own American
scene betrays. And no doubt rightly. Nature, which
wrought us so crudely, put last in Pandora's box not
hope, but fear, our safeguard against our moody selves,
the adjustment which complements so many maladjust-

ments, the fly-wheel to carry over those bursts of impulse that unimpeded so often wreck the generous, the noble, and the brave.

Yet civilization, I suppose, should fill the gaps of nature, or at least such is our hope, and fear has no proper function after we know. But there's the rub, for who can guarantee us knowledge? And so, poor wights, we cling to what custom gives, and insist upon the verity of what we tremble to uncover and forbid others to dispute. The heretic who dares to lay impious hand upon our arks has always been our enemy, and perhaps will be till the last syllable of recorded time. Too often reckless, vain, and shallow, strutting in the glare of the fires he kindles; careless, so he throw large the shadow of his puny self. Yet not always; his kind are also man's best friends, without whom life would be as dead as a pressed flower, yellow and crushed and scentless. Such, when they are true to the faith, put their trust in life, in man's assertion of his right to be, in that old Adam who, from the first flicker of sentience and in the midst of the appalling tragedy of existence, has striven to endure, and in spite of all still goes on. Man's upward course from the first amoeba which felt a conscious thrill, is no more than the effort to affirm the meanings of his own strange self, to divine his significance, and to make it manifest in the little hour vouchsafed him.

A New England rearing is not the likeliest background for such notions. We do not esteem the Puritan for his faith in this world's worth, and we have come, not too respectfully, to question the comfort even of the solaces which he offered when all was done on earth. And so it is written: "Burning at first no doubt would be worst, but time the impression would soften; while those who are bored with praising the Lord, would be more bored with praising Him often." But the Puritan had his ancestors like the rest of us, spiritually as well as biologically, and he was perhaps especially liable to sports and throwbacks. He cannot disown, if he will not boast, his descent from the Stoic, who had no Elysium, even the most decorous and patriarchial; for him life was its own answer. He was a workman who found the stuff and pattern within himself; whose reward was in their union. He knew that outside ourselves there is no value; what we desire is the sole measure of right and wrong, of Heaven and of Hell. He slipped, if slip he did, only because his imagination was too narrow. Man was more richly endowed than he supposed; his hands reach out towards all of nature on which to impose the forms which his busy brain contrives; and so he literally creates his world, fabricating now this, now that, for the mere joy of creation. By some happy chance, that which at first he chooses as a means becomes with use an end, as was foreshadowed even in his appetites. Art, science, polity, even the ministrations to his simplest needs, though mediate in origin, increase "the modest kit" of wants with which he started and open to him endless achievements in the ages that await him. The houses little children make upon the beach are crude and ill-fashioned, and the tide soon comes and sweeps them away, as time will come and sweep away our bravest monuments. But neither time nor tide can spoil the play, nor take away one tittle of the joy that came with making them. What is it that they must pass? I had rather be Apelles than Cheops, or Sappho than an Assyrian scribe. To encumber this earth with the tombs of our dead selves is at best a sodden aspiration.

Are you a member of the Society of Jobbists, or do you know the guild? If not, let me tell you of it. All may join, though few can qualify. Its president is a certain white-haired gentleman, with a keen blue eye, and a dangerous turn for dialectic. But the other members need not and do not fear him, if they keep the rules, and these are very simple. It is an honest craft, which gives good measure for its wages, and undertakes only those jobs which the members can do in proper workmanlike fashion, which of course means no more than that they must like them. Its work is very various and indeed it could scarcely survive in these days, if the better known unions got wind of it, for quarrels over jurisdiction are odious to it. It demands right quality, better than the market will pass, and perhaps it is not quite as insistent as it should be upon standards of living, measured by radios and motor-cars and steam-heat. But the working hours are rigorously controlled, because for five days alone will it labor, and the other two are all the members' own. These belong to them to do with what they will, be it respectable or not; they are nobody's business, not even that of the most prying moralists.

I confess that I have often applied for admission and have been always rejected, though I still live in hope. The membership is not large, at least in America, for it is not regarded with favor, or even with confidence, by those who live in chronic moral exaltation, whom the ills of this world make ever restive, who must be always fretting for some cure; who cannot while away an hour in aimless talk, or find distraction for the eye, or feel agita-

tion in the presence of fair women. Its members have no
program of regeneration; they are averse to propaganda;
they do not organize; they do not agitate; they decline
to worship any Sacred Cows, American or Russian. But
none the less, you must be careful how you thwart them.
They are capable of mischief; for you must not suppose,
because they are amiable and gay and pleasure-loving, because they are not always reverent, that they are not
aware of the silences, or that they do not suppose themselves to have embarked upon a serious enterprise when
they began to breathe. You may go so far with them in
amity and fellowship; you may talk with them till the
cocks crow, and differ as you like and as you can, but do
not interfere with the job, and do not ask for quarter if
you do—you will not get it. For at bottom they have as
much faith as you, and more, for it is open-eyed and does
not wince. They have looked in most of the accessible
closets, and though many are too dark to explore and
they know little about what is in them, still they have
found a good many skeletons, taken them apart, and put
them together. So far as they have got, they are not
afraid of them, and they hope that those they have not
seen may not be worse than the few they have.

The Society goes along quite jauntily; the jobs and the
two days off are all a good deal like play. When you meet
a member, you are aware of a certain serenity that must
come from being at home in this great and awful Universe, where man is so little and fate so relentless. *Fais
ce que voudra* will do as well for their legend as it did for
the Abbey of Thélème. But they study to find out what
they really do want; they remember what Goethe said:
"Let the young man take care what he asks in his youth,

6 3

for in his age he shall have it." It sounds easier than it really is to join the Society. I fancy one must learn the rules apperceptively, for it is no use trying to get them by rote; I have tried that way and it does not work. You had best go to the President, for while some of the other members no doubt are as adept as he, after all he has grasped the underlying idea so well that if you get his exposition, you need not go further. He knows about it all, and he is very willing to take in neophytes.

It is indubitably inscribed in authentic documents that he was born in 1841, and, being a legalistic person myself both by nature and practice, I must accept this for some purposes. But latterly we have got the habit of playing fast and loose with time, and I suspect that somewhere something has got twisted. Secretly I believe that he has spent his time travelling about with inordinate velocity; at least I know that his head at any rate has often been in the stars, and I suppose the rest of him must have gone along. You know that if you can move fast enough, you will keep time back in some curious way that baffles the clocks. At any rate, while we have been working along at mere terrestrial velocities, he has certainly not been growing old. Nobody can say that without flagrant disregard of the obvious, whatever be the records of our wretchedly defective means of counting time. If it be old to degenerate in will, mind, or feeling, patently he is not old. If it be old to be muffled by the body, so that a veil falls between us and our fellows, he is not old. If it be old not to understand youth, its joys, its aspirations, and its generous warmth, he is not old. If we measure youth by the power to assimilate what is new, by freshness of outlook, by sympathy, by

64

understanding, by quickness of response, by affection, by kindness, by gentleness, by magnanimity, he is not old.

Another wrote these words translated from a Greek epitaph; she who for many years most closely shared that life that we have come to honor. Who could as well have said what I have tried to say?

> *A shipwrecked sailor buried on this coast*
> *Bids thee take sail.*
> *Full many a gallant ship, when we were lost,*
> *Weathered the gale.*

I have the honor to present to the School the portrait of Holmes, of the Class of 1866.

SOURCES OF TOLERANCE
[1930]

"SOURCES OF TOLERANCE" was delivered before the Juristic Society of the University of Pennsylvania Law School, June 1930. It is reprinted with permission from the University of Pennsylvania Law Review, November 1930 (Vol. LXXIX, pp. 1–14).

I am going to ask you to go with me, not into questions which have direct relation to the law or to government, but to those which concern the mental habits of our people, since these, indirectly at any rate, in the end determine its institutions. This is not an easy, maybe it is an impossible undertaking, but at any rate, nobody can very effectually challenge what you say about such vague things, and you are exempt from the need of citation—blessed exoneration to a judge. It may be worth discussion, if only for discussion's sake. At least it can serve to bring out differences of opinion.

By way of prelude may I then ask you for a moment to go back in our country for nearly a century and a half? We were substantially a nation of farmers; towns were few; cities, as we should now rate them, did not exist. Life was, as we like to believe, simple. Maybe it was not so in fact, for simplicity depends rather on one's inner state of mind; but at any rate it was less pressed and hurried; people did not think so much about how complicated they were, and less dissipated their attention. The political notions of the time were divided into two contrasting groups which it has been the custom to associate with the great names of Jefferson and Hamilton. It is easy to associate Jefferson's ideas with those of Rousseau, from whom on the outside they seem to have been drawn. This, as I understand it, is wrong, but he had drunk deeply at the springs of Physiocracy, and in any event he believed in the basic virtue of mankind, once set free from artificial restraints. He found his ideal in a community of independent families, each intrenched in its farm, self-subsistent, independent, needing no regulation, and tolerant of little interference, especially by government. Those who invoke his name today must be shocked at his scorn of the mob of mechanics and artisans, whose turbulence and separation from some particular plot of earth unfitted them in his eyes for sharing in the Good Life. A nation in which information, or what passes as such, can be instantaneously sent from one end to the other, in which the craving for conformity demands uniformity in belief, which for that reason wears the same clothes, reads the same print and follows the same fashions, amusements and conventions, would have seemed to him scurvy and sordid. He would have found little in the America of today to justify that Utopia of which he had dreamed.

The extraordinary richness of his own nature, his omnivorant interest in all the activities of man, no doubt colored his picture of a life on the land; yet it also enabled him to transmute into a rosy ideal the dumb aspirations of his people, and so they looked to him for their leadership for a quarter of a century after his accession to power, and if we count Jackson as his dubious disciple, for that much longer. Clearly there was something in his outlook which responded to the needs of those among whom he lived.

Hamilton was a horse of another color, always an exotic, succeeding in his statecraft only because of the disorders which immediately followed the Revolution; whose genius needed the cloak of Washington beneath which his real work was hid for near a century. He was no Utopian; he did not believe in the perfectibility of human nature. Government was a combination of those interests in the community which collectively would be irresistible; a combination resting upon self-interest. When he secured the passage of the Constitution, it was by means of such a combination; the landed class, the manufacturers and the public creditors. In the doubtful contest for ratification, as Beard has shown, it was these votes which eventually won, and it was under the aegis of Washington that he managed to carry on for those critical eight years. With the constant movement of the frontier westward, the underlying, but less articulate, aspirations of a rural people finally asserted themselves, after Adams had run off Hamilton's momentum.

The animosity between the two men was well founded and inevitable. They represented, and we are right still to take them as our most shining examples of, two theories of human society; that which demands external control, and that which insists upon the opportunity for personal expression. Jefferson's victory seemed to him to be the sanction of all that the Revolution had implied; the liberation of a free people from the domination of greed and corruption, opening vistas of human felicity not theretofore known on earth. For its fuller expression he was willing, forced by a sad necessity, to sacrifice his constitutional scruples and forever compromise his party by the acquisition of Louisiana. To Hamilton, Jefferson's accession was the beginning of the end, the last step in a plunge towards anarchy. The squalid political quarrel for the domination of the rump of Federalism which ended in his death, had for him a deeper significance than the leadership in a party then apparently writhing to dissolution. The Eighteenth Brumaire was five years past, and though the Coronation at Notre Dame was still some months away, recent events already foreshadowed it. In the final breakdown of that Jacobinism which he and his associates thought certain and early, the need would arise for some transatlantic Bonaparte to gather the shreds of society, and build a state upon surer foundations than that weak instrument in which at heart he had never really believed. To prevent Federalism, the sacred chalice, from passing into the obscene hands of a turncoat and a traitor was worth the chance that cost him his life.

Each man would have said that he was the champion of liberty, and each would have been right. To one the essential condition of any tolerable life was the free expression of the individual, the power to lead his life on his own terms, to enjoy the fruits of his industry, to garner the harvest of his hands and brain, without subtraction by a horde of office-holders, locusts who laid waste the land and spread the venal doctrine of their right to eat what others had sown, the blight, the virus, of a society of honest men, enjoying the earth which God, at least in this blessed country, had patently spread out for their satisfaction. The other saw in all this no more than the maunderings of a toxic dream. What was the assurance of man's capacity to deal with his own fate? Was it not clear that virtue and intelligence among the sons of Adam was as rare as physical prowess, indeed much rarer? Liberty could not rest upon anarchy; it was conditioned upon an ordered society, in which power should rest where power should be, with the wise and the good, who could be at least presumptively ascertained as those who in the battle of life had already given some signs of capacity. It was an empty phantom to assume some automatic regulation by which without plan and direction public affairs manage themselves. The concerns of a great people are not all individual; they have collective interests without which their life can scarcely rise above that of savages, each shifting for himself, without comfort, security, or the leisure which alone makes existence endurable. Jacobins might bawl of liberty, but really they meant no more than the tyranny of their own domination over the mob.

Placed as we now are, with an experience of over a century behind us, we can say that the future was apparently to justify Hamilton as against his great rival. Our knowledge of the ways of Nature, our command of her energies, and the materials which she has set so freely at our hands, has made it no longer possible to think of a society of families, isolated and non-communicating, each weaving its own fate independently of the rest. We have fabricated a nexus of relations which makes even rural life impossible as Jefferson understood it. The motor, the airplane, the telephone and telegraph, the radio, the railroad, the Linotype, the modern newspaper, the "movie"—and most horrible, the "talkie"—have finally destroyed it. Liberty is irretrievably gone in any sense that it was worth having to him. A farmer must have complicated machinery; he depends upon markets thousands of miles away; he will win by a crop shortage in India, and lose by a fall in industrial shares. He must "listen in" on Amos an' Andy, have camping places in the National Parks and tour in the Ford in winter. So be it; I welcome his larger life, but it has its price; he is tied to all men, as all men are tied to him, in a web whose threads no eye can follow and no fingers unravel.

Nor would there still be many, though doubtless some there are, who would deny that government must be the compromise of conflicting interests, as Hamilton supposed. While there lingers in political platforms and other declamatory compositions the notion that each man, if only he could be disabused of false doctrine, would act and vote with an enlightened eye to the public weal, few really believe it. We know well that an objective calculus of human values is impossible, and if it were available, would be so thin and speculative that men would not accept it. For any times that can count in human endeavor, we must be content with compromises in which the more powerful combination will prevail. The most we can hope is that if the maladjustment becomes too obvious, or the means too offensive to our conventions, the balance can be re-established without dissolution, a cost greater than almost any interests can justify. The method of Hamilton has had its way; so far as we can see must always have its way; in government, as in marriage, in the end the more insistent will prevails.

Liberty is so much latitude as the powerful choose to accord to the weak. So much perhaps must be admitted for abstract statement; anything short of it appears to lead to inconsistencies. At least no other formula has been devised which will answer. If a community decides that some conduct is prejudicial to itself, and so decides by numbers sufficient to impose its will upon dissenters, I know of no principle which can stay its hand. Perhaps indeed it is no more than a truism to say so; for, when we set ourselves this or that limitation, religion for example, we find that we wince in application. Who can say that the polygamy of the Mormons was not a genuine article of that faith? When we forbade it in the name of our morals, was it not an obvious subterfuge still to insist that we recognized religious freedom? Should we tolerate suttee? If we forbid birth-control in the interest of morals, is it inconceivable that we should tax celibacy? We call that conduct moral about whose effect upon our common interest we have unusually strong convictions. We do not hesitate to impose this upon those who do not share our views; and tolerance ends where faith begins. Plato may have been right about the proper relations of the sexes; we should not allow his experiment to be tried. I do not see how we can set any limits to legitimate coercion beyond those which our forbearance concedes.

And yet, so phrased, we should all agree, I think, that the whole substance of liberty has disappeared. It is intolerable to feel that we are each in the power of the conglomerate conscience of a mass of Babbitts, whose intelligence we do not respect, and whose standards we may detest. Life on their terms would be impossible to endure; of their compunctions we have no guarantee. Who shall deliver us from the body of this death? Certainly there was a meaning in Jefferson's hatred of the interposition of collective pressure, though he extended it to so much of what we now accept as government. We may believe that his emphasis was wrong; that it required a great war eventually to clear away the centrifugal tendencies that underlay it; but shall we not feel with him that it is monstrous to lay open the lives of each to whatever current notions of propriety may ordain? That feeling was the energy that lay back of the first ten amendments to the Constitution, which were really a part of the document itself. Impossible though they be of literal interpretation, like a statute, as counsels of moderation rather than as parts of our constituent law, they represent a mood, an attitude towards life, deep rooted in any enduring society.

Jefferson thought that they could be made to prevail by weakening the central power, but he was too astute an observer to rely upon political device alone. It was in the social, not in the political, constitution of his society that real security lay. For it was impossible to sweep a community of small eighteenth century farmers with mob hysteria. His dislike of cities was in part at any rate because they were subject to just such accesses. He did not, and he could not, see that time was to make rural life as susceptible to moral epidemics as the city mobs which he feared and mistrusted. He set his faith upon isolation and isolation in the end has failed him. The shores are no longer studded with rows of solid columns to break the waves of propaganda; they are not studded with anything whatever, and the waves sweep over them without obstacle and run far up into the land. The question I wish to put before you, which all this introduction is to prepare, is this—which I trust you will forgive me

73

for putting in colloquial form—how far is liberty consistent with the methods of the modern "high-power" salesman? If it is not, what is to be done about it? Being Americans, we are not likely to agree that nothing can.

It has always interested me to read of the observations of those patient anthropologists who associate intimately with our cousin, the chimpanzee. I know a woman who endured the embrace of her son's pet for two hours, lest if disturbed in its caresses it might furiously strangle her. Devotion could scarcely ask more. We may learn much of ourselves from what are now, I believe, called the "conduct patterns" of the anthropoids, but it will not interest me so much as if the study could be of the herds. What I want to know is, why we have become so incurably imitative. I can improvise reasons, but you know how worthless that kind of anthropology is, so I shall spare you. But you will agree about the fact I fancy; you will agree that ideas are as infectious as bacteria and appear to run their course like epidemics. First, there is little immunity, nearly all individuals are susceptible, so that the disease spreads like a prairie fire. Next, a period where the curve of infection, as the pathologists say, remains level; this may last a long time. Last a decline of the curve which, so far as is known, nothing can check. The virus has lost its potency, or some immunity has established itself in a wholly mysterious way.

Ideas, fashions, dogmas, literary, political, scientific, and religious, have a very similar course; they get a currency, spread like wildfire, have their day and thereafter nothing can revive them. Were the old questions ever answered? Has anyone ever proved or disproved the right of secession? Most issues are not decided; their importance passes and they follow after. But in their day they rack the world they infest; men mill about them like a frantic herd: not understanding what their doctrines imply, or whither they lead. To them attach the noblest, and the meanest, motives, indifferent to all but that there is a cause to die for, or to profit by. Such habits are not conducive to the life of reason; that kind of devotion is not the method by which man has raised himself from a savage. Rather by quite another way, by doubt, by trial, by tentative conclusion.

In recent times we have deliberately systematized the production of epidemics in ideas, much as a pathologist experiments with a colony of white mice, who are scarcely less protected. The science of propaganda by no means had its origin in the Great War, but that gave it a greater impetus than ever before. To the advertiser we should look for our best technique. I am told that if I see McCracken's tooth-paste often enough in street cars, on billboards and in shop windows, it makes no difference how determined I may be not to become one of McCracken's customers, I shall buy McCracken's tooth-paste sooner or later, whether I will or no; it is as inevitable as that I shut my eyes when you strike at my face. In much the same way political ideas are spread, and moral too, or for that matter, religious. You know the established way of raising money for the School of Applied and Theoretical Taxidermy. One employs a master mind in group suggestion, with lieutenants and field workers. The possible "prospects" are bombarded with a carefully planned series of what for some unknown reason is called "literature"—leaflets, pictures, pathetic appeals, masterful appeals, appeals to patriotism. Shall

American animals suffer the indignity of inadequate stuffing, having themselves given their lives to the cause? Will not you as a loyal American do your bit too; they having made the last supreme sacrifice? Taxidermy is a patriotic duty; are you for taxidermy? If not, you are against it, a taxidermical outlaw at best, at worst a taxidermical Laodicean. Brother, show your colors, join some group, at all costs join, be not a non-joiner, a detestable, lily-livered, half-hearted, supercilious, un-American, whom we would exile if we could and would not pass if he sought entrance.

I submit that a community used to be played on in this way, especially one so large and so homogeneous as we have become, is not a favorable soil for liberty. That plant cannot thrive in such a forcing bed; it is slow growing and needs a more equitable climate. It is the product, not of institutions, but of a temper, of an attitude towards life; of that mood that looks before and after and pines for what is not. It is idle to look to laws, or courts, or principalities, or powers, to secure it. You may write into your constitutions not ten, but fifty, amendments, and it shall not help a farthing, for casuistry will undermine it as casuistry should, if it have no stay but law. It is secure only in that *constans et perpetua voluntas suum cuique tribuendi*; in that sense of fair play, of give and take, of the uncertainty of human hypothesis, of how changeable and passing are our surest convictions, which has so hard a chance to survive in any times, perhaps especially in our own.

There are some who, looking on the American scene, see remedy in trying to introduce and maintain local differences. Especially in matters of government, let us be astute to preserve local autonomy, not to concentrate all power in our capital. There are reasons enough for this in any case, but as a relief from the prevalent mood it seems to me a delusion. That served very well in Jefferson's time; it will not do today. We cannot set our faces against a world enraptured with the affluence which comes from mass production; and what has served so magically in material things, is it not proved to be good for our ideas, our amusements, our morals, our religion? The heretic is odious in proportion as large industry is successful. Rapidity of communication alone makes segregation a broken reed; for men will talk with one another, visit one another, join with one another, listen collectively, look collectively, play collectively, and in the end, for aught I know, eat and sleep collectively, though they have nothing to say, nothing to do, no eyes or ears with which to enjoy or to value what they see and hear. You cannot set up again a Jeffersonian world in separate monads, each looking up to heaven. For good or evil, man, who must have lived for long in groups, likes too much the warm feeling of his mental and moral elbows in touch with his neighbors'.

Well, then, shall we surrender; shall we agree to submit to the dictation of the prevalent fashion in morals and ideas, as we do in dress? Must we capture surreptitiously such independence as we can, "bootleg" it, as it were, and let the heathen rage, the cattle mill, the air resound with imperious nostrums which will brook no dissidence? Maybe it will come to that; sometimes I wonder whether to be a foe of war, for example—which might be thought a blameless disposition—is not a stigma of degeneracy. Again I have pondered on what it is to be a Bolshevik, and once I learned. There was a time when Congress thought it could reach the salaries of my brothers and myself by an income tax, until the Supreme Court manfully came to our rescue. A judge of much experience was talking with me one day about it; I was wrong enough in my law, as it afterwards turned out, and disloyal enough in temper to my class, to say that I thought the tax valid. "Do you know anything about it?" he asked with some asperity. "No," said I, "not a thing." "Have you ever read Taney's letter?" "No," said I again, for I was innocent of any learning. "Why, they can't do that," said he; "they can't do that, that's Bolshevism." And so it turned out, to my personal gratification, since when, freed from that Red Peril, I have enjoyed an immunity which the rest of you, alas, cannot share. Far be it from me to suggest that there are graver thrusts at the structure of society than to tax a Federal judge. Properly instructed, I have recanted my heresy, and yet there hangs about "Bolshevism" a residual vagueness, a lack of clear outline, as of a mountain against the setting sun; which only goes to show, I suppose, that a fundamentally corrupt nature can never be wholly reformed.

As I say, we may have to lie low like Bre'r Rabbit, and get our freedom as best we can, but that is the last resort. Perhaps if we cannot build breakwaters, we may be able to deepen the bottom. The Republic of Switzerland is cut into deep valleys; it has been a traditional home of freedom. Greece is made in the same way; to Greece we owe it that our civilization is not Asian. Our own country has not that protection; and in any event, of what value would it be in these later days, when Fords climb Pikes

Peak and Babe Ruth is the local divinity at once in San Diego and Bangor? But what nature has not done for us, perhaps time can. I conceive that there is nothing which gives a man more pause before taking as absolute what his feelings welcome, and his mind deems plausible, than even the flicker of a recollection that something of the sort has been tried before, felt before, disputed before, and for some reason or other has now quite gone into Limbo. Historians may be dogmatists, I know, though not so often now as when history was dogma. At least you will perhaps agree that even a smattering of history and especially of letters will go far to dull the edges of uncompromising conviction. No doubt one may quote history to support any cause, as the devil quotes scripture; but modern history is not a very satisfactory side-arm in political polemics; it grows less and less so. Besides, it is not so much history one learns as the fact that one is aware that man has had a history at all. The liberation is not in the information but in the background acquired, the sense of mutability, and of the transience of what seems so poignant and so pressing today. One may take sides violently over the execution of Charles the First, but he has been dead a long while; the issue is not bitter unless we connect it with what is going on today. Many can of course do this, but that in itself requires considerable knowledge of intervening events, and those who can achieve a sustained theory are almost entitled to their partisanship, in reward of their ingenuity. After all, we can hope only for palliatives.

With history I class what in general we call the Liberal Arts, Fiction, Drama, Poetry, Biography, especially those of other countries; as far as that be possible, in other

79

tongues. In short, I argue that the political life of a country like ours would get depth and steadiness, would tend to escape its greatest danger, which is the disposition to take the immediate for the eternal, to press the advantage of present numbers to the full, to ignore dissenters and regard them as heretics, by some adumbration of what men have thought and felt in other times and at other places. This seems to me a surer resort than liberal weeklies, societies for the promotion of cultural relations, sermons upon tolerance, American Civil Liberty Unions. I know very well how remote from the possibilities of most men anything of the kind must be, but good temper, as well as bad, is contagious. And today in America vast concourses of youth are flocking to our colleges, eager for something, just what they do not know. It makes much difference what they get. They will be prone to demand something they can immediately use; the tendency is strong to give it them; science, economics, business administration, law in its narrower sense. I submit that the shepherds should not first feed the flocks with these. I argue for the outlines of what used to go as a liberal education—not necessarily in the sense that young folks should waste precious years in efforts, unsuccessful for some reason I cannot understand, to master ancient tongues; but I speak for an introduction into the thoughts and deeds of men who have lived before them, in other countries than their own, with other strifes and other needs. This I maintain, not in the interest of that general cultural background, which is so often a cloak for the superior person, the prig, the snob and the pedant. But I submit to you that in some such way alone can we meet and master the high-power salesman of political patent medicines. I come to you, not as an advocate of education for education's sake, but as one, who like you, I suppose, is troubled by the spirit of faction, by the catch-words with the explosive energy of faith behind them, by the unwillingness to live and let live with which we are plagued. It is well enough to put one's faith in education, but the kind makes a vast difference. The principles of a common pump are in my opinion not so important politically as Keats's *Ode on a Grecian Urn*, to crib a phrase from Augustine Birrell.

May I take an illustration nearer to the field with which you are especially concerned? I venture to believe that it is as important to a judge called upon to pass on a question of constitutional law, to have at least a bowing acquaintance with Acton and Maitland, with Thucydides, Gibbon and Carlyle, with Homer, Dante, Shakespeare and Milton, with Machiavelli, Montaigne and Rabelais, with Plato, Bacon, Hume and Kant, as with the books which have been specifically written on the subject. For in such matters everything turns upon the spirit in which he approaches the questions before him. The words he must construe are empty vessels into which he can pour nearly anything he will. Men do not gather figs of thistles, nor supply institutions from judges whose outlook is limited by parish or class. They must be aware that there are before them more than verbal problems; more than final solutions cast in generalizations of universal applicability. They must be aware of the changing social tensions in every society which make it an organism; which demand new schemata of adaptation; which will disrupt it, if rigidly confined.

This is only an illustration of the much wider question

81

of our political life at large. I submit that the aim is not so fanciful as it may seem; though at the moment I agree the outlook is not promising. Young people are not much disposed to give their time to what seems like loose browsing in the past. Though there are signs of a turn, of the significance of the insignificant, I shall try no forecast. All I want to emphasize is the political aspect of the matter, of the opportunity to preserve that spirit of liberty without which life is insupportable, and nations have never in the past been able to endure.

Jefferson is dead; time has disproved his forecasts; the society which he strove to preserve is gone to chaos and black night, as much as the empire of Genghis Khan; what has succeeded he would disown as any get of his. Yet back of the form there is still the substance, the possibility of the individual expression of life on the terms of him who has to live it. The victory is not all Hamilton's, nor can it be unless we are all to be checked as anonymous members regulated by some bureaucratic machine, impersonal, inflexible, a Chronos to devour us, its children. We shall not succeed by any attempt to put the old wine in new bottles; liberty is an essence so volatile that it will escape any vial however corked. It rests in the hearts of men, in the belief that knowledge is hard to get, that man must break through again and again the thin crust on which he walks, that the certainties of today may become the superstitions of tomorrow; that we have no warrant of assurance save by everlasting readiness to test and test again. William James was its great American apostle in modern times; we shall do well to remember him.

Surely we, the children of a time when the assump-

tions of even the science of our fathers have been out-
worn; surely we ought not to speak in apocalyptic verities,
nor scourge from the temple those who do not see with
our eyes. All the devices of our ingenuity, all our command over the materials of this earth, all the organization and differentiation of our industry and our social
life, all our moral fetishes and exaltations, all our societies to ameliorate mankind, our hospitals, our colleges,
our institutes—all these shall not save us. We shall still
need some knowledge of ourselves, and where shall we
better look than to the fate of those who went before?
Would we hold liberty, we must have charity—charity
to others, charity to ourselves, crawling up from the
moist ovens of a steaming world, still carrying the passional equipment of our ferocious ancestors, emerging
from black superstition amid carnage and atrocity to our
perilous present. What shall it profit us, who come so
by our possessions, if we have not charity?

83

9

TO YALE LAW GRADUATES
[1931]

LEARNED HAND, graduate of Harvard College and the Harvard Law School, addressed the Yale Law School graduates, class of 1931, on June 17 of that year. But before that representatives of the Harvard and Yale Law Schools had been sitting together on the United States Court of Appeals for the Second Circuit. President Calvin Coolidge elevated Learned Hand from the Federal District Court in New York in 1924 and appointed Dean Thomas Walter Swan of the Yale Law School to the same Court of Appeals bench in 1927.

Those of us who have come to years of discretion and more, must often take to retrospect, and seek to appraise the outcome of our lives. Most of a lawyer's time—and with your permission I will include a judge's—consists of activity which seems to have small value and small bearing on the greater issues of the community in which he lives. True, it concerns the individuals whom he touches oftentimes in their deepest interests, but it is hard to believe that the results are important more largely. Moreover, we have our first duty to protect ourselves and those dependent on us; to get a competency honestly is always hard enough; never more so than just now. It must at times seem to us that after all our profession is very much like any other gainful calling, of only transient importance to others, justified by no more than the immediate necessities which surround mankind from the

84

cradle to the grave. Of what meaning are those high-flown adjurations with which our ears were filled when we first tried our wings?

The Good Life, we are told by the greatest of sages, is the noble employment of leisure. True, no doubt, though I fancy that leisure must be taken *alio intuitu*, not in the sense, for example, of Mr. Aldous Huxley, who humorously observes that of all things leisure would be for most men a curse. What Aristotle meant, I suppose, is that the Good Life begins only when one's satisfactions are not derivative, but immediate; that what one gives one's time to should be an end in itself, not a means. All else are slaves; for it makes small difference whether we work under compulsion of violence, or starvation, or the fear of being accounted failures. Only he is free whose efforts are called out by what seems to him a good of itself, by the belief that he is impressing upon the stuff of this world some idea authentically his own. Though we may all have to submit to some slavery, the measure of our freedom is the measure of this success, of so much as we can truly call our own. It is hard for most of us to believe that, so taken, the lawyer's is the Good Life.

It is at times like these when we meet together to take stock, as it were, that we may consider how far we are missing the forest for the trees, and possibly take heart from the more real, though more distant, outlook from which our eyes are turned most of the time. The astronomers have of late been disposed to give mankind a vast scope for its activities; our charter is for all substantial purposes perpetual; so far as we can see the physical conditions of life on the planet may remain for practical purposes unchanged during periods which make our recent emergence into civilization no more than a moment ago. Moreover, if we look back upon only so short a time as three or four centuries, we have ground for thinking that something like what we fondly call Progress, is not only within our compass, but even probable. I know how tenuous is our hold on what we have; nobody who has lived through the last twenty years can be forgiven an easy optimism based upon the assumption of the automatic advancement of mankind. We cannot hide our perils under a fatuous belief in what we choose to call Evolution, as though the stars in their courses or Nature upon this earth were concerned with what we did, how we fared, or whether we live or die.

Yet we should not forget the command we have obtained over the forces which surround us, and the mastery that command may give us in ordering our fate. Whatever our folly, we have at least been wise to learn the secrets of how things actually go on, and if we can only better find what we really are and what we truly want, there is good promise for a future which shall make our past and present appear like Hobbes's vision of the Life of Nature. Nobody can have even a smattering of the new science—that revolution in which we move about so unconsciously—without believing that we may be at the morning of a new understanding, bringing with it capacities for a life for all men which would have seemed to our forefathers a will-o'-the-wisp, a chase for the rainbow's pot of gold. For, though the superior may scorn it, in the long last, control over the material resources about us is the foundation of the Good Life; were we once to tap freely the energies which are so abundantly wasted all around us, we should be set free from necessity, and might learn to find ourselves, so far as we have any selves to find.

It seems to me that the chief obstacle to our success lies not in our powers, were we able to use them, but in the make-up of those same selves which remain so little changed amid our new methods and accomplishments. It is our human wills that are at fault, not our minds or our energy. It is possible that we may decide upon another orgy of slaughter and destruction, and while I do not take too seriously the lurid threats of mutual annihilation which one sometimes reads, it is certainly open to doubt how often men may continue to enjoy the pastime of murder, arson and spoil without lapsing into anarchy and chaos. Nobody can, and nobody today does, feel that security which was the convention at the turn of the last century. We shall succeed in using those powers for a happy future only in case we learn so far to forbear with one another, so much to eschew greed and aggression, that we give ourselves the chance to do what lies within us. The condition of our survival in any but the meagerest existence is our willingness to accommodate ourselves to the conflicting interests of others, to learn to live in a social world.

It is here that we can find a scope and meaning in our work as lawyers which raises it out of the dusty routine of gaining our living. For the law is no more than the formal expression of that tolerable compromise that we call justice, without which the rule of the tooth and claw must prevail. Much has been said and written, much indeed in that school which claims you as her children, of a new approach to law. We are told that the judge must divine the spirit of his time and fearlessly pro-

claim it; even that the demand for any pre-existing rules
to circumscribe his choice and direct the result is an
anachronism, a lapse into that adolescent mood which
craves support because it has never learned to stand
alone. Perhaps so. I confess that for myself the problem
seems chiefly political. In much a judge may undertake
the part of protagonist of the *Zeitgeist*; he may properly
suppose himself adequately fitted to represent all those
interests which must be composed, and to declare the
composition. In much he surely may not, and the path
of temperance and of wisdom is to leave the solution to
other organs of government where the opposing interests
may more adequately count in their mutual impact. In
any case for my present purpose one may have it either
way, so long as somewhere the conscience of men may
have continuous and organic expression, informed by experience, purged by mistake, a fixed resolution to accord
to each his own. Despite its inconsistencies, its crudities,
its delays and its weakness, law still embodies so much
of the results of that disposition as we can collectively
impose. Without it we cannot live; only with it can we
insure the future which by right is ours. The best of
man's hopes are enmeshed in its success; when it fails
they must fail; the measure in which it can reconcile our
passions, our wills, our conflicts, is the measure of our
opportunity to find ourselves.

And so when at times we come together as now, and
wonder how far each one of us can render to his more
aspiring self some account which shall pass muster, let
us not despair, if we are faithful to our trust. For, as you
know, it is not in books that the law can live, but in the
consciousness of the profession as a whole. Judges,

dressed with their brief authority, may seem to speak more finally, but it is only for the moment. In the end they take their cues from the bar and the great schools, like this, which slowly form the moulds. It is the bar which makes the statutes, which fabricates the adjustments they express. In thousands of chambers, committee rooms and lecture halls, the spirit of the law becomes incorporate; and neither you, nor I, nor any other individual, shall have much part in it. We are the workers in the hive; we shall not be missed, nor shall we be able to point at the end to any perceptible contribution. But the hive goes on, an entity, a living thing, a form, a reality. So far as we cannot severally sink our fate in its fate, we shall not have our reward. Our selves are like flames, now dwindling to a spark, seen, but lightening nothing, now flaring to encompass all about, comprehending as much as we may choose to adopt as our own.

When our lights burn low, when we seem to stand futile and without meaning, used up in the senseless strife of interest and passion, concerned with nothing better than to get for others what perhaps they should not have, let us look up to the great edifice which our forebears have built, of which we are now the guardians and the craftsmen. Though severally we may perhaps be paltry and inconsequent, for the present it is we who are charged with its maintenance and its growth. Descended to us, in some sort moulded by our hands, passed on to the future with reverence and with pride, we at once its servants and its masters, renew our fealty to the Law.

10

DEMOCRACY: ITS PRESUMPTIONS
AND REALITIES
[1932]

THIS keen inquiry into the presumptions and realities of democracy was delivered as an address at the twelfth annual dinner of the Federal Bar Association, March 8, 1932, in Washington. It is reprinted with permission from the Federal Bar Association Journal, March 1932 (Vol. I, No. 2, pp. 40–5).

The fathers who contrived and passed the Constitution were wise in their generation; as time passes, we come more and more to realize their powers of divination. And yet, as has been so often observed, they were curiously blind to the way in which the government they set up was to work; they apparently had no intimation of the role that party was to play. In this they were proper children of their time; for, though Britain was already in fair train to develop party out of faction, the spirit of the century chose to ignore it. If you set men free from the restraint of prince and priest, and gave them an opportunity to decide their own fate, they would almost automatically come to an understanding of their true needs, and the needs of one were the needs of all. True, the Fathers were deeply preoccupied with the possibility that their work might be overthrown by faction and popular tumult, or by the despotism which these engender, and against these they provided the elaborate system which we have come to know so well. But, given time, with its opportunity for deliberation, the mass of mankind was assumed to be, broadly speaking, homogeneous; at least, government as a compromise between more or less permanent and competing groups, seems not to have been contemplated. This was a strange inadvertence. Even while the Constitution was being framed, Hamilton at least understood that to pass it he must secure the concurrence of special interests which, though they overlapped, he drew into concert by holding out a different bait to each. Perhaps the greatest testimony to his genius is the skill with which he welded them together, and passed what would probably have failed to command a majority of the votes of even the limited numbers who then had the suffrage. But that the work of government should be carried along by the same means by which it had been instituted, nobody seems to have foreseen. Within a decade all were undeceived, since when we have become accustomed to parties as essential to our institutions.

A party system was still compatible with the underlying ideas of the Eighteenth Century, out of which it had developed. The government, by which I mean those who have present power, is to be watched and checked by an opposition which will succeed, when it can demonstrate that those who now hold office are not acting for the public weal and that it is likely to do better. This presupposes rather that that weal is a matter on which all will judge alike, and in which all share in the same way, than that society will array itself into classes, pressing their several demands, indifferent to the general welfare, and establishing an equilibrium only by compromises in which they alone share. Bipartisan democracy presup-

poses the individual, whose welfare is identical with that
of the community in which he lives, the absence of
coherent social classes, a basic uniformity of interest
throughout.

It seems a strange idea to us now. We have come to
think of the problem of democracy as that of its minorities, a repellant notion, which has predisposed many peoples to throw it over and meet the difficulties by substituting less responsive control, exempt from the discord
and distraction of purpose that is apparently inherent in
a representative state. Even here among us, if your experience is like mine, there is an undercurrent of protest,
a discontent which I cannot help finding ominous. In
what I have to say, I want to suggest that the result is
not as bad as it seems, and that, good or bad, we still de-
rive from it advantages which are irreplaceable in any
other system. If you insist, I shall ask no more than that
you agree with Dean Inge that even though counting
heads is not an ideal way to govern, at least it is better
than breaking them. We do more than count; we measure political forces by the aggressiveness and coherence
of conflicting classes, and this, though it may be the
despair of the reformers, I should like to put in a more
respectable light. It may not be an ideal, I shall argue
that it is a tolerable, system; that it can insure continuity
and give room for slow change, since it allows play to
the actual, if unrecognized, organs of society.

One difficulty at any rate in the traditional theory is
inherent; it arises from our necessary preoccupations and
our incapacity to understand and deal with the multitude of questions that increasingly call for answer in a
desperately complicated world. I do not know how it is

with you, but for myself I generally give up at the outset.
The simplest problems which come up from day to day
seem to me quite unanswerable as soon as I try to get
below the surface. Each side, when I hear it, seems to me
right till I hear the other. I have neither the time nor the
ability to learn the facts, or to estimate their importance
if I knew them; I am disposed to accept the decision of
those charged with the responsibility of dealing with
them. My vote is one of the most unimportant acts of
my life; if I were to acquaint myself with the matters
on which it ought really to depend, if I were to try to
get a judgment on which I was willing to risk affairs of
even the smallest moment, I should be doing nothing
else, and that seems a fatuous conclusion to a fatuous
undertaking. Because, if all were done, for what after
all does my single voice count among so many? Surely
I can play my part better in the society where I chance
to be, if I stick to my last, and leave governing to those
who have had the temerity to accept the job. Distracted
by the confusion, and conscious that I can reach no
sound opinion, I turn away from any share in it and go
about my business. I am aware of those protests of my
youth, lingering in memory, calling upon me to gird my
loins and fall to. But then I reflect; excellent citizens
banded to secure good government; youths full of aspiration and high resolve, ready to turn their swords against
the giants; election returns leaving all outside the breast-
work, shining examples of the noble dead. This is not an
uncommon mood; indeed, the apathy of the modern voter
is the confusion of the modern reformer. I live where
that apathy seems to have attacked even the deepest
ganglia; no disclosures, no scandals, can stir the voters

from their inertia. Doubtless things might become uncomfortable enough to arouse them, but, given reasonable opportunity for personal favors, and a not too irksome control, they are content to abdicate their sovereignty and to be fleeced, if the shepherds will only shear them in their sleep.

That was not the presupposition of our traditional democracy, which assumed an intelligent attention and capacity in public affairs, and a will directed towards the general good. We have surely outgrown the conditions it assumed, and the theory has ceased to work. In Europe they have tried another scheme, partly on paper, partly in practice. Recognizing that most men are bound in the end to look out for themselves, and to know more about their own affairs than anything else, they have either deliberately or by unconscious acceptance, recognized that government will inevitably react to the pressures of economic or social classes, which thus have become internal organs of the state. True, there must be some central control, a brain, as it were, where cross-impulses may neutralize each other; and indeed, so far as this has been omitted, as in theory at times it appears to have been, the machinery is incomplete. But granted such a nexus, there is much in modern politics which seems to present just that picture. I think that in spite of our reluctance, we are coming to the same situation here; have come to it, indeed.

It would indeed be the plainest folly to pretend that such a system works for the best; we see about us everywhere evidences to the contrary. We lose the forest for the trees, forgetting, even so far as we think at all, that we are trustees for those who come after us, squandering

94

the patrimony which we have received. It seems scarcely better statecraft to turn over a society to the scramble of organized minorities than to leave it to be looted by bands of mercenaries under partisan chiefs. We must confess our apostasy; but before we abandon the ritual, is it not best to consider in what the faith has failed, and whether we may not use the old formulas with another meaning? The notion of a common will has teased political philosophers from the outset. It gets its completest expression in the Hegelian State which made its highest bid for dominance during the Great War and failed; the State, as an entity, an organism apart from those who compose it, a creature to which they owe unquestioning allegiance, and which may dispose of them at its own inscrutable pleasure. In theory that form of idolatry has never got much hold on men who speak English; in practice, the modern cult of the nation is hardly distinguishable; it veils itself behind the fiction of a common will. Just where that will resides, or how it is made manifest, is not too plain; like other deities, it is wise not to expose itself too freely. Is it for example to be found in a referendum? Perhaps so; I can think of no complete incarnation. If you put a question for categorical answer to a multitude, you may say that the majority has expressed itself. You may be wrong; in any case your assurance is factitious; men often answer for reasons quite alien to the issue; they seldom have anything that can truly be called an opinion. Their leaders take sides as their interests direct, and they follow because they are used to follow. Indeed it may be better so. You remember Private Willis in *Iolanthe*: "But then the prospect of a lot of dull M.P.'s in close proximity, each thinking for himself, is what no man can face with equanimity." We recently had a referendum in New York about extending the forest preserve. The city voted for it by a large majority; yet as I walk the streets I do not see afforestation written with conviction on the harried faces of my fellow-citizens. I suspect that the powers sent out word—for what subtle reason I do not know—that that amendment was to pass, and pass it did. Was there a common will in New York about adding to the forest preserve? I doubt it. Moreover, granting that at times we do so get an expression of a genuine opinion, belief, attitude—call it what you will—it must be sporadic and limited; one cannot carry on government by referendum—surely not among one hundred and twenty million people. They must act by deputy, and how much common will is there then?

You are familiar enough with the mechanism. Every man who aspires to office wants, if he is worth his salt, to be returned. Why else should he go in; why accept an interruption in his normal vocation, long enough to disrupt it, but not to achieve substantial results elsewhere? And how can he be returned? He looks upon an inert mass of constituents, who care little for themselves as citizens at large, but very much for this measure or that, which affects them in their livelihood. Make me prosperous in my job, and I will take care of myself in my other relations. How much of the history of tariff legislation, for instance, can be written in those words? To promote their special interests they form groups with inconveniently long memories, before which their memories as undifferentiated voters are like the spring snows. The common will as the official sees it, is not common at all; it is a complex of opposing forces, whose resultant has no relation to the common good, but which will nevertheless decide whether he goes back or not. That mechanical equation is his master; he is not the mouth-piece of the people's voice, or any other Hegelian Absolute, realizing its eternal essence in the solution of opposites. And so the common good is squeezed out, and enterprises of great pith and moment fall by the way. The more compact, determined and relentless the groups with which he must deal, the more they have to say in his fate. He must pick his way nicely, must learn to placate though not to yield too much, to have the art of honeyed words but not to seem neutral, and above all to keep constantly audible, visible, likable, even kissable. There are indeed more exhilarating moments when he may strike boldly, but they are not frequent and the effect is apt to be transitory; they are not so good as a supply of advice to mothers which comes in every evening just after bed-time stories.

That, I agree, is not a pretty picture; it did not intrude into the inspired reveries of Thomas Jefferson; though it has hag-ridden the thoughts of his political descendants, and gives them pause. Is there any answer? I suspect not; but there may be solace. After all, silken purses come only from busy silk-worms; we must weave with what we have. The millennium is still beyond the horizon; just beyond, if you insist, but not yet in sight. Have we the qualities of our defects? In the first place, why must we hold altogether illegitimate the advantage that cohesion, assiduity and persistence bring in government as elsewhere? By what right do we count those who have not the energy or intelligence to make themselves felt, equiv-

alents of those who have? I have yet to learn that political masses must be weighed by counting molecules
and disregarding atomic weights. In any society, I submit, the aggressive and insistent will have disproportion-
ate power. For myself, I confess I should like it otherwise; I prefer the still small voice of reason, but then I
am timid and constitutionally incompetent in such matters. But, though I would build the world anew and
nearer to the heart's desire, if I could, I do not propose
to cry for the moon. In a world where the stronger have
always had their way, I am glad if I can keep them from
having it without stint.

It seems to me, with all its defects, our system does
just that. For, abuse it as you will, at least it gives a
bloodless measure of social forces—bloodless, have you
thought of that?—a means of continuity, a principle of
stability, a relief from the paralyzing terror of revolution.
I have been where this was not true; in lands where one
felt the pervasive foreboding of violence, of armed suppression, the inability of minorities to exert just those
peaceful pressures, that seem to us so vicious; where government is conducted not by compromise, but by coup
d'état. And I have looked back with contentment to my
own country, distracted as she might be by a Babel of
many voices, uncertain of her purposes and her path;
where yet there can be revolution without machine guns,
and men may quit a public office and retain a private life.
Given an opportunity to impose our will, a ground where
we may test our mettle, we get the sense that there is
some propriety in yielding to those who impose upon us.
There has been an outlet, a place of reckoning, a means
not of counting heads, but of matching wits and courage.

If these are fairly measured, most of us acquiesce; we are conscious of a stronger power which it is idle to resist, until we in turn have organized in more formidable array and can impress ourselves in turn. And so I will not declaim against the evils of our time, the selfishness of class struggle, the disregard of the common good. Nor will I forsake the faith of our fathers in democracy, however I must transmute it, and make it unlovely to their eyes, were they here to see their strangely perverse disciple. If you will give me scales by which to weigh Tom and Dick and Harry as to their fitness to rule, and tell me how much each shall count, I will talk with you about some other kind of organization. Plato jumped hurdles that are too high for my legs; maybe you can help me over, or lower them. But unless you do, I will stand in the place that I am accustomed to. I will say that there must be a trying-out of men, according to their qualities as God has made them; that it is a precious inheritance, which we must not abjure, that that chance exists; that we must write down our miscarriages to our own flaccid selves. Meanwhile we shall not bottle up the gases and prepare for the inevitable explosion.

And so when I hear so much impatient and irritable complaint, so much readiness to replace what we have by guardians for us all, those supermen, evoked somewhere from the clouds, whom none have seen and none are ready to name, I lapse into a dream, as it were. I see children playing on the grass; their voices are shrill and discordant as children's are; they are restive and quarrelsome; they cannot agree to any common plan; their play annoys them; it goes so poorly. And one says, let us make Jack the master; Jack knows all about it; Jack will tell us

what each is to do and we shall all agree. But Jack is like
all the rest; Helen is discontented with her part and
Henry with his, and soon they fall again into their old
state. No, the children must learn to play by themselves;
there is no Jack the master. And in the end slowly and
with infinite disappointment they do learn a little; they
learn to forbear, to reckon with another, accept a little
where they wanted much, to live and let live, to yield
when they must yield; perhaps, we may hope, not to take
all they can. But the condition is that they shall be willing at least to listen to one another, to get the habit of
pooling their wishes. Somehow or other they must do this,
if the play is to go on; maybe it will not, but there is no
Jack, in or out of the box, who can come to straighten
the game.

We are meeting tonight just ninety-one years from the
day on which one first saw the light, who for far more
than the ordinarily allotted span has played a high and
shining part among us. Seventy years after he lay mor-
tally wounded, as they thought, on a defeated field, he
was still in the service of his country, lending lustre to
that court which we all delight to honor. At last he has
sheathed his sword, and takes his leisure like the gallant
soldier that he is. Another takes his seat, happily his
rightful heir, his one authentic successor. There is no
tribute we can give him which he has not had; no honor
which we shall do more than repeat. What perhaps we
can do is to try to understand his message, the upshot of
his life. In this we are apt to go astray; we have no right
to impute to him the version we may carry off, for he
wrote not for the mass. Them that have eyes to see, let
them see; them that have ears to hear, let them hear. It

is a hard saying, and most of all do I doubt my own capacity as interpreter. And yet, in one way or another, we
must all assume that role; for we cannot ignore what he
said; we must read and write our own gloss. To me at any
rate it seems that that message is not unlike in spirit what
I have been trying to say. Man may be a little lower than
the angels, but he has not yet shaken off the brute. His
passions, his thinking, his body carry their origins with
them; and he fails, if he vaingloriously denies them. His
path is strewn with carnage, the murderer lurks always
not far beneath, to break out from time to time, peace
resolutions to the contrary notwithstanding. What he
has gained has been with immeasurable waste; what he
shall gain will be with immeasurably more. Trial and
error is the confession, not indeed of an impotent, but of
a wayward, creature, blundering about in worlds not
realized. But the Absolute is mute; no tables come from
Sinai to guide him; the brazen sky gives no answer to
his prayers. He must grope his way through the murk, as
his remote forerunners groped, in the dank, hot world in
which they moved. Look where he will, there are no im-
mutable laws to which he can turn; no, not even that in
selfless abnegation he must give up what he craves, for
life is self-assertion. Conflict is normal; we reach accom-
modations as wisdom may teach us that it does not pay
to fight. And wisdom may; for wisdom comes as false
assurance goes—false assurance, that grows from pride in
our powers and ignorance of our ignorance. Beware then
of the heathen gods; have no confidence in principles
that come to us in the trappings of the eternal. Meet
them with gentle irony, friendly scepticism and an open
soul. Nor be cast down; for it is always dawn. Day breaks

forever, and above the eastern horizon the sun is now about to peep. Full light of day? No, perhaps not ever. But yet it grows lighter, and the paths that were so blind will, if one watches sharply enough, become hourly plainer. We shall learn to walk straighter. Yes, it is always dawn.

11

HOW FAR IS A JUDGE FREE
IN RENDERING A DECISION?
[1935]

"How Far Is a Judge Free in Rendering a Decision?"
was presented on May 14, 1933 over a nation-wide radio
network of the Columbia Broadcasting System. It was
printed as Lecture No. 14 in Law Series I (pp. 1–6) of
the National Advisory Council on Radio in Education.
The council was formed three years earlier, with Robert A.
Millikin as president, "to further the art of radio broadcasting in education." Learned Hand's part in the program is reprinted with permission of the University of
Chicago Press, which published it.

I have chosen as a subject tonight, how far a judge is
free in rendering a decision, because I know that in many
people's minds there is much confusion about it. To
some it seems that a judge ought to look to his conscience and follow its dictates; he ought not to be bound
by what they call technical rules, having no relation to
natural right and wrong. Others wish him to observe very
strictly what they consider the law, reading it as though
it were all to be found in written words, and never de-
parting from the literal meaning. They demand this of
him because they say, and rightly, that he ought not to
usurp the power of government, and they believe that to
exercise his own judgment as to the justice of the cause
would be just such a usurpation. I believe that neither
side is right, and, although I am afraid that the subject

will seem abstract and dry, still it is important, and it is well for us to try to come to some understanding about it. The first thing is to find out what we mean by law.

Legal philosophers have disputed for more than two thousand years about what law means. Some have thought that it includes the customs or usages which are generally current in a society; others have held that it should be limited to those rules which will be enforced by the government. The question is perhaps one of words, but as I am speaking of civilized modern society, it will be more convenient to use the word in the second sense. Law does not mean then whatever people usually do, or even what they think to be right. Certainly it does not mean what only the most enlightened individuals usually do or think right. It is the conduct which the government, whether it is a king, or a popular assembly, will compel individuals to conform to, or to which it will at least provide forcible means to secure conformity. If this is true, there must be some way to learn what is this conduct. The law is the command of the government, and it must be ascertainable in some form if it is to be enforced at all.

The only way in which its will can be put is in words, and in modern and civilized societies these are always written. They are in the form of statutes enacted formally, or they are in books which report what has been decided before by judges whom the government gave power to decide. There is no inevitable reason why that should be law which has been decided before, and in many countries this is not true. But it is true in ours, as it is in most countries which Englishmen settled and

104

where English speech prevails. Perhaps it ought not to be, but it is. In all civilized, and for that matter in practically all uncivilized, countries, there are judges who are charged with the duty of saying what the law means, that is, what the government has in fact commanded. When these judges have spoken, the force behind the law will be used.

It seems a simple matter, especially when the law is written down in a book with care and detail, just to read it and say what is its meaning. Perhaps this could be made as easy as it seems, if the law used language coined expressly for its purposes, like science, or mathematics, or music. But that would be practically undesirable, because while the government's commands are to be always obeyed, still they should include only what is generally accepted as just, or convenient, or usual, and should be stated in terms of common speech, so that they may be understood by those who must obey, and may not appear foreign to their notions of good or sensible conduct. Besides, even if the law had a language of its own, it could not provide for all situations which might come up. Nobody is so gifted with foresight that he can divine all possible human events in advance and prescribe the proper rule for each. Take, for example, a collision between two motor-cars. There is no way of saying beforehand exactly what each driver should do or should not, until all the circumstances of the particular case are known. The law leaves this open with the vague command to each that he shall be careful. What being careful means, it does not try to say; it leaves that to the judge, who happens in this case to be a jury of twelve persons, untrained in the law. That is a case where the appeal is almost entirely to the conscience of the tribunal.

The judge must therefore find out the will of the government from words which are chosen from common speech and which had better not attempt to provide for every possible contingency. How does he in fact proceed? Although at times he says and believes that he is not doing so, what he really does is to take the language before him, whether it be from a statute or from the decision of a former judge, and try to find out what the government, or his predecessor, would have done, if the case before him had been before them. He calls this finding the intent of the statute or of the doctrine. This is often not really true. The men who used the language did not have any intent at all about the case that has come up; it had not occurred to their minds. Strictly speaking, it is impossible to know what they would have said about it, if it had. All they have done is to write down certain words which they mean to apply generally to situations of that kind. To apply these literally may either pervert what was plainly their general meaning, or leave undisposed of what there is every reason to suppose they meant to provide for. Thus it is not enough for the judge just to use a dictionary. If he should do no more, he might come out with a result which every sensible man would recognize to be quite the opposite of what was really intended; which would contradict or leave unfulfilled its plain purpose.

Thus, on the one hand, he cannot go beyond what has been said, because he is bound to enforce existing commands and only those; on the other, he cannot suppose that what has been said should clearly frustrate or leave unexecuted its own purpose. This is his frequent position in cases that are not very plain; that is to say, in the greater number that arise. As I have said, there are two extreme schools, neither one of which is really willing to apply its theory consistently, usually applying it when its interests lie along the path it advocates. One school says that the judge must follow the letter of the law absolutely. I call this the dictionary school. No matter what the result is, he must read the words in their usual meaning and stop where they stop. No judges have ever carried on literally in that spirit, and they would not be long tolerated if they did. Nobody would in fact condemn the surgeon who bled a man in the street to cure him, because there was a law against drawing blood in the streets. Everyone would say that the law was only meant to prevent street fighting, and was not intended to cover such a case; that is, that the government which passed that law, although literally it used words which covered the case, did not in fact forbid necessary assistance to sick people. An obviously absurd extreme of that school was where a guilty man escaped, because the indictment left out the word "the," alleging that what he did was "against the peace of state," instead of "against the peace of *the* state." The statute had said that to convict a man the indictment must read like that, but the statute did not mean every syllable it contained.

It is easy to seize on such instances and say that judges are always too literal and that what is needed are men of more common sense. Men of common sense are always needed, and judges are by no means always men of common sense. They are quite like the rest of us. But it is also easy to go wrong, if one gives them too much latitude. The other school would give them almost complete latitude. They argue that a judge should not regard the law; that this has never really been done in the past, and that to attempt ever to do it is an illusion. He must conform his decision to what honest men would think right, and it is better for him to look into his own heart to find out what that is. As I have already said, in a small way some such process is inevitable when one is interpreting any written words. When a judge tries to find out what the government would have intended which it did not say, he puts into its mouth things which he thinks it ought to have said, and that is very close to substituting what he himself thinks right. Let him beware, however, or he will usurp the office of government, even though in a small way he must do so in order to execute its real commands at all.

In our country we have always been extremely jealous of mixing the different processes of government, especially that of making law, with that of saying what it is after it has been made. This distinction, if I am right, cannot be rigidly enforced; but like most of those ideas, which the men who made our constitutions believed in, it has a very sound basis as a guide, provided one does not try to make it into an absolute rule, like driving to the right. They wanted to have a government by the people, and they believed that the only way they could do it, was by giving the power to make laws to assemblies which the people chose, directly or at second hand. They believed that such assemblies would express the common will of the people who were to rule. Never mind what they thought that common will was; it is not so simple as it seems to learn just what they did mean by it, or what anybody can mean. It is enough that they did not mean by it what any one individual, whether or not he was a judge, should think right and proper. They might have made the judge the mouthpiece of the common will, finding it out by his contacts with people generally; but he would then have been ruler, like the Judges of Israel. Still, they had to leave him scope in which he in a limited sense does act as if he were the government, because, as we have seen, he cannot otherwise do what he is required to do. So far they had to confuse lawmaking with law-interpreting.

But the judge must always remember that he should go no further than he is sure the government would have gone, had it been faced with the case before him. If he is in doubt, he must stop, for he cannot tell that the conflicting interests in the society for which he speaks would have come to a just result, even though he is sure that he knows what the just result should be. He is not to substitute even his juster will for theirs; otherwise it would not be the common will which prevails, and to that extent the people would not govern.

So you will see that a judge is in a contradictory position; he is pulled by two opposite forces. On the one hand he must not enforce whatever he thinks best; he must leave that to the common will expressed by the government. On the other, he must try as best he can to put into concrete form what that will is, not by slavishly following the words, but by trying honestly to say what was the underlying purpose expressed. Nobody does this exactly right; great judges do it better than the rest of us. It is necessary that someone shall do it, if we are to realize the hope that we can collectively rule ourselves. And so, while it is proper that people should find fault when their judges fail, it is only reasonable that they should recognize the difficulties. Perhaps it is also fair to ask that before the judges are blamed they shall be given the credit of having tried to do their best. Let them be severely brought to book, when they go wrong, but by those who will take the trouble to understand.

12

TO THE HARVARD ALUMNI
ASSOCIATION
[1936]

ALWAYS a devoted son of his alma mater, Learned Hand
served as president of the Harvard Alumni Association in
1935–6. The address which he gave in this capacity at the
1936 commencement, on June 18, appeared in the Harvard Alumni Bulletin, July 3, 1936 (Vol. XXXVIII, pp.
1195–7), from which it is reprinted with permission.

My gay, youthful, and irrepressible predecessor in this
office told you last year that he would vary the tradition
by which the president of the alumni was permitted to
preach a little sermon on Commencement Day. I shall
not follow his example. I shall restore the ritual; the
blood of a Baptist preacher runs in my veins, and I cannot tell when again I shall have so large and goodly an
audience as this; the temptation is too much. Let me reassure you, however; I am convinced that no souls are
saved after the first five or ten minutes, so that your
ordeal, whatever else it may be, will be short.

I shall borrow my text from the shield of the University, not "Veritas," as perhaps you may assume, for I
confess that that is a little threadbare, and our historian
assures us that it has not constantly perched upon our
banner; there was a period when it flew away, to return
perhaps a hundred years ago. Rather I shall select our
other legend, "Christo et Ecclesiae," and ask you to consider what it can mean to a secular university in the 20th

century. Those resolute men who founded Harvard and chose those words certainly meant by them much that we should not accept today; but that is not important, if there be an enduring truth that we can gather from them; if we can safely put new wine into the old bottles. To the Puritan Community of Saints this life on earth was no more than a trial and preparation for eternity; its values lapsed into insignificance before the awful realities of Heaven and Hell; and man's nature was corrupt until redeemed, and could be redeemed only by ineffable Grace. Yet when all was said, redemption was only a return to man's pristine innocence, and salvation was not an alien mould into which the soul was forced, but the harmonious development of what had all along been its proper form and pattern. And so I think that when the founders of this institution dedicated it to Christ and His Church, they showed their faith that there was a learning, and that there were studies, through which men might learn the soul's real structure; her needs and her possibilities. It was for these and for no merely practical, temporary, and casual ends that they planted this, the first flower of their wilderness; it was in solemn consecration to the salvation of mankind.

Is there anything in this which is still relevant to us today, whose background and whose beliefs have so much changed? May I illustrate from my own experience? Some years ago I went through one of the great moving picture factories at Hollywood; I was first shown the settings and allowed to watch a scene out of a play as it was being rehearsed, over and over again. Then I was taken to the recording machines in charge of dignified, intelligent young mechanicians, more properly scientists, of the lower ranks perhaps, but still deserving that high title. The contrast was, to me at any rate, so depressing that I have never forgotten it. Who could resist the inspiration of the magic by which light and sound were converted into some other essence, instantaneously transported, and made permanent upon a tiny celluloid strip? When one reflected upon the years of devotion and ingenuity, of seething imagination, and of patient verification which lay behind these results, it seemed an honor merely to be one of a species which could do such things. What a piece of work is Man!

But the other side of the shield was as dreadful as the first was inspiring; for the only uses to which this wizard seemed to know how to put his divine powers were beyond endurance tawdry, trite, dreary, and childish. Of what value was it to scale the heavens, to descend to the bowels of the earth, to practise alchemy and all the necromancer's art, if the end were to be so pitiful as this? The whole seemed to have been designed on the theory that one thing was as good as another provided it could, and would, be consumed. That was the vital fallacy. There is no democracy among human values, however each may cry out for an equal vote. It is the business of the soul to impose her own order upon the clamorous rout; to establish a hierarchy appropriate to the demands of her own nature, and by the mere fiat of her absolute choice, if that be based upon self-knowledge. That self-knowledge is the sole legitimate purpose of a university, to achieve and to impart. And the quest for it comprehends whatever is in the earth and the waters and the sky, and in the minds of men and of the angels; for the soul is of this world and cannot safely assume in advance what will prove alien to her, not yet knowing herself. What seems remote today may be intimate and crucial tomorrow. It is the cause; it is the cause that counts; and that must not be acquisition or affluence or power; but that, knowing herself, the soul shall be free, free to be herself; that, should she achieve success and learn the pattern of her needs, she may safely trust her will. In the Abbey of Thélème, where all were gracious, harmonious, joyous, and wise, there were no orders and no laws, save one: "*Fais ce que voudra.*" I would write that on the gates of every university; and I would shape the curriculum solely to teach and learn what those words really mean.

And with this I shall end, conscious indeed that I may seem to have strived after a paradox, but unrepentant of my inconsistency, and indeed protesting that there has been none. For I insist that our forebears meant that salvation was not to be gained by propitiating demons, or averting evil, or conforming with tradition, or by escape into action, or by any other anodyne or evasion. They founded this institution in the faith that by enlightenment men would gain insight into their own being, and that in proportion as they succeeded, they should be free to follow their hearts' desire. A communion of those who lived by that measure, would it not be the City of God, over whose portal there might be written: "Christo et Ecclesiae"?

13

AT THE HARVARD TERCENTENARY
OBSERVANCE
[1936]

THE greatest academic occasion in the long and rich experience of Learned Hand was the observance of the three-hundredth anniversary of the founding of Harvard, culminating in a three-day celebration, September 16–18, 1936. He had been president of the Alumni Association until June 1936; and was on that account one of the speakers at the Tercentenary. His address, delivered on September 18, appeared in the Harvard Alumni Bulletin, September 30, 1936 (Vol. XXXIX, pp. 37–40), from which it is reprinted with permission.

If one of the founders of this College were to reappear here today, it is doubtful whether he would not regret his endeavors, and wish that his work had long since passed into chaos and black night. True, much would fascinate and bewitch him; the variety of the searches into so many fields, the ingenuity with which nature has been trapped to reveal her secrets, the imagination and patience of the search, the commonwealth of scholars who open their discoveries to the world that there may be no monopoly of learning. He would be astounded at the command over the earth and its resources which such studies as are here pursued had given to mankind; he would think it magic that through them men had learned to transport themselves so swiftly, to talk and to write, and to see instantaneously at any distance; by an alchemy of which he had only dreamed, to transmute substances, to divine the location of metals and of hidden sources of energy. Looking more widely, he would be amazed at the cleanliness of cities, at the certainty with which a continuous supply of food was provided, at the hospitals open to all, where the body is painlessly relieved of many of its torments and its ailments are subtly unravelled and often cured. He would be delighted at the ways by which knowledge of the past could be deciphered from broken stones, potsherds, and ruined walls; he would feel the sweep of his antiquity and the drama of his history, when he found how bit by bit its mosaic was being sagaciously filled out. All this and much more he would feel, and it would exhilarate him and make him thankful that he had had any part in a venture which could so contribute to man's freedom and enlightenment, to his command over his fate, to his independence of chance.

But when the first shock was past, and after he had become habituated to the pageant of these wonders, another feeling would succeed, if he had been a true child of his time. He would remember the purpose with which he and his fellows had founded this pious testimonial to their faith. It was to inculcate a knowledge of God and of His ways, of man's duty and of his dependence. All this he would find absent; it would seem to him as though a rich table had been spread, and youth were invited to choose from it at random; as though there were no direction, nothing to guide it to an understanding of its duties, its interests, or its fate. Worse than that, there would appear to be a positive, though implicit, assumption that neither duties, interest, nor fate could in fact be comprehended; for everywhere he would infer that the knowledge of truth, if not truth itself, was assumed to be an accidental acquisition, depending upon how far happy intuition might turn out to be verified by experiment, so far as experiment could be so conducted as to be a valid test, which was seldom the case. For the rest, youth was left to its own devices because nobody had a substitute which he would guarantee, or indeed even venture, to put forward. Our founder, seeing his College, which he had hoped would help towards an understanding of divine truth, thus reduced to a Tower of Babel, might well wish that he had spared his pains, and even regret that he had been called back at all for a glimpse of their profanation.

I remember, when I was at this College many years ago, going to a lecture by President Eliot about the early teaching of Louis Agassiz. He said that Agassiz used to give each pupil a piece of stone and tell him to examine it, and report to him what he found. One boy came back in a few hours ready to answer. "Not yet," said Agassiz, "come back in a fortnight." The boy told his father, who was much disgusted: "That is absurd," he said, "that is the way a puppy learns." "Yes gentlemen," said to us that serene, majestic presence, "Yes gentlemen, that is the way a puppy learns, and that is the way each one of us must learn." Probably you will agree. In that symbol we have conquered, and it has become our gospel. Truth can be ascertained only through trial and error; no education is worthy the name which does not acquaint the student, in however small a field, with that method at first hand. Only so can he escape from leading strings.

Yet in another sense the boy's father was right. So far

as we can tell, the native powers of mankind have not improved for thousands of years; our remote ancestors were as good as we. If a child today knows more than Aristotle it is only because he is the inheritor of a mass of acquired and ordered experiences. Life is too short, and experiment too costly, for the individual to verify an appreciable part of what the race has learned; he must be content to depend upon authority and can hope for no longer contribution of his own than to establish the hall-marks by which he may divide the true prophets from the false.

Empiricists in theory we may boast ourselves, bound to accept nothing that will not withstand all tests; but practically, we are condemned to be authoritarians, and must guide our lives by the authentic deliverances of accredited sages. That would not be so bad, if the inward universe of will and feeling remained our own. And so indeed it seems at first to do; we love, we desire, we welcome, we reject, all as the spirit listeth. There is nothing good or bad but thinking makes it so; our choices are underived; as to them we recognize no authority. Nor need it concern us though their origin be in our bodies and their occurrence be dependent upon the outside world. It is enough if we are unaware of the impact of influences felt to be alien and coercive; freedom we need not trouble to distinguish from the consciousness of freedom. Here at last we can be ourselves.

If man were an ephemera, living for an hour, he might reason so. Each choice would then be without significance beyond itself, without implication or consequence; the absolute self-affirmation of a god. But he lives in time and amid his kind; he looks before and after, his days are bound each to each, and he has his being only as a member of a group. That continuity and that communal nature clip his wings and cage his flights. Not only to predict the future consequences of his conduct, but to appraise them in advance after he has done so, he must resort to the experience of others. It is true that when I choose between present goods—between push-pin and poetry let us say—I am dealing directly with absolute data, the irreducible atoms of the moral universe. Incommensurable they may be, but I measure them; my choice is the deepest manifestation of my being; no mediation is necessary, and nothing more is to be said. But when I choose between my present and my future good, or between my own welfare and another's, I am conscious of no such self-sufficiency. Be my will as pure as a saint's, how am I to weigh your advantage against my own? I can have no intuitive warrant for knowing that what is good for me is good for you. Or how is my own ghostly future to take on a body that I can match against the poignant demands of the moment? Perhaps I shall exact an undue discount of the absent good, or perhaps I shall overvalue it; I must in any event have recourse to some arbiter outside my immediate self, which can make these phantoms real. I must recognize an authority just as though I were dealing with the outside world; in fact that is what I am dealing with. And so the wise have taught since the first syllable of recorded time. The individual must not be left to his own moral devices; somewhere, somehow, he must be able to find a rule, a plan, a course, a map, to show him the path of his salvation. Our founder seems then to have been justified; there must be oracles to which youth may repair, and whose message we may and should inculcate. We cannot leave it to the bias of the immediate; liberty is an illusion, useful only when antiquated authority is to be overthrown, but of itself a signal for chaos and a symptom of decay.

Is there no answer? Perhaps not; not at least over the whole of that vast future which lies before us. Conceivably the time may come when the heart shall be so understood, and men shall have become so benign, that there will be a gentle rule which each will feel to be his own; when there will be not even a wilful handful to rebel against standards in perfect conformity with a common human nature. We have no glimmering of the infinite varieties of those patterns which the future has in store. Besides, what is it we wish to preserve? Is it disregard of the wisdom of the ages? Is it insensibility to the welfare of our fellows? Is it yielding to the moment's impulse against the counsels of prudence? What is this freedom which escapes all bounds, and would set its face against an ordered universe? The less of it, the better. And yet, and yet, when all is said; when the counsels of prudence and the admonitions of virtue have been heeded; when the future has been discounted, and the claims of others have been measured; "though reason chafe, there comes a voice without reply," deep from the recesses of our being. Inarticulate, primitive, animal perhaps, but imperious, not to be denied. The core of life remains untouched, the kernel from which the rest has come. Absolute, unbound, knowing no loyalties but a single loyalty, admitting no coercion, its very essence in its affirmation, the self asserts its unassailable right to create all values, what it chooses alone is good. Others may command, it may be forced to comply; but within, its rule is unimpaired; it knows no compromise; it brooks no equal. That is the unbending spirit we would foster; that is the freedom we wish to insure. These would be mad, whirling words to our founder, justifying his worst fears; the insolent defiance by a puny creature of his Maker, through whose grace alone he might hope to escape damnation. Perhaps he would be right; but even on his own premises that is not too clear. For why did that doctrine on which he set his faith spread over the world? Was it not just because it whispered in the weary ears of the downtrodden that each life was sacred, that each fate was momentous? A sparrow cannot fall without God's will. Can that be sacred which another bids? Can that be momentous which is derived? The command alone can be sacred; the original alone can be momentous. Implicit was the belief that man, and man alone, creates the universe of good and evil; that beyond and beneath all commandments is the commandment, "Be Thyself."

Three hundred years hence men may once again gather here on a mission like ours; we cannot foreshadow their faiths, their hopes, their compromises, their loyalties. Could we return, these would seem to us strange and perverse, as ours will seem to them, brought as they will be out of limbo for the curious. Complaisance may be the order of that day; all may freely acknowledge the mild rule of all. Nature then will know "such harmony alone could hold all Heaven and Earth in happier union," and "Heaven, as at some festival, will open wide the gates of her high palace hall." We shall appear thin and childish, defiant out of fear for our petty selves which stood in need only of enlightenment. So be it. Life is a dicer's throw; and reason, a smoky torch. We move by what light we have; but some light we need to move at all. That commandment then be ours; with it we will grope our way. A long procession of future generations will weigh our faith, and we shall never know the verdict. Nor need we care. Yonder our oriflamme unfurls.

14

FOREWORD TO THE *HARVARD LAW REVIEW*, VOLUME L
[1936]

His *long interest in the* Harvard Law Review, *as demonstrated by his own important contributions to its pages, made Learned Hand the ideal choice for author of the foreword to mark the appearance of the fiftieth volume. This issue appeared in November 1936, with his inspiriting preface on pp. 1–3. It is reprinted with permission. Earlier contributions of Learned Hand to the* Harvard Law Review *are listed on p. 13 of this book.*

With this number the fiftieth volume of the *Review* begins. It is the plan to give over the whole of it to a series of surveys, devoted, with one or two exceptions, to some particular subject, and written by a specialist. These will undertake to review the progress of the law during the last fifty years, and as a whole they should constitute a fairly complete legal picture of the period. It has been one that deserves some such analysis and commemoration; during it there have been the beginnings of outlooks and attitudes of whose consequences we can have not the slightest intimation. The legal relations between the individual and the community which arise out of the production and distribution of property, comprise by far the greater, and more important, part of the law; subtract these and very little content would be left. The theory of feudalism was that property was held conditionally on the performance of social duties; I call them social because although there was not as yet properly any "state" as we now know it, one's legal duties to one's lord were as nearly social as could then be; and while these were for the most part military, defense and aggression were the chief communal activities. After gunpower and the long-bow had in the fifteenth century destroyed the bases of that system, though it continued vestigially for several centuries, its rationale disappeared; and while the Tudors were forging the English commonwealth, legal theory created no new nexus of property and duties; the notion that tenure was conditional upon the performance of prescribed activities was for the most part gone. So far as it remained, as it always has, through the public administration of the squirearchy, it was no part of legal theory.

It was obviously impossible that the American colonists of the seventeenth century should have maintained, even if they had inherited it, a tradition of communal servitudes, so to say; the conditions would have made it unreal. The individual asked little of society, and himself created whatever value his meager possessions acquired. On the contrary he established, and handed on, a notion of society as an aggregation of monads, legally bound together as lightly as possible and for few common purposes; that was indeed the ideal of Thomas Jefferson, and in 1886 it was still in outline the prevailing belief. It might have yielded sooner than it did, had it not been for the authority of the English economists of the second quarter of the nineteenth century, whose interpretation of the Industrial Revolution was so palatable to a community, much of it still actually pioneer, and all of it of pioneer mentality. But yield it did not; and much of it even yet endures. It is quite true that there had always remained certain kinds of property whose tenure was conditional upon public service; but they had never been important until after the Civil War, when the railroads became the only means for the carriage of goods, and their operation was absolutely vital to the areas which they served. Yet it was less than fifty years ago that the Interstate Commerce Commission was established. Moreover, when the Supreme Court in Munn v. Illinois (94 U.S. 113 [1876]) in 1876 declared that one might assume public duties by devoting one's property to a public use, though one enjoyed no special franchise, it astounded the profession and opened new vistas of which indeed we have by no means yet seen the end.

While it is a mistake to assume that technological changes, even when revolutionary, inevitably presuppose new legal adaptations, in the last century they created a wholly new social structure out of which new legal relations became imperative. Every smallest step of modern industry depends upon a co-operation whose maintenance and regulation is the very stuff of law. Furthermore, it was during the last half century that the practice became common, by means of the private corporation, to conduct industry without personal liability. True, it has always been possible to impose any desired conditions upon the corporate property itself, but the need is doubled when responsibility is so slackened, and when it becomes possible for managers to seize the stewardship of enormous congregations of plant and tools without effective control from within. The modern shareholder who, properly enough, looks upon himself as not charged with the duties of a management which he cannot master and would be helpless to direct if he could, has had therefore to accept public regulation to an extent which his grandfather with some justice would have resented, and of which he has surely yet seen but a small part. The period to be treated in these articles has therefore been the seeding-time for a crop of new ideas, based upon a revolutionary outlook. Final adjustments, if any are to be final, are certainly far in the future, but whatever the course may be, these years will be looked back upon as those in which the questions to be answered were emerging, and becoming clamorous. Nor does it seem to me that this movement was confined to public law. I agree that the general formulation of what, for example, will excuse the nonperformance of a contract, is not closely related to the enmeshed interdependence of modern industrial life. But the actual application of the formula may turn very largely upon just that, and upon how far individual conduct should be permeated with communal compunctions. This volume ought, therefore, to have a value for the future, which is not yet apparent to us; it will certainly have an interest quite different, and to me much greater, than, for example, a similar series of surveys for the period between 1836 and 1886. It was a happy decision so to celebrate the Fiftieth Anniversary of the *Review*.

15

IN MEMORY OF CHARLES NEAVE
[1938]

CHARLES NEAVE (1868–1937) was one of the country's
most distinguished patent lawyers. Born in Cincinnati,
he studied at Yale University and the Massachusetts Institute of Technology and then was graduated from Harvard College. He was counsel for and a director of the
General Electric Company and a member of the corporation of M.I.T. His New York law firm was Fish, Richard-
son & Neave. He served as president of the New York
Patent Law Association and it was at a memorial service
held by that organization that Learned Hand spoke these
words of tribute to his close friend.

When I came to the bench many years ago, Charles
Neave was already at the height of his powers. He was
tall and handsome—as you all remember; his presence
was at once impressive; his manner was quiet and reserved; he never raised his voice, or resorted to any ora-
torical tricks, relying always upon the force of his reason-
ing. He could condense what he had to say into the most
surprisingly small compass, both in his arguments and
in his briefs; whether this was the result of much labor,
or of an amazing facility, I was always puzzled to know.
He could make plain—or at least it seemed so to his hearers—complicated questions in chemistry and electricity,
with a clarity that was unequalled in my experience.
With the courage which only comes of justified self-
confidence, he dared to rest his case upon its strongest

point, and so avoided that appearance of weakness and uncertainty which comes of a clutter of arguments. Few lawyers are willing to do this; it is the mark of the most distinguished talent.

We shall not see his better in his field; indeed he had few, if any, equals. We cannot regret the end of such a life; we feel the separation, we can regret that he had no years after the strain of labor had ceased; but there is a perfection in its complete self-expression, as of some noble work of art, which does not depend upon duration. I ask you to rise and drink a toast with me to his memory.

16

MR. JUSTICE CARDOZO
[1939]

BENJAMIN NATHAN CARDOZO (1870–1938) served as Associate Justice of the United States Supreme Court for six years beginning in 1932, when he was appointed by President Herbert Hoover to succeed Justice Oliver Wendell Holmes, Jr. Cardozo had already won renown as the distinguished Chief Judge of the New York Court of Appeals at Albany, the highest of New York state courts, and as author of several brilliant books on jurisprudence. These included: The Nature of the Judicial Process (1921), The Growth of the Law (1924), The Paradoxes of Legal Science (1928), and Law and Literature (1931). On the Supreme Court, Justice Cardozo regularly did far more than his share of the work. His death brought such deep regret that in January 1939 the Columbia, Yale, and Harvard law-school journals joined in publishing simultaneous issues in tribute to him. Learned Hand's contribution to the symposium is reprinted with the permission of all three. The citations are: Harvard Law Review, Vol. LII, pp. 361–3; Yale Law Journal, Vol. XLVIII, pp. 379–81; Columbia Law Review, Vol. XXXIX, pp. 9–11.

The antinomy at the basis of a judge's work has been so often discussed that I can justify no more than a bare restatement of it. His authority and his immunity depend upon the assumption that he speaks with the mouth of others: the momentum of his utterances must be greater than any which his personal reputation and character can command, if it is to do the work assigned to it—if it is to stand against the passionate resentments arising out of the interests he must frustrate. He must pose as a kind of oracle, voicing the dictates of a vague divinity—a communion which reaches far beyond the memory of any now living, and has gathered up a prestige beyond that of any single man. Yet the customary law of English-speaking peoples stands, a structure indubitably made by the hands of generations of judges, each professing to be a pupil, yet each in fact a builder who has contributed his few bricks and his little mortar, often indeed under the illusion that he has added nothing. A judge must manage to escape both horns of this dilemma: he must preserve his authority by cloaking himself in the majesty of an overshadowing past; but he must discover some composition with the dominant trends of his time—at all hazards he must maintain that tolerable continuity without which society dissolves, and men must begin again the weary path up from savagery.

This was the problem that fascinated Cardozo throughout his life; about it he wrote with much beauty, insight and feeling. His solution of the contradiction was his great contribution to his time. Do not understand me to suppose that there is a solution in the sense that one finds an answer to a problem in algebra or geometry. There is no such solution; there seldom is to any of the real problems of life. But there are ways of going about a solution, and to find the right way constantly teased him. A judge must think of himself as an artist, he said, who, although he must know the handbooks, should never trust to them for his guidance; in the end he must rely upon his almost instinctive sense of where the line lay between the word and the purpose which lay behind it; he must somehow manage to be true to both. There were indeed times when I dared to question the paths by which he reached his goal, but it seems to me that almost never did I venture to say that he came out at the wrong place. His results had an unerring accuracy, which, in my case at any rate, usually left me altogether reconciled, and which curiously contrasted with his tentative, at times almost apologetic, approaches to them. He never disguised the difficulties, as lazy judges do who win the game by sweeping all the chessmen off the table: like John Stuart Mill, he would often begin by stating the other side better than its advocate had stated it himself. At times to those of us who knew him, the anguish which had preceded decision was apparent, for again and again, like Jacob, he had to wrestle with the angel all through the night; and he wrote his opinion with his very blood. But when once his mind came to rest, he was as inflexible as he had been uncertain before. No man ever gave more copiously of himself to all aspects of his problem, but he knew that it was a judge's duty to decide, not to debate, and the loser who asked him to re-open a decision once made found a cold welcome.

In all this I have not told you what qualities made it possible for him to find just that compromise between the letter and the spirit that so constantly guided him to safety. I have not told you, because I do not know. It was wisdom: and like most wisdom, his ran beyond the reasons which he gave for it. And what is wisdom—that gift of God which the great prophets of his race exalted? I do not know; like you, I know it when I see it, but I cannot tell of what it is composed. One ingredient I think I do know: the wise man is the detached man. By that I mean more than detached from his grosser interests—his advancement and his gain. Many of us can be that—I dare to believe that most judges can be, and are. I am thinking of something far more subtly interfused. Our convictions, our outlook, the whole make-up of our thinking, which we cannot help bringing to the decision of every question, is the creature of our past; and into our past have been woven all sorts of frustrated ambitions with their envies, and of hopes of preferment with their corruptions, which, long since forgotten, still determine our conclusions. A wise man is one exempt from the handicap of such a past; he is a runner stripped for the race; he can weigh the conflicting factors of his problem without always finding himself in one scale or the other. Cardozo was such a man; his gentle nature had in it no acquisitiveness; he did not use himself as a measure of value; the secret of his humor—a precious gift that he did not wear upon his sleeve—lay in his ability to get outside of himself, and look back. Yet from this self-effacement came a power greater than the power of him who ruleth a city. He was wise because his spirit was uncontaminated, because he knew no violence, or hatred, or envy, or jealousy, or ill-will. I believe that it was this purity that chiefly made him the judge we so much revere; more than his learning, his acuteness, and his fabulous industry. In this America of ours where the passion for publicity is a disease, and where swarms of foolish, tawdry moths dash with rapture into its consuming fire, it was a rare good fortune that brought to such eminence a man so reserved, so unassuming, so retiring, so gracious to high and low, and so serene. He is gone, and while the west is still lighted with his radiance, it is well for us to pause and take count of our own coarser selves. He has a lesson to teach us if we care to stop and learn; a lesson quite at variance with most that we practice, and much that we profess.

17

ON RECEIVING AN HONORARY DEGREE
[1939]

THE degree of Doctor of Laws was awarded to Learned Hand by Columbia University (1930), Yale (1931), the University of Pennsylvania (1933), Amherst (1938), Dartmouth (1938), Harvard (1939), Princeton (1947), New School for Social Research (1949), New York University (1951), Cambridge University (1952), University of the State of New York (1952), and University of Chicago (1952). The Harvard citation, read on June 22, 1939, described him as: "A judge worthy of his name, judicial in his temper, profound in his knowledge; a philosopher whose decisions affect a nation." His address appeared in the Harvard Alumni Bulletin, July 7, 1939 (Vol. XLI, pp. 1129–31), from which it is reprinted with permission.

Santayana has spoken somewhere of the "deadly significance of symbols." They are not always deadly; we in this country have just had an example of two gracious living symbols of good-will and amity.

Still, we are not likely to disagree with Santayana's phrase in general; certainly when we turn our eyes to the East, we see symbols of deadly import—the Sickle and Hammer, the Swastika and the Lictor's Axe. These, whatever their followers profess, in fact threaten our civilization, because they stand for a denial of its basic axiom: that the good life of a society is the sum of the lives of the individuals who make it up, and that it has no other meaning. Our danger is real enough, but I rather think that the peril is not where we often put it.

Let me illustrate from my own experience. At the beginning of the Great War it looked as though Germany would have a swift and easy victory. For myself I did not fear that the Germans would then come and subjugate our country; what gave me a deeper chill was lest the example of what such a complete subjection of the individual to the mass could accomplish might convert mankind—us along with it—to a discipline after the German pattern; lest, for my own time at any rate, all that made life worth living—the habits and feelings in which I had grown up—should disappear. It was not the violence of our enemies that would undo us, I thought, but our own spiritual weakness, the shallowness of our convictions.

That same distrust is, I believe, at the bottom of much of the panic which from time to time now takes hold of us at the totalitarians of today. In our heart of hearts we doubt our capacity to withstand their blandishments; we are afraid that we may wake up to find ourselves disciples of the hated gospel. There is no fury like that against one who, we fear, may succeed in making us disloyal to beliefs we hold with passion, but have not really won. So let us not be too hard on those who insist upon fighting heresies with weapons borrowed from the heretics. At least, this is not the place to try to define the limits of free speech, or to inquire what are the best means of checking modern refinements of propaganda. That is a part of the art of government, and, like other arts, government must be content to proceed by compromise.

Yet, however tolerant we may be of the means, we ought not to lose sight of the end, or imagine that any compromise is without its price, or that payment of that price is more than deferred, because it is not due at once. Our democracy rests upon the assumption that, set free, the common man can manage his own fate; that errors will cancel each other by open discussion; that the interests of each, even when unguided from above, will not diverge too radically from the interests of all. That may be an illusion; it may be, in the words of Ortega y Gasset, "a discipline too difficult and complex to take firm root on earth." But still we do profess it, and while we do, let us not disguise from ourselves that, so far as we set up official orthodoxies, however vague in content, we falsify the underlying presupposition of our state. Peccadilloes, though venial, have an unpleasant way of coming back in formidable guise; their gravity we cannot reckon at the moment.

How shall we, then, be on guard that the means shall not swallow up the end, and that our defences shall not leave us nothing to defend? Somewhere we must keep burning the ideal which alone justifies the concessions we must make; especially we must foster those among us who furnish forth that ideal. And where shall we find a better exemplar of those qualities of heart and mind on which in the end a democratic state must rest than in the scholar? I am not thinking of the patience and penetration with which he must be endowed, or of the equipment he must have; but of the consecration of his spirit to the pursuit of truth. No one can keep a mind always open to new evidence, always ready to change its conclusions, who has other allegiance or commitments. Upon the failure of this necessary detachment right judgment is most often wrecked; its achievement most strains our animal nature; it is the last habit to be acquired and the first to be lost.

Now I am not so simple as to suppose that the detachment of a true scholar is ever likely to be the portion of the common man; and for that matter it would not be desirable in most practical activities; life is made up of a series of judgments on insufficient data, and if we waited to run down all our doubts, it would flow past us. But the rock on which a democratic state is most apt to split is that passion of faction which will admit no mediation, and demands the extinction of all opposition. Unless some means is found to assuage its violence, the state dissolves and re-emerges as an autocracy; and there are no such means except insofar as the state is made up of those, to some degree practised in the habit of suspended judgment, and possessing a spirit capable of disinterested scrutiny.

High among these will stand the scholar, if he be faithful to his creed; and it is with the consciousness of his supreme value that we have become so sensitive—sometimes I wonder whether we may not have become oversensitive—to all coercion from without, which, however remotely, can impinge upon him. We insist upon his fullest measure of protection against all such; and I shall take as much for granted, because I want to speak of something else. I am thinking of what the scholar imposes upon himself; better, perhaps, of what he may fail to impose upon himself; of those abnegations which are the condition of his preserving the serenity in which alone he can work; I am thinking of an aloofness from burning issues, which is hard for generous and passionate natures, but without which they almost inevitably become advocates, agitators, crusaders, and propagandists.

You may take Martin Luther or Erasmus for your model, but you cannot play both roles at once; you may not carry a sword beneath a scholar's gown, or lead flaming causes from a cloister. Luther cannot be domesticated in a university. You cannot raise the standard against oppression, or leap into the breach to relieve injustice, and still keep an open mind to every disconcerting fact, or an open ear to the cold voice of doubt. I am satisfied that a scholar who tries to combine these parts sells his birthright for a mess of pottage; that, when the final count is made, it will be found that the impairment of his powers far outweighs any possible contribution to the causes he has espoused. If he is fit to serve in his calling at all, it is only because he has learned not to serve in any other, for his singleness of mind quickly evaporates in the fires of passions, however holy.

Many years ago in this place I sat under men who resisted all such allurements; men who believed that the pursuit of knowledge was enough to absorb all their powers and more. They taught me, not by precept, but by example, that nothing is more commendable, and more fair, than that a man should lay aside all else, and seek truth; not to preach what he might find; and surely not to try to make his views prevail; but, like Lessing, to find his satisfaction in the search itself. These men did not seek to rebuild the world nearer to the heart's desire; they were content to be themselves, confident that, if they were faithful in that, their light would shine, steady and far. Like others, I have not been true to what they taught me; I have strayed from their ways; yet in days of discouragement, when all the uses of this world seemed weary, stale, flat, and unprofitable, the memory of these teachers of mine has returned again and again to freshen, and renew, my spirit. Unafraid before the unknown universe; indifferent to the world's disparagements, and uncorrupted by its prizes; ardent and secure in that faith by which alone mankind in the end can live; they were themselves the best lesson that I took away. And now in return, because I can do no more, I come to lay a tribute of gratitude and reverence before the shades of these, my masters then, my masters always.

18

FOREWORD TO WILLISTON'S *LIFE AND LAW*
[1940]

SAMUEL WILLISTON, born in Cambridge, Massachusetts, in 1861, was graduated from Harvard College in 1882 and from the Harvard Law School in 1888. He began legal practice in Boston on graduation and joined the Harvard law faculty in 1890. Appointed Weld professor of law in 1903, he became the Dane professor in 1919. He was acting dean in 1909 and became emeritus professor in 1938. Among his many services to the legal profession was his leadership of the uniform-laws movement. He drafted measures for uniform laws of sales, warehouse receipts, bills of lading, and certificates of stock. He also wrote books on sales, contracts, and bankruptcy. To Williston's autobiography, Life and Law (1941), Learned Hand, one of his early students in the Harvard Law School, contributed the foreword. This is reprinted with the permission of the publisher, Little, Brown & Company.

When Samuel Williston began to teach in the Harvard Law School in 1890, he found as associates three of the great names that had originally grouped themselves about Langdell at the Harvard Law School—Thayer, Gray and Ames. Langdell had arrived at the case-system because he thought of law as a set of principles to be derived from the reports by the process of induction; he appealed to the analogy of the physical sciences, and it may be that it was this that, some years before, had so much impressed President Eliot of Harvard University, who had himself been a chemist. This is not the place to discuss the validity of the analogy, but it is hard to resist the belief that this basic concept had something to do with the persistency with which he sought to find uniformity amid the decisions, which were by hypothesis the phenomena for his inductions. It often led him altogether to disregard the judges' reasons, and to substitute, in justification of their results, explanations entirely foreign to anything that had ever been in their minds. Ames was a great legal historian, who had traced many doctrines from their seeds to fruition; he was given to finding the leaf and flower more perfect in the bud than was always obvious to others. In practice, the law which he taught had an esoteric flavor somewhat like Langdell's. Both were great men; but both were disposed to search for, and find, underlying syntheses that were at times authentic with them.

Thayer and Gray were of another stripe. They did indeed recognize that law must pretend to generality, if it is to have an authority greater than the personal word of the judge, but they were content to accept the variants with the theorem, and to let consistency take care of itself as best it could; and Gray expressed this outlook in lectures of charm and humor, to which—it seems to me— nothing that has followed has added, and from which nothing has taken away. Williston instinctively found himself ranged with Thayer and Gray, although his subject might well have led him in the other direction. Consent had for many years been the cornerstone for much of the political thinking of the time; and to make it serve, the judges had gone to great lengths to discover in contracts an initial acceptance of consequences they felt bound to impose upon the promisor. It assuaged harsh results, if one could say that the sufferer had agreed to them in advance, and sophistry, as ever, was a facile handmaiden to authority. It is a commonplace that men's thinking is conditioned by their passional make-up, and it was inevitable that Williston should have refused to accept scholastic overlays, however currently imposing. His direct and penetrating mind was free to act as a solvent upon any such plating, because he was not overawed by authority, but more particularly because he had no interest in subtleties for their own sake, or enough interest in formal symmetry to obscure what lay before him. He was an innovator throughout his subject, but by steps, and in response to an intellectual detachment which stifled overwhelming loyalties or the afflatus of revelation. Such men certainly never figure among the Luthers of this world, and no doubt the world owes much to its Luthers; abuses get deeply rooted and entwine so much that to tear them out will fetch along much that is good. The eruptive energy necessary can apparently be nurtured only upon burning concepts, arrived at intuitively, coming with the impact of absolute certainty. But whatever their services, revolutionaries obstruct the path to truth; the qualities which clear it are wholly inconsistent with theirs; scepticism, tolerance, discrimination, urbanity, some—but not too much—reserve towards change, insistence upon proportion, and, above all, humility before the vast unknown.

In the author of this book these qualities were happily fused, as he who reads it will learn. He will find the picture of one who had neither vanity, nor its counterpart, self-depreciation; neither pedantry, nor intellectual slackness; neither worship for the past, nor a heart open to each new-comer: it will not be hard to see why the serene spirit—even under its frequent load of illness—should have ended by making its possessor one of the great figures of his calling, final authority when he speaks. But one thing he will not find, for it is reserved to us who were his pupils; he will not come to know him as a teacher. For that, one should have sat under that unperturbed young man; one should have felt the impact of the apparently effortless self-possession which, though it never imposed itself, always won. For, while this Socrates of ours never coerced our assent, like his prototype he did not let us alone until we had peered into the corners of our minds, and had in some measure discovered the litter they contained. Such self-revelation was indeed often painful—is painful still—but out of it came a gratitude which has endured; still endures after the initial difference in years has been foreshortened almost to the vanishing-point. We would give much to keep this memory; we do not shame ourselves in acknowledging that we have never shaken free from the dominance then secured; it has been a happy subjection, dishonoring neither side. And this book in which he tells us of himself is for all of us a fortunate occasion; once more it gives us an opportunity to salute our master.

19

LIBERTY
[1941]

THE *Elizabethan Club at Yale University invited Learned Hand to be its speaker on the occasion of its thirtieth anniversary dinner, May 10, 1941. His address appeared in the* Yale Alumni Magazine, *June 6, 1941 (Vol. IV, No. 20, pp. 10–12), from which it is reprinted with permission.*

I have chosen for the subject of my talk, "Liberty." When I say that I chose it, I am not speaking quite the truth; rather it chose itself. I was so acutely aware of the quicksands and wastes which await the explorer in that region that I tried to avoid an expedition into it. Perhaps a judge is especially aware of these; his colleagues are constantly assuring him that all he needs is to avoid license and anarchy on the one hand, and tyranny and despotism on the other; if he will only stick to that simple admonition he is sure to arrive. That is not very encouraging as a starter; but what gives the task its real difficulty is that the word is so charged with passion. About none is written a more fiery record of suffering and heroism; it is the center and the kernel of that inner life for which men will fight and die who will fight and die for anything. Furthermore, and perhaps for that reason, it has been the rallying cry of those who hold quite opposite beliefs; one can say of it after Lincoln: "Both sides pray to it and each invokes its aid against the other." Few stop to ask what they mean, and those who do soon find the answer baffling and uncertain. Why then should I venture to talk about it here tonight? Only because I could not help it. In such a world as this, so wretched and so riven, where men and women are suffering misery, mutilation, and death in the name of Liberty—whatever it may be—how can anyone be content who does not try to come to at least a tentative conclusion with himself about it? And so, although I am conscious of the small chance of success where so many have failed, I shall ask you to bear with me as I too try my luck with this Sphinx, whom like her prototype if I answer I answer at my peril.

I do not know how it is with you, but my own first spontaneous response to the word is negative; I think that I am free when I can do what I want; this tiny protoplasmal center of radiant energy demands that alien impacts shall not thwart its insistences and its self-assertions. What are these? We can start with a dictum attributed to Lawrence Henderson that they consist in the performance of our accustomed rituals. (Those of you who have read Trotter's *Instinct of the Herd* will perhaps remember analogues drawn from the accepted social observances of man's best friend, the Dog, which I forbear to quote.) Henderson's definition would be entirely satisfactory to anthropologists, who, very properly, refuse to play favorites among the conventions of mankind. It is as authentic a denial of freedom to compel a Bushman to look at his mother-in-law during the period of his wife's gestation, as it is to deny Colonel Lindbergh the privilege of assuring us of the speedy and certain collapse of Great Britain. Each has a vested right in his freedom grounded in the deepest of foundations, the current liturgies of the society to which he belongs. Since, so conceived, Liberty is negative, one freedom is as good as another; there is no objective standard except for blind partisans of the status quo whatever it may be. The rite of burying the aged alive, whatever the aged may say against it, has equal sanction with that of providing a college education for those who are not fit to receive one.

Let us then look for an objective standard. Surely we can safely begin with the satisfaction of our primitive needs. We must eat, sleep, be clothed and sheltered, and have our mates and our children. It is irrelevant that the Universe so often denies us these; we are considering hindrances by our fellows. Shall we say then that, so far as they deny us such goods, they deny our Liberty? "Do not waste our time in trivialities," you will answer, "we must of course yield these in part, and other desires scarcely less imperious; but by doing so we create civilized society so that our life shall not be 'short, brutish, and nasty.' Why go over that old stuff again? It was what Holmes meant when he said he liked to pay taxes because he felt he was buying civilization." No doubt; but if we press the inquiry a little further it gets more real. To say that we must compromise leaves all practical questions unanswered. Kant may have been right when he said that our conduct must be such that it can be made a universal rule; but that does not help us to find any particular rule; perhaps there are not any. If we declare that a freeman will yield so far, but only so far, as, having with entire detachment weighed his own good against his neighbor's, he finds the neighbor's better, that does not tell us how he is to decide which of the two is in fact the better. Of course there is the initial obstacle that entire detachment is an obvious fiction. To proceed at all we must set up some persons in our society with authority—like Plato's "Guardians" for instance, to whom we can depute the weighing of one good against another. The outlook has never been very propitious that we can find any such guardians, but for my purposes it is not important; for if we secured absolute detachment and impartiality, we should have got no further than to face the real problem.

Let me start with an example drawn from Plato's own city; not because we need doubt the answer, but because it illustrates the incommensurability of the elements that must be measured. When at times I hear, as we all do, some cultivated snob vaporing about the perfection of life in Athens, say from 480 to 430 B.C., and how it was the apex of civilization, someone is sure to interject that it was not so at all; rather that Athens was a hideous nightmare; that these supposed specimens of ultimate human perfection were shameless exploiters of a far greater number of other men whose misery, when matched against their own splendors, makes Stygian blackness to the eyes of all just and humane persons. When such a Thersites disturbs the complacency of the cultivated snob, sometimes I feel like siding with the snob—even now when the dawn of social justice has broken into bright unclouded day. I should not do so by way of challenge to the challenger's conclusion, but I should ask him to tell me the processes by which he reached it. I should say that of course I recognized that the exploitation of the weak, taken by itself, was undiluted evil; and that in its more aggravated form we need not even discuss it—for instance, the often lamented lot of those unfortunate men who were worked to death in the mines of Laurium no doubt outweighed an infinity of noble employment of leisure. I should ask him to put aside such concrete incidents disturbing to philosophic speculation and consider the issue abstractly. Supposing that an ethical or hedonistic calculus were possible, and supposing that there were no other means than the exploitation of the exploited by which the lives of the Athenian citizens could have been what they were, and supposing that these were as perfect as both he and the cultivated snob seemed to agree they were; how he could guess which way the beam would tip if one put the lives of the citizens in one scale and the good things of which they deprived their slaves in the other. I should tell him that, though I was sure of the answer, I had always been a little baffled to know how such a balance could be struck; but that, like Socrates, I was confident that he must know, since he seemed so certain. And if he, rightly angry at this offensively insincere humility, were to answer, as I suspect he might, that injustice could never be right, and that there were some things which everyone knew, among which was that oppression and justice were inherently antithetical, I should not feel that he had thoroughly illuminated all the dark places.

At any rate I know that, whatever he said, he could not tell me how to strike such a balance. While each of us can do it for himself here and now, he finds trouble even for himself when he includes his own future; and when we come to deal with a community, a community of say one hundred and thirty million persons, how can we possibly proceed? What we do in fact is to assume that all are alike; that what is a good for A is a good for B, and that A's preference—A's better—will be B's. Perhaps one cannot conduct a democracy on any other assumption; but not only is it not true in fact; but whatever its truth, it is impossible to make people believe it. They will do so in the abstract, but they fall into endless dispute in application, and the effort is apt to end either in mutual paralysis of action, or a seizure of power by a part. The resulting confusion and discord have therefore often suggested this solution: instill in all a faith that each achieves his personal and individual best by submerging himself in common aspirations, a common fate, a common self. There would be no denial of Liberty in that; nobody would feel himself under alien domination; each would realize himself in all, and all in each.

"Old stuff again," you will say, "it sounds good but you know it cannot be done; people are too different, and that is all there is to it. Once you try to make them alike you have more trouble on your hands than when you started." On the contrary I am disposed to believe that perhaps it can be done, for a time anyway, and for a very large proportion at least of a large community. Certainly I am not so sure as I used to be that it cannot be done. There are more and more signs about us that our increasingly efficient and pervasive apparatus of mass suggestion is planing off individual differences, and making us more and more facile for mass manipulation. We need not look to Russia and Germany, or to their pathetic Italian imitator; we need not leave home at all. Indeed, something of the kind was possible long before the days of the tabloid, the radio, the moving picture, and the motor car. Sparta was an instance; so was Rome for a while; and Islam in the 8th Century, Spain in the

16th, and France in the 18th. And it has always been possible to create nonpolitical groups with corporate selves. Man is a gregarious animal, extremely sensitive to authority; if it will only indoctrinate him thoroughly in his childhood and youth, he can be made to espouse any kind of orthodoxy—whether of belief or feeling. There were philosophical prophets of the Absolute Collective Self long before Hegel and Fichte. In his early manhood Plato had seen the Athenian democracy crumble from faction; he concluded that only under the Spartan model could mankind achieve that justice which was the end of society as it was of the individual. Again and again the same theme has recurred thereafter.

Now, as a practical means of realizing common purposes nothing comparable exists, as we are now learning to our cost. Lord Lothian shortly before his death—and very near, I think, to where we now are—forcibly admonished us of this. "You cannot match the power of such a people as the Germans, unless you are willing to sink your separate interests in your common cause and accept sacrifices such as they accept by means of a faith of equal fervor." Hitler is quite right in predicting the doom of democracies as he understands democracies; I wish it were more certain that he misunderstands them. A society in which each is willing to surrender only that for which he can see a personal equivalent, is not a society at all; it is a group already in process of dissolution, and no one need concern himself to stay its inevitable end; it would be a hard choice between it and a totalitarian society. No Utopia, nothing but Bedlam, will automatically emerge from a regime of unbridled individualism, be it ever so rugged.

What then, you will ask, am I really talking about? If it be true that any orthodoxy can be implanted in us, provided we are caught and schooled while young, or provided even in our later years that we are subjected to the everlasting iteration of sacred rubrics, in school, in press, in moving picture, and by radio; and if, when we have been so "conditioned," we feel authority to be no restraint but rather a means toward the realization of our deeper self; and if something of the sort is essential to survival in a robbers' world, where the strong are sure to win; if all these things be true, why should we boggle about any other Liberty; what more do we need? That other societies so organized have been predatory, does not mean that we need be predacious; our communal self can become the chalice for a more exquisite liquor of civilization than the troubled world has yet seen. In our Father's house are many mansions; we will occupy one where life shall be seemly and noble and forbearing and happy and gay; yet strong enough withal to resist any aggression.

Some day such a vision may come true; the future may have in store aeons of beatitude in which men shall find utter self-realization and utter self-expression in the utter self-surrender of the hive; I do not forget the words of the collect: "Whose service is perfect freedom." Be that as it may, it is not on the score of its impracticability that I do not welcome that prospect; but because I believe that its realization would suppress the most precious part of our nature. To put it very badly, and perhaps a little contentiously, it is man's inherent willfulness that I would preserve, and in which I wish to set the stronghold of that Liberty I prize; that stone which social reformers have always rejected I would make the head of the corner.

I cannot tell why to me personally such a society seems stifling; I only know that although with Epictetus I can say: "If I were an ant, I should play the part of an ant," in fact I am not an ant, and if I try to play the part of an ant I know that I shall end in the care of a psychoanalyst. I will own that when on occasion I visit my simian cousins in captivity, the spectacle does not refresh me. Not only have they a distressing lack of reserve, but their restlessness affects me with a homeopathic uneasiness. Kipling seems right, and I wince that we have so many family traits in common. My kinship with them becomes even more distasteful when I pass to the cages of the great cats, who lie there serenely with their steady yellow eyes, calm, self-secure, fearing nothing. Why must my cousins and I be so agitated; why this ceaseless, errant curiosity; pausing only for an instant and then off to something new? It is all very trying; and yet here will I pitch my tent. James Harvey Robinson used to say that we rose from the ape because like him we kept "monkeying around," always meddling with everything about us. True, there is a difference, because although the ape meddles, he forgets, and we have learned, first to meddle and remember, and then to meddle and record. But without the meddling nothing would have happened of all that glorious array of achievement: battleships, aeroplanes, relativity, the proton, neutron, and electron, T.N.T., poison gas, sulfathiazole, the Fifth Symphony, The Iliad, The Divine Comedy, Hamlet, Faust, The Critique of Pure Reason, Das Kapital, The Constitution of the United States, The Congress of Industrial Organizations, Huey Long, and The New Deal. All these from just "monkeying around"!

My thesis is that any organization of society which depresses free and spontaneous meddling is on the decline, however showy its immediate spoils; I maintain that in such a society Liberty is gone, little as its members may know it; that the Nirvana of the individual is too high a price for a collective Paradise. I maintain this primarily as an authentic demand of the spirit—*animula vagula blandula* . . . *quae nunc abibis in loca*—and I maintain it too as practical sagacity. Because, once you get people believing that there is an authoritative well of wisdom to which they can turn for absolutes, you have dried up the springs on which they must in the end draw even for the things of this world. As soon as we cease to pry about at random, we shall come to rely upon accredited bodies of authoritative dogma; and as soon as we come to rely upon accredited bodies of authoritative dogma, not only are the days of our Liberty over, but we have lost the password that has hitherto opened to us the gates of success as well. Even in that very technology on which they so much pride themselves, the totalitarians in the end will fail; for they stand upon the shoulders of generations of free inquiry. No doubt they will try to keep their hands off materially profitable activities; but they will finally learn that you cannot put men's minds in watertight compartments; you cannot have a nation, each one of whom is half slave and half free, any more than you can have a nation in which half are wholly slave and half are wholly free. Where heterodoxy in what

men prize most is a crime, fresh thinking about anything
will disappear. Even the loaves and fishes will not be
multiplied.

As I predicted, I have brought down a very small
quarry. We started to find some positive content for
Liberty, and all we have discovered is that it does not
follow because we are not conscious of constraint that
we are not constrained. Yet little as that seems, it is not
I think an altogether contemptible result, for behind it
lies a faith. It is the faith that our collective fate in the
end depends upon the irrepressible fertility of the individual, and the finality of what he chooses to call good.
It is the faith that neither principalities, nor powers, nor
things present, nor things to come, can rightfully suppress that fertility or deny that good. It is the faith in
the indefectible significance of each one of us, inherited,
if I understand it aright, from One who lived and died
some 1900 years ago in Palestine. It is a faith not easy to
live by, whose credo is full of hard sayings. If you accept
it, it may cast you for the role of Prometheus, a part of
whose lines, you will remember, contain a good deal
about defying the Powers of this World. Those powers
are ruthless, competent, and strong; and among the prop-
erties in the play there are real lightning and a real eagle;
make no mistake about that. Moreover, the audience is
likely to be very small; indeed it is not improbable that
there will be none at all. The only curtain calls you will
get are those you give yourself. But the lead is a man's
part, and perhaps some of us can fill it. Who can tell?

20

THE CONTRIBUTION OF AN INDEPENDENT JUDICIARY TO CIVILIZATION
[1942]

THE *Supreme Judicial Court of Massachusetts observed the 250th anniversary of its founding with impressive ceremonies on November 21, 1942, in Boston. After proceedings in the Courthouse attended by the Governor and other officials of Massachusetts, the presiding judges of other New England state supreme courts and Associate Justice Felix Frankfurter of the United States Supreme Court, a banquet of bench and bar was held at the Copley Plaza Hotel. In salute to the oldest court in America in continuous existence, Learned Hand spoke on "The Contribution of an Independent Judiciary to Civilization." His address appeared in The Supreme Judicial Court of Massachusetts 1692–1942 (pp. 59–67), published by the Massachusetts Bar Association, from which it is reprinted with permission.*

In considering the contributions of an independent judiciary to our kind of civilization, I should like to distinguish between its customary law and constitution on the one hand and what I shall call its "enacted law" on the other. By "enacted law" I mean any authoritative command of an organ of government purposely made responsive to the pressure of the interests affected. I shall assume that before "enacted law" is passed these interests have opportunity in the press, in public meeting, by appearance before committees or the like and in any other lawful way, to exert their influence. "Enacted law" in that sense is ordinarily a compromise of conflicts and its success depends upon how far mutual concessions result in an adjustment which brings in its train the most satisfaction and leaves the least acrimony. I am not sure that an independent judiciary would be desirable in a society where law was enacted by a different process. For example, Gallup polls may in the end become so accurate that, if we should wish a government by referendum, we could accept them as reliable and speedy equivalents. It might be best not to make independent a judiciary called upon to interpret the answers so obtained. Nobody can capture the implications of his purposes, or really know what he wants till they have been tried out in experience; but, although political controversy is poor makeshift, it is the best we can get in advance, and law must speak in futuro. Those vague stirrings of mass feeling which many who pride themselves upon their democracy mistake for the popular will must always be made concrete before they can become law in any practical sense, and the process of definition is as important as the dumb energy which provokes it, perhaps more so. In a society governed by Gallup polls it might be well to submit the judiciary to a Gallup poll, too; the definition of the popular command would be too much like the command itself.

But an independent judiciary is an inescapable corollary of "enacted law" in the sense I am using it. Such laws do not indeed represent permanent principles of jurisprudence—assuming that there are any such—but they can be relatively stable; and, provided that the opportunity always exists to supplant them when there is a new shift in political power, it is of critical consequence that they should be loyally enforced until they are amended by the same process which made them. That is the presupposition upon which the compromises were originally accepted; to disturb them by surreptitious, irresponsible and anonymous intervention imperils the possibility of any future settlements and pro tanto upsets the whole system. Such laws need but one canon of interpretation, to understand what the real accord was. The duty of ascertaining its meaning is difficult enough at best, and one certain way of missing it is by reading it literally, for words are such temperamental beings that the surest way to lose their essence is to take them at their face. Courts must reconstruct the past solution imaginatively in its setting and project the purposes which inspired it upon the concrete occasions which arise for their decision. To interject into the process the fear of displeasure or the hope of favor of those who can make their will felt, is inevitably to corrupt the event, and could never be proposed by anyone who really comprehended the issue. This was long held a truism, but it must be owned that the edge of our displeasure at its denial has of late been somewhat turned. In the name of a more loyal fealty to the popular will, we are asked to defeat the only means by which that will can become articulate and be made effective. To this, the first aspect of our question, I submit that there is but one answer: an unflinching resistance.

The respect all men feel in some measure for customary law lies deep in their nature; we accept the verdict of the past until the need for change cries out loudly enough to force upon us a choice between the comforts of further inertia and the irksomeness of action. Through the openings given by that disposition, the common law has been fabricated bit by bit without express assent and under the ministrations of those who have always protested that, like the Bourbons, they learn nothing and forget nothing. Logically, the irresponsibility of an independent judiciary is here an anomaly, like the common law itself; in a pitilessly consistent democracy judges would not be making law at all. Why then do we not resent it? In earlier times when the parturition of statutes was slow and painful, judicial license was tolerated partly for that reason and partly because judges fairly represented the governing classes. While the king was supreme, or nearly so, he could remove them at pleasure, and even when, after the fall of the Stuarts, they began to hold upon good behavior, they were still for long in harmony with those who had succeeded to the reins. Occasionally—Lord Mansfield is the classic example—they could without offence make radical changes in the customary law. That is no longer true; both the need and the unison have gone; legislation has become easy, judges no longer speak for the ruling classes. The price of their continued power must therefore be a self-denying ordinance which forbids change in what has not already become unacceptable. To compose inconsistencies, to unravel confusions, to announce unrecognized implications, to make, in Holmes' now hackneyed phrase, "interstitial" advances; these are the measure of what they may properly do, and there is not indeed much danger of their exceeding this limit; rather the contrary, for they are curiously timid about innovations. A judge who will hector the bar and browbeat the witnesses and who can find a warrant in the Fourteenth Amendment for stifling a patently reasonable legislative experiment, will tremble at the thought of introducing a new exception into the hearsay rule. And so, although precisions and purists might repine, in the end things work out very well as they are, for the advantages of leaving step by step amendments of the customary law in the hands of those trained in it, outweigh the dangers.

You may well think that I have so far been merely skirmishing in a rather obvious effort to avoid the main engagement. For, unless I am deceived, those who proposed the subject of the evening were really thinking about judges and constitutions, perhaps more especially the United States Constitution; and unless I am a skulker, I must now advance to the attack. Nevertheless, I shall first attempt one more diversion. A constitution is primarily an instrument to distribute political power; and so far as it is, it is hard to escape the necessity of some tribunal with authority to declare when the prescribed distribution has been disturbed. Otherwise those who hold the purse will be likely in the end to dominate and absorb everything else, except as astute executives may from time to time check them by capturing and holding popular favor. Obviously the independence of such a tribunal must be secure; and there seems to be nothing to add to what I have been saying about "enacted law." I do not mean that courts should approach such constitutional questions as they approach statutes, and they have never done so when they knew their business; constitutions can only map out the terrain roughly, inevitably leaving much to be filled in. The scope of the interstate commerce power of Congress is an ever present instance. It is impossible to avoid all such occasions, but it was a daring expedient to meet them with judges, deliberately put beyond the reach of popular pressure. And yet, granted the necessity of some such authority, probably independent judges were the most likely to do the job well. Besides, the strains that decisions on these questions set up are not ordinarily dangerous to the social structure. For the most part the interests involved are only the sensibilities of the officials whose provinces they mark out, and usually their resentments have no grave seismic consequences.

But American constitutions always go further. Not only do they distribute the powers of government, but they assume to lay down general principles to insure the just exercise of those powers. This is the contribution to political science of which we are proud, and especially of a judiciary of Vestal unapproachability which shall always tend the Sacred Flame of Justice. Yet here we are on less firm ground. It is true that the logic which has treated these like other provisions of a constitution seems on its face unanswerable. Are they not parts in the same document? Did they not originally have a meaning? Why should not that meaning be found in the same way as that of the rest of the instrument? Nevertheless there are vital differences. Here history is only a feeble light, for these rubrics were meant to answer future problems unimagined and unimaginable. Nothing which by the utmost liberality can be called interpretation describes the process by which they must be applied. Indeed if law be a command for specific conduct, they are not law at all; they are cautionary warnings against the intemperance of faction and the first approaches of despotism. The answers to the questions which they raise demand the appraisal and balancing of human values which there are no scales to weigh. Who can say whether the contributions of one group may not justify allowing it a preference? How far should the capable, the shrewd or the strong be allowed to exploit their powers? When does utterance go beyond persuasion and become only incitement? How far are children wards of the state so as to justify its intervention in their nurture? What limits should be imposed upon the right to inherit? Where does religious freedom end and moral obliquity begin? As to such questions one can sometimes say what effect a proposal will have in fact, just as one can foretell how much money a tax will raise and who will pay it. But when that is done, one has come only to the kernel of the matter, which is the choice between what will be gained and what will be lost. The difficulty here does not come from ignorance, but from the absence of any standard, for values are incommensurable. It is true that theoretically, and sometimes practically, cases can arise where courts might properly intervene, not indeed because the legislature has appraised the values wrongly, for it is hard to see how that can be if it has honestly tried to appraise them at all; but because that is exactly what it has failed to do, because its action has been nothing but the patent exploitation of one group whose interests it has altogether disregarded. But the dangers are always very great. What seems to the losers mere spoliation usually appears to the gainers less than a reasonable relief from manifest injustice. Moreover, even were there a hedonistic rod by which to measure loss or gain, how could we know that the judges had it; or—what is more important—would enough people think they had, to be satisfied that they should use it? So long as law remains a profession (and certainly there is no indication that its complexities are decreasing) judges must be drawn from a professional class with the special interests and the special hierarchy of values which that implies. And even if they were as detached as Rhadamanthus himself, it would not serve unless people believed that they were. But to believe that another is truly a Daniel come to judgment demands almost the detachment of a Daniel; and whatever may be properly said for the judges, among whom there are indeed those as detached as it is given men to be, nobody will assert that detachment is a disposition widespread in any society.

It is not true, as you may be disposed at first blush to reply, that all this can be said with equal force of any other decision of a court. Constitutions are deliberately made difficult of amendment; mistaken readings of them cannot be readily corrected. Moreover, if they could be, constitutions must not degenerate into vade mecums or codes; when they begin to do so, it is a sign of a community unsure of itself and seeking protection against its own misgivings. And that is especially true of such parts of a constitution as I am talking about; these particularly must be left imprecise. If a court be really candid, it can only say: "We find that this measure will have this result; it will injure this group in such and such ways, and benefit that group in these other ways. We declare it invalid, because after every conceivable allowance for differences of outlook, we cannot see how a fair person can honestly believe that the benefits balance the losses."

Practically, it is very seldom possible to be sure of such a conclusion; practically, it is very seldom possible to say that a legislature has abdicated by surrendering to one faction; the relevant factors are too many and too incomparable.

Nor need it surprise us that these stately admonitions refuse to subject themselves to analysis. They are the precipitates of "old, unhappy, far-off things, and battles long ago," originally cast as universals to enlarge the scope of the victory, to give it authority, to reassure the very victors themselves that they have been champions in something more momentous than a passing struggle. Thrown large upon the screen of the future as eternal verities, they are emptied of the vital occasions which gave them birth, and become moral adjurations, the more imperious because inscrutable, but with only that content which each generation must pour into them anew in the light of its own experience. If an independent judiciary seeks to fill them from its own bosom, in the end it will cease to be independent. And its independence will be well lost, for that bosom is not ample enough for the hopes and fears of all sorts and conditions of men, nor will its answers be theirs; it must be content to stand aside from these fateful battles. There are two ways in which the judges may forfeit their independence, if they do not abstain. If they are intransigent but honest, they will be curbed; but a worse fate will befall them if they learn to trim their sails to the prevailing winds. A society whose judges have taught it to expect complaisance will exact complaisance; and complaisance under the pretense of interpretation is rottenness. If judges are to kill this thing they love, let them do it, not like cowards with a kiss, but like brave men with a sword.

And so, to sum up, I believe that for by far the greater part of their work it is a condition upon the success of our system that the judges should be independent; and I do not believe that their independence should be impaired because of their constitutional function. But the price of this immunity, I insist, is that they should not have the last word in those basic conflicts of "right and wrong—between whose endless jar justice resides." You may ask what then will become of the fundamental principles of equity and fair play which our constitutions enshrine; and whether I seriously believe that unsupported they will serve merely as counsels of moderation. I do not think that anyone can say what will be left of those principles; I do not know whether they will serve only as counsels; but this much I think I do know—that a society so riven that the spirit of moderation is gone, no court can save; that a society where that spirit flourishes. no court need save; that in a society which evades its responsibility by thrusting upon the courts the nurture of that spirit, that spirit in the end will perish. What is the spirit of moderation? It is the temper which does not press a partisan advantage to its bitter end, which can understand and will respect the other side, which feels a unity between all citizens—real and not the factitious product of propaganda—which recognizes their common fate and their common aspirations—in a word, which has faith in the sacredness of the individual. If you ask me how such a temper and such a faith are bred and fostered, I cannot answer. They are the last flowers of civilization, delicate and easily overrun by the weeds of our sinful human nature; we may even now be witnessing their uprooting and disappearance until in the progress of the ages their seeds can once more find some friendly soil. But I am satisfied that they must have the vigor within themselves to withstand the winds and weather of an indifferent and ruthless world; and that it is idle to seek shelter for them in a courtroom. Men must take that temper and that faith with them into the field, into the market-place, into the factory, into the council-room, into their homes; they cannot be imposed; they must be lived. Words will not express them; arguments will not clarify them; decisions will not maintain them. They are the fruit of the wisdom that comes of trial and a pure heart; no one can possess them who has not stood in awe before the spectacle of this mysterious Universe; no one can possess them whom that spectacle has not purged through pity and through fear—pity for the pride and folly which inexorably enmesh men in toils of their own contriving; fear, because that same pride and that same folly lie deep in the recesses of his own soul.

21

MR. JUSTICE BRANDEIS
[1942]

LOUIS DEMBITZ BRANDEIS (1856–1941) was a native of Louisville, Kentucky, and a graduate of the Harvard Law School. He began law practice in St. Louis in 1878. His work as a "people's attorney" in Boston and elsewhere in many important cases involving consumers attracted the admiration of Woodrow Wilson, who wanted him in the Cabinet in 1913. When Brandeis published in 1914 Other People's Money, a powerful analysis of the use and influence of finance on politics and life in the United States, Wilson was more determined than ever to draft Brandeis into his New Freedom Administration. The perfect opportunity came in a vacancy on the Supreme Court, and on January 28, 1916, Wilson made the appointment. Before the nomination was twenty-four hours old it was evident that it would be confirmed, if at all, only after a long and bitter struggle. Seven past presidents of the American Bar Association declared Brandeis unfit for the Supreme Court. These included William Howard Taft, Elihu Root, Joseph H. Choate, and Moorfield Storey. The president of Harvard, A. Lawrence Lowell, joined the opposition, but this was countered happily by a strong endorsement from President Emeritus Charles W. Eliot. The battle raged for three months, and sixteen hundred pages of testimony were taken at hearings. Then, on May 5, 1916, Wilson sent to the chairman of the Senate Judiciary Committee a letter that remains a classic statement of qualifications for public service, particularly on the Supreme Court. A few days later the subcommittee voted, 3 to 2, on straight party lines, for confirmation. The vote in committee, on May 24, was 10 Democrats for confirmation to 8 Republicans opposed. The latter included Borah of Idaho, who years later said this was one of two votes he most regretted in his long career in the Senate. Confirmation was by vote of 46 to 22, with only three Republicans in the affirmative: Norris of Nebraska, La Follette of Wisconsin, and Poindexter of Washington. Those opposed included Harding of Ohio, Lodge of Massachusetts, Curtis of Kansas, Cummins of Iowa, Fall of New Mexico, and Sutherland (later Justice) of Utah. The twentieth anniversary of Brandeis's entry upon judicial duties, his retirement three years later and his death, on October 5, 1941, were occasions for mounting appreciation of his contributions to American economics, government, and jurisprudence. A memorial service was held in the Supreme Court on December 21, 1942. Learned Hand's address on that occasion appeared in the Proceedings of the Bar of the Supreme Court, 317 U.S. xi–xiv.

A man's life, like a piece of tapestry, is made up of many strands which interwoven make a pattern; to separate a single one and look at it alone not only destroys the whole, but gives the strand itself a false value. So it must be with what I say today; this is no occasion to appraise the life and work of the man whose memory we have met to honor. It would be impossible at this time to do justice to the content of so manifold a nature and so full a life; its memorial stands written at large, chiefly in the records of his court; perhaps best preserved in the minds of living men and women. Before passing to my theme, I can therefore do no more than allude to much that I can ill afford to leave out: for instance, to his almost mystic reverence for that court whose tradition seemed to him not only to consecrate its own members, but to impress its sacred mission upon all who shared in any measure in its work, even menially. To his mind nothing must weaken its influence or tarnish its lustre; no matter how hot had been the dispute, how wide the final difference, how plain the speech, nothing ever appeared to ruffle or disturb his serenity, or to suggest that he harbored anything but regard and respect for the views of his colleagues, however far removed from his own. Nor can I more than mention the clear, ungarnished style which so well betrayed the will that lay behind; the undiverted purpose to clarify and convince. How it eschewed all that might distract attention from the thought to its expression. The telling phrase, the vivid metaphor, the far-fetched word that teases the reader and flatters him with the vanity of recognition—these must not obtrude upon that which alone mattered: that conviction should be carried home. So put it that all your hearers shall not be aware of the medium; so put it that they shall not feel you, yet shall be possessed of what you say. If style be the measure of the man, here was evidence of that insistence upon fact and reason which was at once his weapon and his shield. Others too must speak of the fiery nature which showed itself when stirred, but which for the most part lay buried beneath an iron control; of that ascesis, which seemed so to increase that towards the end one wondered at times whether, like some Eastern sage, the body's grosser part had not been quite burnt away and mere spirit remained; of those quick flashes of indignation at injustice, pretense, or oppression. These and much more which would make the figure stand out more boldly against its background, I shall not try to portray. I must leave them to others who can speak more intimately and with more right.

At the risk of which I spoke a moment ago, I mean to choose a single thread from all the rest, which I venture to believe leads to the heart and kernel of his thinking and—at least at this present—to the best of his teaching. I mean what I shall describe as his hatred of the mechanization of life. This he carried far indeed; as to it he lived at odds with much of the movement of his time. In many modern contrivances which to most of us seem innocent acquisitions of mankind—the motor car for instance—he saw a significance hostile to life's deeper, truer values. If he compromised as to a very few, the exceptions only served to emphasize the consistency of his conviction that by far the greater part of what passes for improvement and is greedily converted into necessity, is tawdry, vain and destructive of spiritual values. In addition, he also thought that the supposed efficiency with which these wants were supplied was illusory, even technologically. He had studied large industrial aggregations as few have and was satisfied that long before consolidation reached its modern size, it began to go to pieces at the top. There was a much earlier limit to human ability; minds did not exist able to direct such manifold and intricate structures. But that was only an incident; the important matter was the inevitable effect of size upon the individual, even though it neither limited nor impaired

efficiency. Allied with this was his attitude towards concentration of political power which appeared so often in
what he said from the bench. Indeed, his determination
to preserve the autonomy of the states—though it went
along with an unflinching assertion of federal power in
matters which he reckoned truly national—amounted
almost to an obsession. Haphazard as they might be in
origin, and even devoid of much present significance, the
states were the only breakwater against the ever pound-
ing surf which threatened to submerge the individual
and destroy the only kind of society in which personality
could survive.

As is the case with all our convictions, the foundation
of all this lay in the vision of the Good Life. It is, I
know, a little incongruous to quote another's vision of
the Good Life who was in most respects at the opposite
pole of belief and feeling, but nevertheless there comes
to my mind a scrap from the inscription above the gate
of the Abbey of Thélème:

Here enter you, pure, honest, faithful, true

.   .   .   .

Come, settle here a charitable faith,
Which neighborly affection nourisheth.

He believed that there could be no true community
save that built upon the personal acquaintance of each
with each; that thus alone could character and ability be
rightly gauged; without that "neighborly affection"
which would result, no "faith" could be nourished,
"charitable" or other. Only so could latent richness
which lurks in all of us come to flower. As the social
group grows too large for mutual contact and appraisal,

life quickly begins to lose its flavor and significance. Among multitudes relations must become standardized; to standardize is to generalize, and to generalize is to ignore all those authentic features which mark, and which indeed alone create, an individual. Not only is there no compensation for our losses, but most of our positive ills have directly resulted from great size. With it has indeed come the magic of modern communication and quick transport; but out of these has come the sinister apparatus of mass suggestion and mass production. Such devices, always tending more and more to reduce us to a common model, subject us—our hard-won immunity now gone—to epidemics of hallowed catchword and formula. The herd is regaining its ancient and evil primacy; civilization is being reversed, for it has consisted of exactly the opposite process of individualization—witness the history of law and morals. These many inventions are a step backward; they lull men into the belief that because they are severally less subject to violence, they are more safe; because they are more steadily fed and clothed, they are more secure from want; because their bodies are cleaner, their hearts are purer. It is an illusion; our security has actually diminished as our demands have become more exacting; our comforts we purchase at the cost of a softer fibre, a feebler will and an infantile suggestibility.

I am well aware of the reply to all this; it is on every tongue. "Do not talk to us," you say, "of the tiny city utopias of Plato or Aristotle; or of Jefferson with his dream of proud, honorable isolation; however circumscribed. Those days are gone forever, and they are well lost. The vast command over Nature which the last century gave to mankind and which is but a fragmentary earnest of the future, mankind will not forego. The conquest of disease, the elimination of drudgery, the freedom from famine, the enjoyment of comfort, yes even that most doubtful gift, the not-too-distant possession of a leisure we have not yet learned to use—on these, having once tasted them, mankind will continue to insist. And, at least so far as we have gone, they appear to be conditioned upon the co-operation and organization of great numbers. Perhaps we may be able to keep and to increase our gains without working on so fast a scale; we do not know; show us and we may try; but for the present we prefer to keep along the road which has led us so far, and we will not lend an auspicious ear to jeremiads that we should retrace the steps which have brought us in sight of so glorious a consummation."

If it is hard to see any answer to all this, the day has clearly gone forever of societies small enough for their members to have personal acquaintance with each other, and to find their station through the appraisal of those who have any first-hand knowledge of them. Publicity is an evil substitute, and the art of publicity is a black art; but it has come to stay; every year adds to its potency and to the finality of its judgments. The hand that rules the press, the radio, the screen and the far-spread magazine, rules the country; whether we like it or not, we must learn to accept it. And yet it is the power of reiterated suggestion and consecrated platitude that at this moment has brought our entire civilization to imminent peril of destruction. The individual is as helpless against it as the child is helpless against the formulas with which he is indoctrinated. Not only is it possible by these means

to shape his tastes, his feelings, his desires and his hopes;
but it is possible to convert him into a fanatical zealot,
ready to torture and destroy and to suffer mutilation and
death for an obscene faith, baseless in fact and morally
monstrous. This, the vastest conflict with which mankind has ever been faced, whose outcome still remains
undecided, in the end turns upon whether the individual can survive; upon whether the ultimate value
shall be this wistful, cloudy, errant You or I, or that
Great Beast, Leviathan, that phantom conjured up as an
ignis fatuus in our darkness and a scapegoat for our
futility.

We Americans have at last chosen sides; we believe
that it may be idle to seek the Soul of Man outside Society; it is certainly idle to seek Society outside the Soul
of Man. We believe this to be the transcendent stake;
we will not turn back; in the heavens we have seen the
sign in which we shall conquer or die. But our faith will
need again and again to be refreshed; and from the life
we commemorate today we may gain refreshment. A
great people does not go to its leaders for incantations or
liturgies by which to propitiate fate or to cajole victory;
it goes to them to peer into the recesses of its own soul,
to lay bare its deepest desires; it goes to them as it goes
to its poets and its seers. And for that reason it means
little in what form this man's message may have been;
only the substance of it counts. If I have read it aright,
this was that substance. "You may build your Towers of
Babel to the clouds; you may contrive ingeniously to
circumvent Nature by devices beyond even the understanding of all but a handful; you may provide endless
distractions to escape the tedium of your barren lives;

173

you may rummage the whole planet for your ease and comfort. It shall avail you nothing; the more you struggle, the more deeply you will be enmeshed. Not until you have the courage to meet yourselves face to face; to take true account of what you find; to respect the sum of that account for itself and not for what it may bring you; deeply to believe that each of you is a holy vessel unique and irreplaceable; only then will you have taken the first steps along the path of Wisdom. Be content with nothing less; let not the heathen beguile you to their temples, or the Sirens with their songs. Lay up your Treasure in the Heaven of your hearts, where moth and rust do not corrupt and thieves cannot break through and steal."

22

AT THE FIFTIETH ANNIVERSARY COMMENCEMENT
[1943]

THE class orator of the Harvard Class of 1893 returned to Cambridge for the fiftieth commencement reunion and ceremony, on May 26, 1943. This is the address that Learned Hand delivered for the golden anniversary of his class.

Mr. Toastmaster and Friends: There really is not a great deal more that I can say to you than what I have already put into the few words that I wrote for the last report. Anything else will be mere elaboration. I suppose it is the usual, shall I say, fate of all people who get to be as old as we, to look back and to think, perhaps in an illusory way, of the associations they had when they were young, which I suppose at that time almost universally they did not realize, but of which, as they come to the end, they feel the depth and meaning. Perhaps this has no more meaning than the fact that, when the roll is pretty well near its end, they are apt to look on life as no more than the development of what was inevitable at the start. When we do look back to those years—I don't know how you feel—but for myself I feel how wonderfully rich it was. I have heard a great many young people, who got half way between their start and their graduation—extremely cultured young persons at that—who have said to me: "We went to Harvard College and we stayed a couple of years, but there didn't

seem to be anything they had to offer and so we quit."
Well, I just have not known what they meant, because
from my own experience this seemed to me so utterly un-
true. I was a green boy from a small provincial town;
nobody could have been greener than I, or more unsophisticated. Perhaps that may account for the fact that
I enjoyed it all so much, and when I have heard these
youngsters say they didn't find anything there I have
been stupefied; I have not known what they were talking
about. Because for me—and most of you I fancy will
agree—to come here, and find those wonderful tables
spread before us with all the viands of the mind and of
the feelings and of the emotions—all that was past and
the hope of what was to come—to have those spread before us and offered to us by men who were devoted to
trying to make us see what was in this world, what this
universe really was, and what it might be if we could
only comprehend it—I say to have that opportunity; I
have never been able to understand how anyone could
pass that up and say that there was nothing for him in it.
I don't understand it now. Perhaps you think that that
is nothing more than sentimentality; and perhaps you are
right. I don't know; I will not judge; but that is the way
it was to me; and I hope that is the way it was to you.

DeLancey Howe has resurrected out of oblivion something I said about our teachers. I will not try to repeat
it now, except to say that that is how I feel, and I believe that is how you feel. Those devoted men who believed in the pursuit of knowledge—perhaps in no more
than the pursuit of knowledge—but the pursuit of knowledge, whether it be its own end or whether it be a means
to make life more worth living: who believe that that is

the noble employment of leisure. I am tempted to call them great men, and some of them were; but, great or not, the impression that they left on me—and I dare say on you: what I got from them has given its value to anything I have ever been able to do since. It was that sense —I don't want to call it vision—it was that sense of value, sense of what is really worthwhile, which has impressed me in those moments few enough, in which I have been loyal to it, and has helped me through.

Lapsley said—and I agree with him—that these things are incommunicable, and perhaps they should be; perhaps it is an error to try to reduce them to more than that understanding which lies too deep for words. But I shall try at least to put in words this much, being not unaware of the danger. These men did communicate to us, though not didactically. They certainly did not try to preach. I don't think that people ought to preach the truth; it is like bringing up children; those of you who have had children know that you teach them by example, by a kind of osmosis. What is it that those men left with us—what was the ineradicable tradition? That is what I am trying to get at. I think it is the same thing which this terrible calamity that has come upon us has brought to us: the sacredness of each individual. We cannot, we must not try to force the individual to our own image, to our own pattern. Now, in the minds of all of you you will at once say: "That is impossible and he doesn't realize the implications and the double meaning of what he is saying." I do. I can't go into it here, and I don't suppose I could explain it; but I think that that is really the question with which now in mortal agony the world is wrestling, and I am sure that the defeat of

Germany will not alone be its solution. There is a passage, a little quatrain of a not very great poet, which has always to me been very deeply significant, and I like to use it on occasions like this. Perhaps you have not known it. It is from William Watson.

> Momentous to himself, as I to me,
>   Hath been each man that ever woman bore;
> Once in a lightning flash of sympathy
>   I felt that truth an instant, and no more.

I wonder whether what we are about and what we hope may come can be translated into a hope that the lightning flash of sympathy may endure for more than for an instant; I wonder whether it may become a steady glow to guide us always. At least to me, that is what those four years that we spent together have meant. I believe they really bound us. This is their significance, now that we are old. We are not through; I don't even think we are what Holmes said in his valedictory. Do you remember it? He said that when the horses had finished the race they ran a final run on the track; and then he quoted from that passage of Virgil which ends: "Death plucks me by the ear and says: 'Live, I am coming.'" I am not yet ready to resign in that spirit; we have a duty to perform. I wish I felt sure that, if it had fallen to me I should have been able to discharge the same duty as those young Americans are discharging theirs who are called to give their lives and are giving them so unsparingly and so nobly. That has not been our portion; and now we are old. But I don't think our duty or our power has necessarily gone; and I do think that with reverence we can still show the light if we have it; and that it still burns. It is shining within us, and if I have interpreted aright what it means, we can be messengers each one in his way, and nothing we do will be entirely without effect. For, when all is said, as my friend George Rublee likes to put it, the only success is to be a success as a person; and it is still not too late for that.

23

PHILIP LITTELL
[1944]

PHILIP LITTELL (1868–1943) was born in Brookline,
Massachusetts, and was graduated from Harvard in 1890.
He was on the editorial staff of the Milwaukee Sentinel
(1890–1901), the New York Globe (1910–13), and the
New Republic (1914–23). He wrote Books and Things
(1919) and This Way Out (1928). His home was in
Cornish, N.H., where he was a neighbor and a friend of
the Hands at their summer home, Low Court. At his
death the Century Association of New York, of which
Littell was a member, asked Learned Hand to prepare the
memorial. It was incorporated in a ceremony, on January 13, 1944, for members who had died in 1943, and was
printed in a volume issued by the Merrymount Press,
Boston.

Philip Littell had been a member of the Association
for only about three years when he died, and during
most of that time he was too ill to come to the Clubhouse. He was, however, a friend of many of us, and
probably known to most. His talents were many and varied; wit, acumen, wisdom, wide familiarity with all English literature and an extraordinary memory all combined
to make him one of the most gifted literary critics of his
time. Aside from his work in his earlier years upon daily
newspapers, the greater part of what he wrote was in the
New Republic for its first five or six years, a good deal of
which was later republished in a separate volume. This

included not only literary comment, but general observations, gay, ironic, observant and charming. *This Way
Out*, a book on the Garden of Eden and the Expulsion,
was full of beauty, pathos, tenderness, satire, and fancy.

He was generous and helpful without measure to
younger writers, never sparing of his time; showing them
their strength and weakness in a way possible only to one
who had his understanding and learning. But it was in
his friendships and other personal relations that his life
was most remarkable, and in which he most expressed
himself. More or less continuously for nearly thirty years
he had been an invalid; in the last five or more years he
was confined substantially to the house. Always, to the
very end when he was nearly completely incapacitated,
he was the center of a circle of friends and acquaintances
who found in him an inexhaustible source of gaiety, enlightenment and refreshment. About him there was not
the faintest suspicion of invalidism; he succeeded, even
after illness upon illness came upon him, in so entirely
detaching himself from his infirmities that his associates
were unaware that he was not in the same health as they.
In the memory of those who loved him, and who knew
how perfect had to be the suppression to eliminate all
shadow of ill health, this will always seem an achievement amazing and unequalled in their experience.

In company, his address was urbane, courteous, and a
little grave. He greatly excelled in talk, though at times
it was not easy for those less quick and subtle than he to
catch the allusions of his wit. He was an attentive listener;
it was an undeviating part of his courtesy never to interrupt. He was considerate of others' arguments, but usually enough superior to his opponents to be devastating;

and indeed, having entered the lists, though invariably kind, he neither asked, nor gave, quarter on the issue. He loved children and became passionate even to fury at injustice or cruelty done them; as indeed he could become at all wrongs to the weak and helpless. He gave and received love from more persons than is the fate of all but very few; to his familiars the joy and freedom of his perfect companionship will never be surpassed.

24

PHILHELLENE EDITORIAL
[1944]

GREECE was in dire straits in 1944 and Learned Hand
was one of many Americans who joined in helping out
the small but ancient nation. As a member of the board
of trustees of the American Friends of Greece, he made
a statement that was printed as an editorial in the Philhellene, an occasional publication of that organization,
issued in New York. His message was dated March 20,
1944.

If all were for the best in a best of all possible worlds,
we need have no fear for the future of the Greek people.
Such heroism, such constancy, such martyrdom for the
right, could only end in restoration, security, plenty, and
inward accord, combining to bring on a golden hereafter,
stretching out indefinitely. Alas, the forecast is far different. Even if we pass over the period immediately following an armistice, even if we assume that the factions
which now so ominously threaten have composed their
differences and that some measure of inner concord has
been established, even if we imagine the ravages of the
Herrenvolk have been repaired, how can we assure this
gallant people of its future in the world of nations?
What can we say to any small nation: to the Belgians,
to the Dutch, to the Danes, to the Norwegians? That passion of national identity, which suffering has made so
much the fiercer, demands not merely recognition, but
independence, "sovereignty," the right to manage one's

own affairs without dictation, without interference, without surveillance. Which of us complacent citizens of a great power would accept less? By what right do we arrogate to ourselves what we deny to others? And yet which of us but in our heart of hearts knows that all this cannot be? Not for them; not indeed for us. Even in the past, small nations were seldom safe nations, although some of them did manage some measure of safety. Leonidas might have held out, if he had guarded the path to his rear; and Greece was never conquered till she fell from within. The Swiss could defend their mountains; the Dutch could flood their pastures. But today there can be no exceptions, for nothing can protect us against attack from above; and small nations will exist only at the sufferance of those who support great air fleets. Neither terrain nor distance is any longer a barrier, and destruction is a matter of minutes.

Faced with this, many good men can see no escape but in an all comprehensive community; an organization in which the rights of all nations shall be equal, and shall be protected by the common might. This is no place to argue whether that is possible; for, even assuming that it is, it is no friend of Greece, or of any other small people, which finds in it an opportunity to realize the autonomy it craves. The notion that there are international principles from which definite national rights can be deduced is an ignis fatuus which will lead us once more to disaster. Power will not be gainsaid; we can only hope that it may learn moderation. But moderation in its exercise is bred by moderation in the demands upon it. We already stand in peril that we have raised hopes which, when we are put to the proof, we shall not fulfill; let us not again default in meeting those expectations which will not unreasonably be drawn from what we say. Let us remember, while the spirit of generosity and sacrifice inspires us, that with the coming of peace we shall inevitably suffer a drop in our potential; we shall sag in our sympathies; we shall find it hard to resist those Sirens who will ask us once more to return to the delights of normalcy. Now, while our hearts are open, do not let us close our minds; in our commitments let us remember the day of performance. It were better we should somewhat disappoint this great and gallant people now, than endure their just resentment later. It is not that there is aught we can give that they do not deserve; it is that in the high tide of our gratitude for what they have done in the common cause, we shall not promise what we shall not carry out.

25

THE DEBT OF THE WORLD TO GREECE
[1944]

THE American Friends of Greece held a rally on March 29, 1944, in New York City. Learned Hand, as a member of the board of trustees of the organization, spoke on "The Debt of the World to Greece." His text was printed in the Philhellene, May–June 1944 (Vol. III, Nos. 5–6).

The Greek People, inspired by their own past and in turn passing on to us that inspiration at a time when we sadly needed their example, have put us deeply in their debt. That debt we have already in some measure recognized, and we shall do more to discharge it later. We have helped to tide them over what there is good reason to believe has been the worst of their ordeal; we shall not stop when peace comes; already plans are in prospect which will help them at least in the most grievous of their future trials. Nothing we can do will be more than their due; let us remember that, but for such as them, we might be in their case. Yet we must not forget that man lives not by bread alone; we must not measure our duty in terms of food shipments, of "reconstruction," of "health centers," even of the dispatch of wise and helpful counsellors and friends. When the awful moment of choice came to that devoted and heroic people, the supreme value which turned the scale was none of these. They knew what their sacrifice was to be; they knew that everything which they have in fact lost would be taken from them. Yet there was something for which they were willing to cast all this away. They were conscious of common traditions, common aspirations and a common fate; they chose to be faithful to those traditions, to realize those aspirations and to meet that fate. They will not believe that it profits them to be restored to all they have lost, if they do not gain the stake for which they played.

Here lies the substance of what they ask of us; it will demand all the intelligence, all the forbearance, all the patience, all the courage, all the wisdom, which we can muster. We are not yet alive to the difficulties; we are too ready to suppose that we can find the solution, if only we bring good will to the search. We are flooded with vague concepts, like "sovereignty," "democracy," "rights of small nations," "equality before the law," put forward as though they had some definite content. The Greeks will not be so put off; complacent generalities, however well meant, will not serve. If we fail, they will not thank us for the shiploads that we have sent them, or for the rehabilitation of their cities and their farms. And they will be right, for we shall not have helped them in what they really fought for. It is too soon even in outline to forecast what this help should be. The airplane alone has gone far to break down the old "frames of reference"; a weapon which, in the hands of a great power, can in a few hours wipe out utterly the defenses of any small people, puts our ingenuity to the supreme test. We shall have to devise altogether new concepts of what we mean by "independence," and "liberty" and "autonomy." The problems which we shall have to face will demand concrete thinking; our answers will inevitably repel and disgust visionaries, who are never content with less than the City of God, who will decry all compromise as treason. Shall we have the selflessness, the patience and the wisdom to fabricate some protection at once adequate and practicable? Shall we succeed in forging a shield for this people behind which they can work out their future? They ask of us, and they ask rightly, not some dream of a better world, some vision of Utopia; but a viable arrangement within which they can live and work with security. They will not be content with counterfeits, however fair and specious. The American people must not delay to search their souls; they must begin to ask themselves how they are prepared to answer.

26

THE SPIRIT OF LIBERTY
[1944]

IN the critical World War II year of 1944 a vast "I Am an American Day" ceremony was held in Central Park, New York City, on May 21. Many thousands of people were present, including a large number of new citizens. Learned Hand's brief address was so eloquent and so moving that the text immediately became the object of wide demand. It was quickly printed and reprinted and also put into anthologies. The impact was so great that the speaker was invited to address a similar gathering the next year.

We have gathered here to affirm a faith, a faith in a common purpose, a common conviction, a common devotion. Some of us have chosen America as the land of our adoption; the rest have come from those who did the same. For this reason we have some right to consider ourselves a picked group, a group of those who had the courage to break from the past and brave the dangers and the loneliness of a strange land. What was the object that nerved us, or those who went before us, to this choice? We sought liberty; freedom from oppression, freedom from want, freedom to be ourselves. This we then sought; this we now believe that we are by way of winning. What do we mean when we say that first of all we seek liberty? I often wonder whether we do not rest our hopes too much upon constitutions, upon laws and upon courts. These are false hopes; believe me, these are false hopes. Liberty lies in the hearts of men and women; when it dies there, no constitution, no law, no court can save it; no constitution, no law, no court can even do much to help it. While it lies there it needs no constitution, no law, no court to save it. And what is this liberty which must lie in the hearts of men and women? It is not the ruthless, the unbridled will; it is not freedom to do as one likes. That is the denial of liberty, and leads straight to its overthrow. A society in which men recognize no check upon their freedom soon becomes a society where freedom is the possession of only a savage few; as we have learned to our sorrow.

What then is the spirit of liberty? I cannot define it; I can only tell you my own faith. The spirit of liberty is the spirit which is not too sure that it is right; the spirit of liberty is the spirit which seeks to understand the minds of other men and women; the spirit of liberty is the spirit which weighs their interests alongside its own without bias; the spirit of liberty remembers that not even a sparrow falls to earth unheeded; the spirit of liberty is the spirit of Him who, near two thousand years ago, taught mankind that lesson it has never learned, but has never quite forgotten;* that there may be a kingdom where the least shall be heard and considered side by side with the greatest. And now in that spirit, that spirit of an America which has never been, and which may never be; nay, which never will be except as the con-

---

* This clause was taken in substance from the following clause in H. G. Wells's *The Outline of History* (volume II, page 632, George Newnes, Ltd., London): ". . . whose pitiless and difficult doctrine of self-abandonment and self-forgetfulness we can neither disregard nor yet bring ourselves to obey." L. H.

science and courage of Americans create it; yet in the spirit of that America which lies hidden in some form in the aspirations of us all; in the spirit of that America for which our young men are at this moment fighting and dying; in that spirit of liberty and of America I ask you to rise and with me pledge our faith in the glorious destiny of our beloved country.

27

A PLEDGE OF ALLEGIANCE
[1945]

LEARNED HAND's second "I Am an American Day" address, before an audience similar to that which heard the first, was delivered in Central Park, New York City, on May 20, 1945.

We meet once more to attest our loyalty, and pledge our allegiance. In the year that has passed we have lost much, and we have gained much. We have lost that great captain, to whose foresight, courage and sagacity it is so largely due that we still stand a free people. We have lost thousands and tens of thousands of our youth who fell in battle; we have the wounded to care for, and the bereaved to comfort, so far as comfort is possible. Against all this we and our Allies have utterly brought down our most dreaded enemy; victory is more than half won. At this moment, solemn and momentous, we have no sense of jubilation; we know that our troubles are not at an end; we know that the punishment of our enemies, however just, is no guaranty of our safety, even after that other victory, which with confidence we expect, shall have followed the victory already gained.

And so, as we renew our mutual fealty, it is fitting that we should pause, and seek to take account of the meaning of our cost and suffering. Was not the issue this: whether mankind should be divided between those who command and those who serve; between those who use others at their will and those who must submit; whether the measure of a man's power to shape his own destiny should be the force at his disposal? Our nation was founded upon an answer to those questions, and we have fought this war to make good that answer. For ourselves and for the present, we are safe; our immediate peril is past. But for how long are we safe; and how far have we removed our peril? If our nation could not itself exist half slave and half free, are we sure that it can exist in a world half slave and half free? Is the same conflict less irrepressible when world wide than it was eighty years ago when it was only nation wide? Right knows no boundaries, and justice no frontiers; the brotherhood of man is not a domestic institution.

No, our job will not end with the sound of the guns. Even in our own interest we must have an eye to the interests of others; a nation which lives only to itself will in the end perish; false to the faith, it will shrivel and pass to that oblivion which is its proper receptacle. We may not stop until we have done our part to fashion a world in which there shall be some share of fellowship; which shall be better than a den of thieves. Let us not disguise the difficulties; and, above all, let us not content ourselves with noble aspirations, counsels of perfection, and self-righteous advice to others. We shall need the wisdom of the serpent; we shall have to be content with short steps; we shall be obliged to give and take: we shall face the strongest passions of mankind— our own not the least; and in the end we shall have fabricated an imperfect instrument. But we shall not have wholly failed; we shall have gone forward, if we bring to our task a pure and chastened spirit, patience, understanding, sympathy, forbearance, generosity, fortitude and above all an inflexible determination. The history of man has just begun: in the aeons which lie before him lie limitless hope or limitless despair. The choice is his; the present choice is ours: it is worth the trial.

Therefore, as we now pledge allegiance to our flag, shall we not see it as more than a symbol for those alone over whom it waves? Shall we not believe that, be we never so prosperous, and safe, and contented, we shall have failed to grasp its meaning, and shall have been truant to its promise, except as we strive to make it a signal, a beacon, a standard, to which the best hopes of mankind will ever turn? In confidence that you share that belief, I now ask you to raise your hands and repeat with me this pledge:

I pledge allegiance to the flag of the United States of America, and to the Republic for which it stands—one nation, indivisible, with liberty and justice for all.

28

SIMON FLEXNER
[1946]

SIMON FLEXNER (1863–1946) was born in Louisville,
Kentucky, and studied medicine at the University of
Louisville while working as a druggist's clerk. After receiving his degree in 1889, he went to Johns Hopkins
University to study under Dr. William Henry Welch.
He did laboratory work in Berlin and then in 1903 assumed the directorship of the laboratories of the Rockefeller Institute for Medical Research in New York. A
decade later he became one of the charter members of
the Rockefeller Foundation, and his name appeared in
the certificate of incorporation. His administrative duties did not keep him from continuing his own research,
including experimental investigation of venoms and study
of the cause and spread of poliomyelitis. A meeting in
memory of Simon Flexner was held at the Rockefeller
Institute on June 12, 1946, at which Learned Hand
spoke, along with John D. Rockefeller, Jr., Raymond B.
Fosdick, and others. His address is reprinted from a book-
let of the memorial, published by the Merrymount Press,
Boston (pp. 7–12).

You have not asked me to join with you this afternoon
because of anything I can say about Simon Flexner's
place in medicine; but only, I assume, because it seemed
appropriate that someone who was a layman, and had
been for long his friend, by taking part in this symposium might help to fill out the different aspects of his

career. I shall forgo saying anything of my personal relations with him beyond seizing this chance gratefully to acknowledge the many acts of kindness that he did me over more than forty years of uninterrupted friendship. Whenever I asked his advice, he made me feel, not that he was doing me a favor, but that we were jointly interested in a situation to whose solution he might, and believed he could, bring some help; and wise, practical help he invariably did bring. These "little unremembered acts of kindness and love" did not seem such to him; but they did to me, and I come with gladness to add my personal tribute of affection to the memory of a lost and faithful friend, whom I shall not replace. However, this too is not what you have asked of me; but how he appeared to one who had no competence to measure his achievements in his calling. I shall try to describe one trait in his character which in my relations with him most impressed me. It was by no means the only one that did; but since I deem it especially precious, I should like to dwell upon it.

Of those qualities on which civilization depends, next after courage, it seems to me, comes an open mind, and, indeed, the highest courage is, as Holmes used to say, to stake your all upon a conclusion which you are aware tomorrow may prove false. Surely we need no proof in these disastrous days that, if men would only bear and forbear, would only hold their beliefs tentatively and subject to verification, would try to see with others' eyes, the greatest part of this world's woes would be at an end. Now, it would seem—at first blush as we lawyers say—as though the discipline of a scientist was the best assurance we could ask of a disposition not to judge till one had examined, and always to verify before one acted; and so it has indeed always been with the great names in science, as it has been with the truly great names everywhere. But scientists are not exempt from human frailties, and the spirit of tolerance cannot exist without scepticism, and scepticism is a late comer upon the human scene, and will always remain an alien: like all aliens, at best it will always be suspected. Life is the transmission of received symbols into action, and accommodation between the objective significance of the symbols and the conduct they provoke is often remote or non-existent. As William James says somewhere: "Nature tells all frogs to jump for what looks red and take their chances. If it is only red meat, well and good; if it is red flannel on a hook, in the long run also well and good, though not for that particular frog."

I sometimes wonder, if you will forgive me, whether the very severity of the discipline of science may not predispose its pupils to revel in the luxury of conviction, when in other fields they find themselves relieved from the insistent scrutiny which their calling exacts. Doubt being abnormal, human nature has an unlovely way of asserting itself with violence, when outraged by the burden of an eternity of verification. Set free from professional responsibility, one may at last feel that one can be one's real self—yes, that deepest, truest, because that primitive, self. May I call to mind, as an illustration, the attitude some fifty years ago of physicists towards philosophy, which was then driven home upon me, because I had a short and unsuccessful love affair with philosophy at the time? As a lover, I well remember my indignation at the arrogant, and at times, illiterate, hostility against all that went by the name of metaphysics. Eschewing all barren exercises in what seemed to them the most sterile of verbal gymnastics, the physicists of that time lived, contented and assured, in a Lucretian universe of those tidy little marbles, which only needed one perfect and comprehensive Newtonian equation to make precisely ascertainable each moment of the past, and each moment of the future. They had no "blank misgivings of a Creature moving about in worlds not realized"; they never did "tremble like a guilty thing surprised." Dogmatists, dealing in a currency which was sure never to suffer depreciation, they could afford to sweep into the rubbish heap any inane visitants from Laputa, who were still unaccountably allowed to strut upon the boards. Yet how now have all their axioms vanished into Limbo. Could they return, it would be to find all the chessmen gone with which they played their game; and even those neat models forbidden us which, until only a few years ago, we were allowed to use, as helps over hard places. All these replaced by entities, beside which those of the Schoolmen look solid and practicable; all replaced by a nominalistic universe of the purest conceptualistic fabric. It is immoral to ask about the shape or the position of an electron, and indeed it is doubtful whether the question is not nonsense. Moreover, whatever it may be—for with existence it does appear to be endowed—no more wayward creature ever came into the universe of discourse. Indeed, we are assured that it is only because the world is filled with mythical myriads of these capricious witches and their partners, the equally unpredictable protons, that we are not battered about in a perpetual Walpurgisnacht of meaningless agitation.

Jeans appears to have been wrong about God; he is not a Mathematican, only a Statistician, a kind of Sublimated Actuary.

As I knew Simon Flexner, he wholly escaped this snare. Whether it was the struggles of his early years, the necessity of accommodating himself to narrow opportunities and exacting duties, of putting at continual hazard all that he had so hardly achieved, I cannot say. I knew him only after he had won the recognition which followed him through the rest of his life. But after all, was not that just the season to expect a crop of arrogance, self-assurance and complacency? It never appeared; not a single shoot ever pushed its ugly head above the surface. Surely, in medicine you too must be familiar with those laymen who can correct your obvious imbecilities; at any rate we lawyers find on all sides lay answers to our most perplexing problems, which we are assured that we reject only because we are a stiff-necked generation, incapable of change or progress. Not so with him; if I talked my shop he was interested, understanding and sympathetic, with the mellow interest, understanding and sympathy of a spirit, whose horizons encompassed much territory, and which was well aware that of the perils of the soul among the most grievous are pride and certitude. When too he spoke of his own shop, it was the same; lucidly he could explain it in such terms as a layman could comprehend, or at least in such that he left, thinking that he had comprehended. Nor was there shadow of assertion beyond what the evidence seemed to warrant up to that moment. Open, detached, ready to revise, never insistent to convert, no crusader, or the friend of crusades or crusaders. It was on this account that I always came away from him, conscious of that sort of rare communion which, were it common, would at length make this world a home for beings who might justly be called human. One life, I know, does not move us far along the road; but I am convinced that it is only in proportion as we honor and foster such lives that we shall move at all towards freedom. That is not the faith of this generation; in its pathetic pursuit of that ever retreating pot of gold, it puts its trust in loyalties, in creeds, in causes, in regulation, in institutions, in courts, in principles, in propaganda. The one thing to which it will not trust is the vagrant mind and the self-directed soul. So be it, by their fruit ye shall know them; and do we need to be assured that our fruit is bitter?

And so I thank you for letting me have a part with you here. I thank you first in the name of my affection; but even more I thank you in the name of that homage which all of us owe, and, for myself, with a full heart I pay, to the memory of one who was far-sighted and temperate and wise and just.

29

CHIEF JUSTICE STONE'S CONCEPT
OF THE JUDICIAL FUNCTION
[1946]

HARLAN FISKE STONE (1872–1946) was born in Chester-
field, New Hampshire, of a family of New England farmers. He studied at Amherst, where he first met Calvin
Coolidge, who was to appoint him to the Supreme Court
some thirty years later. He took law at Columbia University and began the practice of law in New York City
in 1898. His interests were in considerable part academic,
however, and he began to lecture in the Columbia Law
School in 1899, and became full professor in 1905 and
dean in 1910, a post he distinguished for thirteen years.
In 1924 President Coolidge persuaded him to take the
post of Attorney General in the midst of the reeking
scandals that followed the Harding Administration. He
at once dropped a raft of the hangers-on of the Ohio
gang and put an end to the snooping with which the Department of Justice had terrorized many persons of un-
orthodox views. He had just restored the supremacy of
law and judicial procedure and was about to launch an
antitrust suit against the Aluminum Company of America when President Coolidge nominated him for the Supreme Court. Senator Norris of Nebraska opposed the
appointment as obedient to "special interests and the
corporations." Only six nay votes were cast, and Stone
became a justice in 1925. But far from lining up with
what might have been regarded as the interests of such
former clients as the heirs of J. P. Morgan, he soon
joined with Justices Holmes and Brandeis in dissents.

*With the retirement of Charles Evans Hughes in 1941,
Stone was named Chief Justice by President Roosevelt.
He presided at five trying terms and struggled with the
problem of reconciling constitutional government and
popular liberties with the means to oppose sheer and destructive power. After his death, on an opinion day in
1946, the Columbia Law Review, to which he had contributed many times, issued a memorial number in September 1946. For it Learned Hand wrote "Chief Justice
Stone's Concept of the Judicial Function" (Vol. LVII,
pp. 696–9). The article is reprinted with permission.*

This is not the occasion for a critical estimate of the
place in our time of Chief Justice Stone. Today I wish to
speak only of what I believe was his conception of the
position of a judge in a democratic society, more particularly in such a society when it is organized under a
written constitution whose authoritative interpretation
rests with the courts. When he came into the Supreme
Court in 1925 there had for long been a cleavage, deep,
though somewhat vague in its boundaries, touching what
that place should be; it showed itself chiefly in the interpretation of the Bill of Rights, as we have become
accustomed collectively to call the first eight, and the
Thirteenth, Fourteenth and Fifteenth Amendments to
the Constitution. With the extraordinary industrial ex-
pansion which followed the Civil War, there came in
the seventies and eighties acute industrial and agrarian
tensions, which, though in kind they were not new and
indeed went back to the beginning of the republic and
earlier, had not theretofore been thought to call for

much affirmative governmental regulation. Beginning in the eighties the states strove to relieve these by statutes whose passage the propertied interests, on whom they impinged, were powerless to prevent. They appealed to the Fourteenth Amendment on the score that these measures invaded just those rights of property which the Amendment had been designed to protect. There was no doubt that they did invade those rights as they had theretofore been enjoyed and understood; and the judges, having been for the most part drawn—as was inevitable —from the group whose interests were affected, in entire good faith found ample warrant for the position that such enactments were contrary to the fundamental pre-suppositions of a society based upon that system of free enterprise which the Bill of Rights guaranteed. It was during the nineties that this movement was in its heyday; perhaps it reached its most extreme expression in the Income Tax Decision, in spite of the fact that that involved the Bill of Rights, if at all, only very obliquely.

Not only did this interpretation of the Amendments arouse resentment in the groups which had succeeded in pressing through the laws in question; but the constitutional assumptions on which the decisions were based also called out protests from the profession; on the bench, at the bar, and in the schools. While young Stone was still studying law there were questionings, and at Harvard, Thayer had already become the prophet of a new approach. By the time the future chief justice had become dean the difference was articulate and strident, and he made no secret where his choice lay. After he became a justice of the court his record was uniform in siding with that minority of his brethren who made up for their small number by the weight of their authority. Their notion was that the Bill of Rights could not be treated like ordinary law; its directions were to be understood rather as admonitions to forbearance; as directed against the spirit of faction when faction sought to press political advantage to ruthless extremes. These men believed that democracy was a political contrivance by which the group conflicts inevitable in all society should find a relatively harmless outlet in the give and take of legislative compromise after the contending groups had had a chance to measure their relative strength; and through which the bitterest animosities might at least be assuaged, even though that reconciliation did not ensue which sometimes follows upon an open fight. They had no illusion that the outcome would necessarily be the best obtainable, certainly not that which they might themselves have personally chosen; but the political stability of such a system, and the possible enlightenment which the battle itself might bring, were worth the price. All this Harlan Stone, whether as teacher or as judge, believed with deep conviction, and supported with undeviating loyalty. After many years of discouragement, he saw his school apparently triumphant; it had become the accepted doctrine that statutes were not to be held invalid, so long as anyone could find a reasonable basis for not ascribing them purely to envy or greed; and, as it was seldom, if ever, that this could not be done with any confidence, most statutes were upheld.

There was here, however, a logical dilemma, which, like other political dilemmas, would not be suppressed as new problems arose. The battle had been fought almost exclusively over the institution of property; and, although the changes effected were revolutionary, they had been gradual, and they had not gone beyond what the prevailing fashions had demanded, here and even more in Europe. Nevertheless, the losing school occupied a position from which logically it was hard to dislodge it. It argued that the interpretation of the winners was in effect an abdication of the admitted premise that the Bill of Rights was law, and not merely a counsel of perfection and an ideal of temperance: always to be kept in mind, it is true, but whose infractions were to be treated only as matter for regret. If all it forbade were statutes or administrative excesses which were so utterly outrageous that nobody could give any rational support, it was an idle gesture, for it is nearly always possible to find a plausible justification for any measure that has commanded enough popular support to get itself enacted. The winners answered that, however that might be, it was apparent that any more stringent doctrine than they were willing to admit made the courts a third camera— in fact final arbiters in disputes in which everybody agreed they should have no part. Unless they abstained, the whole system would fall apart; or, if it did not, certainly the judges must be made sensitive and responsive to the shifting pressures of political sentiment, a corrective which few were prepared to accept. Therefore, they argued, theirs was the only possible canon, let political logic find in it what flaws it would.

With the dominance of this second view it might seem that the conflict was over. But the end was not yet; for the latent equivocation involved reappeared as the field of combat changed. Even before Justice Stone became Chief Justice it began to seem as though, when "personal rights" were in issue, something strangely akin to the discredited attitude towards the Bill of Rights of the old apostles of the institution of property, was regaining recognition. Just why property itself was not a "personal right" nobody took the time to explain; and perhaps the inquiry would have been regarded as captious and invidious anyway; but the fact remained that in the name of the Bill of Rights the courts were upsetting statutes which were plainly compromises between conflicting interests, each of which had more than a merely plausible support in reason. That looked a good deal as though more specific directions could be found in the lapidary counsels of the Amendments than the successful school had been able to discover, so long as the dispute turned on property. It needed little acquaintance with the robust and loyal character of the Chief Justice to foretell that he would not be content with what to him was an opportunistic reversion at the expense of his conviction as to the powers of a court. He could not understand how the principle which he had all along supported, could mean that, when concerned with interests other than property, the courts should have a wider latitude for enforcing their own predilections than when they were concerned with property itself. There might be logical defects in his canon, but it deserved a consistent application or it deserved none at all; at any rate it was not to be made into an excuse for having one's way in any given case. Most of all was its even-handed application important to the judges themselves, since only by not intervening could they hope to preserve that independence which was the condition of any successful discharge of their duties.

It was because he was throughout true to this view that, it seems to me, we should especially remember him with gratitude, and honor him as a judge. We face difficulties which are big with portent, and uncertain of solution. Such solutions as will arrive, like all human solutions, will be likely to be inadequate and unfair placebos. But nevertheless they will be compromises, as government almost always must be in a free country; and if they are to be upset under cover of the majestic sententiousness of the Bill of Rights, they are likely to become centres of frictions undreamed of by those who avail themselves of this facile opportunity to enforce their will. What I have said does not touch more than one facet of the career of this great and honorable public servant; but I submit that it is well for us to pause and consider how important in the days ahead may be his attempt to keep alive at the end, as he did at the beginning, the tradition of detachment and aloofness without which, I am persuaded, courts and judges will fail. And make no mistake, that tradition is under attack, even if it be not a frontal attack. We are assured that only the unsophisticated and naive will believe in the reality of detachment and aloofness in judges, or in anyone else. These philosophers believe that they have burrowed too far into the visceral origins of all beliefs and of all convictions to be fobbed off by the ingenuous assumptions of a simpler age. None of us can ever escape covertly seeking our interests; our disguises, be they ever so ingenious, are easily penetrated; our shams are readily exposed. Let us not underrate the power of this attack; let us remember how desperately in our own youth we too dreaded appearing to be without guile; how we longed to be reckoned astute and enfranchised; and let us not forget that youth is the same now as then. Therefore it is fitting for us to meet here today in grateful commemoration of the life of this stalwart, true-hearted, steadfast champion of a faith whose disappearance will in the end bring with it a relapse into the reign of the tooth and claw.

30

THOMAS WALTER SWAN
[1947]

THOMAS WALTER SWAN was born in Norwich, Connecticut, in 1877. He received his bachelor's degree at Yale in
1900 and his law degree at Harvard three years later. He
began the practice of law in Chicago in 1903 and also
lectured in the University of Chicago Law School. In
1916 he was called to the Yale Law School as professor
and dean. He was one of the foremost legal educators in
the country when, eleven years later, he was appointed
to the Federal Court of Appeals for the Second Circuit
(New York, Connecticut, and Vermont) by President
Calvin Coolidge. The Yale Law Journal observed the
twentieth anniversary of his appointment to the bench
with a dedicated issue including an article by Learned
Hand, his friend and colleague on the court. It is reprinted with permission from the December 1947 issue
(Vol. LVII, pp. 167–72).

When President Coolidge appointed Judge Swan to
the Second Circuit, it was in some sense an act of faith.
It is true that, as dean of the Yale Law School for more
than ten years, he had shown uncommon talents as a
leader and a teacher; that under him the school went
forward as it never had before in an equal time, and that
he had shown rare breadth of mind in the appointment
of men who radically differed from his own views. However, the school had taken up all his time and allowed
him no access to courts; and his earlier practice in Chi-

cago—whither he went directly after he had finished his education—had been almost exclusively in chambers. Thus, when he became a judge, his acquaintance with courts had been very largely at second hand; and indeed, so far as concerns the actual trial of causes, such it remains today. It would have been easy, therefore, to assume that such a man, put on an appellate court, would prove to be more a scholar remote from practical affairs and given to speculation, than a judge who would be interested primarily in the just despatch of causes, and who would make no further excursions into the realm of theory than was necessary to support his decisions. Moreover, in 1927 it had not become as common as it now is to look to the schools to fill the bench; the tradition had not so much yielded that the law should grow by accretion, each step preparing for the next, and that courts should be jealous of attempts to lay down doctrines of wide generality. A legal theorist was the last kind of judge whom President Coolidge would have consciously chosen; and, in spite of the possibilities I have mentioned, it at once became evident that he had made no mistake, and that his act of faith had been justified. There had come to the court a judge, not given to remoulding the world nearer to the heart's desire, but one who sought in the body of our inherited law and in the statutes, those guides and directions which were to be both his limitations and his opportunities. On the other hand it also soon appeared that, although he was a "legal" judge in the sense I have just mentioned, he regarded the law, not as a set of fiats to be read literally, and rigidly applied to all occasions embraced within the words and only to those; but as the means of fulfilling the purposes of a living society, which could be comprehended only as they were step by step realized.

In temper and bearing he was transparently made for the office. His manners on the bench were, and are, a model; and—be it said in all humility—often an admonition to others whose composure is not equally proof against irritation. He speaks but little, and is no "ill-tuned cymbal"; he never seeks to bring out in advance what will appear in season; nor does he lead the argument far afield into pastures whence the return is tortuous and uncertain. When he does speak, it is to put a narrow question, directed to inconsistencies already apparent, or to the untoward consequences of that which has been said. He is never in the teacher's chair, nor does he drive counsel to confusion by successive advances, designed to end in rout. His urbanity is almost always unruffled; never, in an experience with him of over twenty years, have I known him to hector a lawyer, or abuse the advantage of his position which denies any retort in kind. He has as little of the bully as of the showman, and he has reaped from the bar the harvest which his courteous and considerate nature has sown. Not that he suffers fools gladly, or is ready to let those wander along who think that they shall be heard for their much speaking. To direct, and if necessary to curtail, argument seems to him as much a part of the judge's duty, as to listen; and listen he always does; or, at least he gives the appearance of listening, for he never adopts the not uncommon device of discouraging prosy advocates by a real, or assumed, show of contemptuous inattention. In conference he is open minded, until he has heard what his brothers have to say, which he considers with respect and at times with too much deference; but, after he has once come to a conclusion, he is tenacious and very seldom yields. He is little given to dissent, being wholly without vanity, and—as it seems to me—not conscious enough of the importance of weakening the force of a wrong decision as a precedent. He is readier than most judges to take seriously petitions for rehearing (especially if he has written the opinion himself); not indeed, because of vacillation or of any shrinking from responsibility, but from an over tender scruple, coupled with entire absence of any pride of opinion. Incidentally, I have, however, never observed that he, more often than other judges, votes to change the original result. On the other hand he is always ready to accept suggestion from his brothers in amending or even in rewriting his opinions, before they are handed down, if he agrees with the substance of the proposal. He will not overrule a precedent, unless he can be satisfied beyond peradventure that it was untenable when made; and not even then, if it has gathered around it the support of a substantial body of decisions based upon it. As a corollary, he is not given to wide commitments when he writes, for he distrusts the guidance which the present evidence and the present argument give, if the issues be amplified beyond what is necessary to dispose of the controversy. He believes that the industry of other suitors to whom they may become vital, if expanded, is likely further to explore and illuminate them. Consistently with this, he does not seek to support his conclusions by resort to broad or speculative general principles; but, like an English judge, looks to the precedents or to the text for his warrant.

He finds his way through thickets of verbiage in statutes

or regulations with more ease than any other judge of my personal acquaintance. In my own case the words of such an act as the Income Tax, for example, merely dance before my eyes in a meaningless procession: cross-reference to cross-reference, exception upon exception—couched in abstract terms that offer no handle to seize hold of—leave in my mind only a confused sense of some vitally important, but successfully concealed, purport, which it is my duty to extract, but which is within my power, if at all, only after the most inordinate expenditure of time. I know that these monsters are the result of fabulous industry and ingenuity, plugging up this hole and casting out that net, against all possible evasion; yet at times I cannot help recalling a saying of William James about certain passages of Hegel: that they were no doubt written with a passion of rationality; but that one cannot help wondering whether to the reader they have any significance save that the words are strung together with syntactical correctness. Much of the law is now as difficult to fathom, and more and more of it is likely to be so; for there is little doubt that we are entering a period of increasingly detailed regulation, and it will be the duty of judges to thread the path—for path there is—through these fantastic labyrinths. Any facility in doing so is of the utmost importance; I envy its possessors, among whom my brother stands in the front rank. Again and again I have found myself utterly bewildered by the involution of phrase with phrase and of term with term, until his kindly light showed the turn which I had missed, and led me out of what had appeared to be a cul de sac. The talent, which can keep in solution, at whatever cost, these many ingredients and carry them all over into a final precipitate, is rare enough; but the talent which can do so without hours of distress and confusion is vouchsafed to only a scanty few.

His style is also a judicial model; simple, clear, severe, trimmed of ornament. He never seeks a display of learning, or a locution or phrase designed to divert his reader's attention from the substance he would convey, and to centre it upon himself; and in this he is protected, as few indeed of us are protected, by as complete an absence of any desire to startle and impress others with his endowments, as I have known on the bench or off. His propositions are well fortified by citation, and, in doubtful cases, he will exhaust the books before he is content with the result. An amusing instance of this was his opinion in what proved later to be the revolutionary case of Erie Railroad Company v. Tompkins. That involved a tort committed in Pennsylvania, whose common law on the point was different from the great body of decisions elsewhere. At first we were going to follow the Pennsylvania decisions for we did not know the others, and the briefs—as is so often the case—were inadequate. After much delving he found that, if we were to apply the "general law"—as we were then bound to do in a "diversity case"—the Pennsylvania rule did not govern; and so we held and were reversed by the epoch-making volte face of the Supreme Court. Had it not been for his hypertrophied judicial conscience, who shall say that we might not still be worshipping the Golden Calf of Swift v. Tyson?

In addition he has—so far as it is given to any of us to have it—that merit which perhaps should rank highest in point of style: i.e. not to be misled into assuming the conclusion in the minor premise—not to beg the question. I can think of no single fault that has done more to confuse the law and to disseminate litigation. One would suppose that so transparent a logical vice would be easily detected; but the offenders pass in troops before our eyes, bearing great names and distinguished titles. The truth is that we are all sinners; nobody's record is clean; and indeed it is only fair to say that much of the very texture of the law invites us to sin, for it so often holds out to us, as though they were objective standards, terms like "reasonable care," "due notice," "reasonable restraint," which are no more than signals that the dispute is to be decided with moderation and without disregard of any of the interests at stake. So inveterate is the disposition to eschew all deduction in such cases, that some ironist might argue that, given the average judicial capacity for self-scrutiny, it is safer not to expose the springs of decision, because the chances of a right result are greater than that its support will endure disclosure. Perhaps so; maybe, for the ingenuous and the artless to beg the question is nature's self-protective artifice. That need not be answered; but as a conscious expedient it would corrupt. Besides, few of us would care to avow that the law prospers only in proportion as those who administer it know not what they do; or that to use its language with full understanding of its purport, will not in the end promote its progress.

So much then for manners, acumen, and style. These count for much in a judge; far more than often we are prepared to admit; but, when all is said, the real test is how truly does he interpret the law. Even as far back as Aristotle judicial interpretation was seen as an essential

in the structure of a civilized society; but it has vexed
men from the beginning and will continue to vex them
till the end, how far the occasion which provoked an
"enactment,"—to adopt his term—and the purpose which
infused it—be it constitution, statute, precedent or regulation—shall prevail to set its limits, or to enlarge its
comprehension. This is not the place to attempt an answer—perhaps there is none anyway—; it is enough that,
whatever it is, in any event it must always be ad hoc. It
is true that in archaic societies law, which is usually itself
a sacred text, is read, like other primitive sacred texts, to
cover every situation which falls within the exact content of the words, and to exclude every situation which
does not. But as soon as a society becomes conscious of
self-direction, it begins to apply in some measure a "literary" canon—to borrow from Matthew Arnold—: that is,
it begins to read the text, not sub specie aeternitatis; but
with the recollection that in origin it served to compose
some existing conflict of interest, and that this should
serve to interpret it. The extent to which such societies
permit their judges to do this is the extent of their confidence in them: more properly, in modern times at any
rate, the measure of their own confidence that they can
trust themselves to select those on whose skill and sagacity they are willing to rely. There are indeed political
philosophers who insist that a judge must inevitably
choose between the dictionary and tabula rasa; but there
is a plain distinction in theory between "interpretation"
and "legislation," as well as a clear boundary in practice.
Let the judge go as far afield as he will, in seeking the
meaning of an "enactment"; if he is honest, he will never
substitute his personal appraisal of the interests at stake,

or his personal preference between them. It is true that he is not engaged in a historical reconstruction, as he is when determining an issue of fact; his task is more difficult, so difficult that it is impossible ever to know how far he has been successful. For it is no less than to decide how those who have passed the "enactment" would have dealt with the "particulars" before him, about which they have said nothing whatever. Impalpable and even insoluble as that inquiry may be, the method which he must pursue is toto coelo different from that open to him, were he free to enforce his own choices.

What then are the qualities, mental and moral, which best serve a judge to discharge this perilous but inescapable duty? First he must be aware of the difficulty and the hazard. He must hesitate long before imputing more to the "enactment" than he finds in the words, remembering that the "policy" of any law may inhere as much in its limits as in its extent. He must hesitate long before cutting down their literal effect, remembering that the authors presumably said no more than they wanted. He must have the historical capacity to reconstruct the whole setting which evoked the law; the contentions which it resolved; the objects which it sought; the events which led up to it. But all this is only the beginning, for he must possess the far more exceptional power of divination which can peer into the purpose beyond its expression, and bring to fruition that which lay only in flower. Of the moral qualities necessary to this, before and beyond all he must purge his mind and will of those personal presuppositions and prejudices which almost inevitably invade all human judgments; he must approach his problems with as little preconception of what should be the outcome as it is given to men to have; in short, the prime condition of his success will be his capacity for detachment. There are those who insist that detachment is an illusion; that our conclusions, when their bases are sifted, always reveal a passional foundation. Even so; though they be throughout the creatures of past emotional experience, it does not follow that that experience can never predispose us to impartiality. A bias against bias may be as likely a result of some buried crisis, as any other bias. Be that as it may, we know that men do differ widely in this capacity; and the incredulity which seeks to discredit that knowledge is a part of the crusade against reason from which we have already so bitterly suffered. We may deny—and, if we are competent observers, we will deny—that no one can be aware of the danger and in large measure provide against it.

My brother is not a man of neutral disposition, but of strong convictions resolutely held; he might be thought likely to allow these to enter into his judicial decisions. I will not say that any of us is without all tincture of such interjections; but he stands among those who are most completely free. In support of this I could adduce the overwhelming testimony of bench and bar, familiar with him and his work. They find in him a rectitude, which goes far beyond the elimination of all personal interest or concern; a rectitude which ignores his own beliefs and his own inclinations, and seeks for its sanction an authority, more commanding than the authority of himself or any other man—the authority of the collective will of a people, manifesting itself in their accredited declarations, as they strive, however blindly and inarticulately, towards their conception of the Good Life. To that authority alone he owns allegiance; and without stint and without alloy he has given himself to ascertain and to realize that conception. This he has done with patience, courage, insight, self-effacement, understanding, imagination, and learning; and his success has been an achievement equalled by only a handful. It is well that we should seize upon a moment, in itself irrelevant, on which to celebrate an anniversary of such a public servant. We are aware that today the foundations of all that we hold dear are in the balance; and we live in just apprehension. Without such servants no society can prosper; without such servants no society can in the end even endure. Let us pause then to acclaim one, who—himself all unaware of his deserts—has so richly earned our gratitude, and whose presence helps us to take heart against our forebodings.

31

CHARLES EVANS HUGHES
[1949]

CHARLES EVANS HUGHES (1862–1948) had one of the most distinguished public careers in the history of the United States. Born at Glens Falls, New York, where his father was a Baptist pastor, he was taught by his mother to read the Bible by the time he was four, and by the age of eight she had grounded him in French and German. From his father he learned Greek. He was graduated from Public School No. 35, New York City, and attended Madison University, now Colgate University, from which he transferred to Brown University, Providence, R.I. He took his law degree at Columbia University, after which he became in 1891 a professor of law at Cornell, but he soon turned to practice in New York. As a rising and at the same time courageous member of the bar, he began a series of brilliant exposés into the financial operations and management of public utilities and insurance companies. He bowed to no pressure and was uninfluenced when uneasy party bosses offered to make him mayor. These bold public services led to his election to the governorship in 1906, and he was reelected in 1908. President William Howard Taft appointed him to the Supreme Court in 1910 and he was making an excellent record on the highest bench when the Republican National Convention nominated him in 1916 for President. By the slender margin of California's delayed electoral vote did he miss the White House. He was Secretary of State from 1921 to 1925, and was the leading figure at the Washington Conference to limit

armaments. *By President Herbert Hoover he was returned*
to the Supreme Court in 1930 to succeed Chief Justice
Taft. Presiding with Olympian dignity but also with kind-
liness, he led the Supreme Court through a very impor-
tant decade, which included the New Deal test cases and
the Roosevelt court-enlargement plan. He retired in 1941
and died in 1948. Learned Hand's tribute is reprinted
with permission from the 1949 Harvard Law School
Yearbook (p. 9).

In our darker moments we wonder whether it may not
be inevitable in our democracy that accession to office
must be through sedulous adulation of our cultus hero,
the "Common Man," endless iteration of accredited
catch-words, cunning use of question-begging sedatives
and promises to every special interest of whatever it asks.
We ask ourselves whether, if so, we shall not in the end
succumb to these evasions of the dire problems that surround us; and whether our shrill disputations will not be
engulfed in the silence of an obscene totalitarianism. At
such seasons it is well for us to remember that more
often than in our melancholy we may fear, there emerge
great figures who owe nothing to the apparatus of organized sycophancy, and rise into respect and power by
the mere force of their character and endowments.
Among such was Chief Justice Hughes, who successively
occupied nearly all the highest offices of state (and
missed the highest of all only by the slenderest margin)
without recourse to the shoddy paraphernalia that so
often open the path to power. The qualities which made
him the inescapable candidate for governor in 1906—un-

welcome as he was to the political hierarchy of the time —were to carry him forward in all the steps of his illustrious career. They were a relentless self-discipline in mastering the details of his subject, a reserve against premature commitment while the matter remained in solution, broad horizons to include all the relevant factors, and at the end a solid assurance in the outcome. However, such gifts would not have brought to him the public trust and confidence which followed him in all his undertakings, had it not been for the high purpose apparent in all his incessant public services. You might differ with him as radically as you chose; you might believe that he had gone clean astray; but to question the sincerity and purity of his motives betrayed either that you had not understood what he was after, or that your own standards needed scrutiny. If any society is to prosper, it must be staffed with servants of such stuff; indeed, if any society is to endure, it must not be without them. Sure-footed time will tread out the lesser figures of our day; but, if our heritage does not perish, the work of this man and his example will remain a visible memorial of one who helped to keep alive and pass on that ordered freedom without which mankind must lapse into savagery, and repeat its slow and bitter ascent to even that level of mutual forbearance and good-will which it has now attained. We who knew him can do no better than to record our gratitude for a life to which we have owed so much.

32

THE ONE CONDITION
[1951]

A FRIEND and participant from the earliest years of the
American Law Institute, Learned Hand spoke extempo-
raneously at its twenty-eighth annual dinner at Mayflower Hotel, Washington, May 18, 1951. He was preceded
by several speakers, including Justice Felix Frankfurter, of
the Supreme Court, who paid tribute to him in connection with the announcement, a short while before, of his
retirement from the bench. The proceedings were recorded by a stenographer, and the closing paragraphs of
Learned Hand's response were printed in an editorial,
"Telling the Bar," in the Washington Post, May 27,
1951.

My friends, our future is precarious. I do not know if
you remember the time 11 years ago in 1940 when we
were here just on the eve of those dreadful days when it
seemed not unlikely that the whole of all which made
life precious might be overwhelmed. Today we stand in
as much danger as we did then; and, although it is not
from us that the heaviest sacrifices are demanded, yet we
have much to answer for. I like to hope—although I
agree that we can have no certainty, still I like to hope
—that we have a good chance, a splendid fighting chance
and much assurance of victory but on one condition:
that we do not go to pieces internally. It is there, I think,
that you and I may be able to help.

Because, my friends, will you not agree that any society which begins to be doubtful of itself; in which one man looks at another and says: "He may be a traitor," in which that spirit has disappeared which says: "I will not accept that, I will not believe that—I will demand proof. I will not say of my brother that he may be a traitor," but I will say, "Produce what you have. I will judge it fairly, and if he is, he shall pay the penalty; but I will not take it on rumor. I will not take it on hearsay. I will remember that what has brought us up from savagery is a loyalty to truth, and truth cannot emerge unless it is subjected to the utmost scrutiny"—will you not agree that a society which has lost sight of that, cannot survive?

And so I say to you that today we stand as we did 11 years ago, perhaps in even greater peril; and I say too that you and I have this which we can contribute and which may be the most important of all. On our people has fallen a responsibility, greater than that of any other people; you and I, loyal custodians of our precious heritage, have our part to perform. You remember in *The Cloister on the Hearth*, in tight moments how Gerard's companion used to say: "*Courage, mon ami, le diable est mort.*" No, my friends, the devil isn't dead; but take heart of grace; we shall get him yet!

33

MORALS IN PUBLIC LIFE
[1951]

NEWSPAPERS and congressional investigations into commercialized gambling, influence in government loans, tax settlements, and other matters disclosed an unusually low state of public morals in 1950–1. Hearings were held by a subcommittee of the Senate Committee on Labor and Public Welfare to see what Congress might do to remedy conditions. Senator Paul H. Douglas, of Illinois, was chairman of the subcommittee, and one of the distinguished citizens he asked to Washington to testify was Learned Hand, who appeared on June 28, 1951.

Senator Douglas. Ladies and gentlemen, we are very privileged this afternoon to have with us I think perhaps the Judge in the United States who is most respected both by lawyers and by the general public, a man who has been on the Federal District, and Circuit Court for over 40 years, a man whose integrity is respected by the entire nation, a man who many of us had always hoped would be a member of the Supreme Court of the United States. It is really a great honor to have you with us, Judge Learned Hand.

STATEMENT OF HONORABLE LEARNED HAND,
CHIEF JUDGE OF THE SECOND JUDICIAL CIRCUIT
OF THE UNITED STATES COURT OF APPEALS,
NEW YORK, NEW YORK.

Judge Hand. I do not know, Senators, exactly how you expect me to proceed. Are you going to ask questions?

Senator Douglas. I would appreciate it if you would proceed in your own way. You have had great experience in life and deep insight into the problems of public officials and the ethical difficulties which come up. I would appreciate it very much if you would talk informally on the basis of your reflection as to some of the concrete ways in which you think we might improve public ethics incidental to the resolution which Senator Fulbright is proposing, and which is the creation of this commission.

Judge Hand. Senator, I understand this is particularly to affect the legislative and executive branches.

Senator Douglas. Senator Fulbright as a lawyer felt reluctant to indicate that there might be anything wrong with the judicial branch.

Judge Hand. There linger in the back of my memory some things that happened very close at home, but they shall not be mentioned.

Senator Fulbright. If there is anything wrong, it has been better concealed, at least. I am not aware of anything wrong.

Judge Hand. All right, then, I will not bring it to your attention. I could a tale unfold.

Senator Douglas. There is a former judge from New York who is serving in the penitentiary.

Judge Hand. He has gone now. I would not say to a greater penitentiary.

To be serious, I hope you believe that I am in earnest, when I say that I really feel, when I come before you here, that I do not know anything about legislative politics, or for that matter, executive politics. When I was young I lived in Albany and tried to get into politics a little bit, but I was no good; and there is now not much that I can think to say which is not platitude. Political activity is a craft; I should like to call it an art. It is like any other craft or art; you have to be experienced in it in order to practice it; and I discount the criticism of those who have not had to deal with the material which is the conduct and actions and responses of the ordinary man —you and I and everyone else. I do not mean to say that such criticism may never have any value; the comments of columnists no doubt do; yet even they speak so often only from their ivory tower.

I hope you will not think that I am slack in my morals when I say that in judging public conduct we should always remember that it has to pass muster with the voters, or it will be an idle gesture. Compromise here, as elsewhere, is a question of more or less; and I am personally disposed to lend a very large measure of forbearance toward much that I might not approve save for the end in view.

I think you will get the drift of what I say; and it really in a way goes a long way towards exhausting all I have got to say. There is, however, one thing I should like to add which I feel deeply and which is indeed only a corollary: we never shall get along in matters of large public interest, if we proceed by generalizations, indeed, if you insist, by principles, put forward as applicable in all circumstances. Human affairs are too complicated for that; we cannot see far enough ahead so to deal with them. Rather let us say with Cardinal Newman: "One step enough for me." The consequence is that the only way that public affairs can be successfully managed is by treating each case by itself; even so, the trouble is far from ended. We must ask what a proposed measure will do in fact. How will the people whom it touches react and respond to it? That is something that theoretically one might be able to forecast, although practically it is largely impossible. But suppose one does find what it will do. Then—and this is the more difficult part—one must make a choice between the values that will be affected, for there are substantially always conflicts of group interests.

All of this may seem to you far afield from public morals; but I think not. It means that we shall not succeed by hitching our wagons to a star, but by a prayerful attempt in each case to make some compromise that will, for a substantial time if possible, effect a settlement.

Senator Douglas. Judge Hand, back about a century and a half ago, as I remember, Jeremy Bentham wrote his book *Principles of Morals and Legislation* in which he laid down his calculus of pleasures and pains, and said the legislator should take as his standard those acts which would diminish the total amount of pain and increase the total amount of happiness for as large a number as possible.

There are certain elements of measure of happiness, but do you think the utilitarian calculus can be used?

Judge Hand. Not practically. Negatively it was a great contribution; for at least it set the theoretical measure between right and wrong; but practically I know of no such calculus, because I do not know how to weigh values against each other. That is really the key to the whole business—morals included.

In legislation, often the best is that compromise between the two which will result in the least friction in application and execution. As I have just intimated, there is a good deal to be said, as a theory of democracy, for that which will find the greatest measure of acceptance in the long run. That approach to political thinking is very offensive to many people; but I can only answer that a number of accredited heroes of the past seem to me to have agreed. They have not been anxious to find, and they did not know how to find, abstract principles valid for all situations. They were very largely compromisers. Erasmus was one, for instance; and I always like to think of a man, not so well known, the Marquis of Halifax, George Savile, who wrote the *Character of a Trimmer*. I should rate Robert Walpole as another; yet he was a maker of the England of the 18th Century. You may think it fantastic of me to include Oliver Cromwell. Let me hasten to say why I do so. He went from step to step, and he did not attempt to deal with his material in general terms. Let me give you, as an instance, one utterance of his which has always hung in my mind. It was just before the Battle of Dunbar; he beat the Scots in the end, as you know, after a very tough fight; but he wrote them before the battle, trying to get them to accept a reasonable composition. These were his words: "I beseech ye in the bowels of Christ, think that ye may be mistaken." I should like to have that written over the portals of every church, every school, and every court house, and, may I say, of every

legislative body in the United States. I should like to
have every court begin, "I beseech ye in the bowels of
Christ, think that we may be mistaken."

Senator *Douglas*. Judge, I wonder if you would
let Senator Fulbright, who is the man responsible for
this resolution, ask you some questions?

Judge Hand. I should be delighted.

Senator *Fulbright*. I am interested, as I know this
committee is, in your reflections on some of the things
which have appeared in our society in recent months.
For example, the revelations in your own city of New
York of this winter involving the college students apparently on a rather large scale. You are familiar with that,
that is, involving the bribery of basketball players, the
wide spread of that medium by gamblers in New York.

Judge Hand. Yes.

Senator *Fulbright*. You are familiar with the Kefauver hearings, I believe.

Judge Hand. In a general way; I did not follow
them.

Senator *Fulbright*. From the press.

Judge Hand. I did not follow them in detail.

Senator *Fulbright*. You are familiar to some extent with the hearings held by the Subcommittee of the
Banking and Currency Committee on the RFC?

Judge Hand. Yes.

Senator *Fulbright*. You are familiar to some extent with the present hearings that were going on yester-
day about the widespread use of narcotics by juveniles?

Judge Hand. Yes.

Senator *Fulbright*. Does that seem to you a normal and natural and inevitable condition in our society?

It may be that being young and inexperienced and a naive young man that these things have made too much of an impression on me, and we should take them as they are. Do you feel that our society is all that we can expect it to be or is there anything that can be done or should be attempted to be done about it?

Judge Hand. That is a dreadfully hard thing to answer. I do not suppose that we have changed very much with time. These things recur, you know. Take the government of the City of New York; there have been periodic arousals when the lid was opened and the people saw what had been happening, and then you have reform movements. You are too young, but I remember Travers Jerome; he did a great deal of good, and we were all keen about him. His efforts quickened into some good administration, but then things slumped back as people got indifferent.

Senator Douglas. Do you think it ever goes back to quite where it was before?

Judge Hand. Yes, I am afraid it does, Senator.

Senator Douglas. Merely a swing in the pendulum back and forth, but no particular progress.

Judge Hand. Perhaps not quite that; but remember that we are all inferior creatures; we are humans and our imperfections will come out in one way or another. I doubt if the political structure of our society makes much difference. How much of the time are not our choices really influenced by our own interests? We cannot expect more of other people than we have ourselves. Possibly things may grow better; but the mills of the gods grind very, very slow.

Senator Fulbright. Judge, do you not think it is

true that there is a difference in the discrimination of some people?

Judge Hand. Yes.

Senator Fulbright. Some people can realize what is in their own interest better than others.

Judge Hand. Yes, of course.

Senator Fulbright. Some take the very short term view which they think is in their own interests but is not in their own interests.

Judge Hand. Of course.

Senator Fulbright. Of course, our experience has been so different, but it was only 25 years ago that I was in college and I played football. I may be biased but certainly I have the definite impression that when I played football it was not accompanied by anything like the professionalism or I would say the hypocrisy or the gambling or the other things that have been revealed recently in these scandals in New York. I may not have known about it. At least it never appeared in the press, as it has this time.

Judge Hand. I have no doubt that is true. I have no doubt that this venality in athletics is new, and I suspect the price has been a great deal increased. I go back so much further than you that in my day there was no money to be made in athletics. Now it has become an opportunity for a great deal of money.

I remember in the case of some of these boys, it was very pitiful, for the bribes offered them must have made a great difference to their families. It was asking a great deal of them not to yield to that temptation. That certainly did not exist in my day, and it did not in yours.

Senator Fulbright. I use it simply as one thing I

am personally familiar with. I am not as familiar with the widespread gambling that has been revealed by Kefauver. However, I do not recall at that time of ever having read about it. It either did not exist or it was better concealed.

Judge Hand. Maybe. We have had that kind of thing in New York, you know.

Senator Fulbright. I do not think New York should be used as the criterion of the United States.

Senator Douglas. I have great respect for my dear friend from Arkansas who is one of the finest members of the Senate, a man with great standards, but I have always understood that there was a place called Hot Springs in Arkansas.

Senator Fulbright. Hot Springs has become an important center in recent years. I am not saying it does not exist. The point I am trying to make is this, and I am quite willing to accept your first admonition that I am mistaken on two counts, that perhaps the world is better than I think it is, and even if it is not, there is nothing you can do about it.

Judge Hand. I do not want to say that nothing can be done about it. I do not want to throw up the fight, if that is what you mean.

Senator Fulbright. I say I am willing to accept that. But I was hoping that a commission of men with far greater experience than I have, and with time to consider these problems, might reassure us on just such fundamental problems because I think such problems have a very direct bearing on the political system of this country.

Judge Hand. They do.

Senator Fulbright. And the efficiencies of the political system and the respect in which the citizens hold it has a very real bearing on whether we survive in this struggle. I am not particularly concerned with the local conditions in New York City. I was only using it as a background to arrive at the main question which concerns us here, which is whether or not our government is functioning as well as it can be made to function, and does it attract and does it have the best men, the best brains that this country is able to produce.

Now, I know there is a tendency to look back in the old days and say in the days of Jefferson we had great men in government, and today they are not great. Perhaps that is inevitable. We think so. But still there is a sneaking feeling in my mind that perhaps there was a little different attitude toward government and government service, that in those days the best men that were available did think it was an honor to serve the country, whereas today they do not think so. We have had witnesses say here positively, I think Mr. Childs, that as a general proposition, the general attitude toward public officials was one of contempt on the part of the American people.

One other witness said, yes, that is true, but as to individuals they have respect. In other words, as I understood the testimony, it would be that the American people think Senators as a whole are contemptible, but that Senator Douglas as an individual is a fine man, or Senator Aiken.

Senator Douglas. There would be some doubt about the first part of your statement.

Senator Fulbright. But the effect of that is that

young people who after all are influenced by the views of their elders will conclude at that crucial period in their lives not to plan to enter public service.

Therefore, the pool of available talent is a very restricted one. That is the sort of question I wondered what you thought about.

Judge Hand. There is no doubt that a good many people do not want to try it because it is very difficult to get a hold on public life and still to keep an ordinary job. Take the law, for instance. I remember that, when I started, I rather had hankerings of that sort, and the man with whom I began, who was one of the men I loved and admired, told me not to do it. I never knew anyone who really got to be something without it costing him too much time out of his profession. It is hard to combine the two. Competition is extremely keen. Unless you are going to make politics a career, it is apt to be prejudicial to your career at the bar and other callings.

Senator Douglas. It is far more prejudicial than other pursuits.

Judge Hand. Is it?

Senator Douglas. The bar is the one profession where you can combine running for elective office much more readily than almost any other occupation there is. A minister cannot run because it splits his congregation. The merchant cannot run because he will lose trade. College professors and teachers generally cannot run. It is only a rare exception. Doctors very seldom run. Possibly an orchardist can run. But law men can, because even when they get defeated they get advertising and even people whose political views are different permit them to run because after all, the lawyer is taking the case and does not believe the political platform which he is advocating.

Senator Aiken. Lawyers frequently seek nomination for the purpose of getting free advertising.

Senator Fulbright. Judge, it sounds to me that both of them are rather indirectly casting some aspersions on our profession.

Judge Hand. Oh, no. When you think, Senator, what the ordinary conventional aspersion on the profession is, I think like Lord Clive, we ought to be amazed at our own moderation, do you not?

Senator Aiken. I would like to ask the Judge a question following up the discussion we had with a witness this morning. The discussion we were having was the advantage of a single administrator over a commission, or vice versa. I would like to know your opinion. Is one man more likely to reach a correct or an unbiased and honest decision than a commission of, we will say, seven or eight men?

Judge Hand. You have got them rather big, but I am very decidedly, judging from my own experience, of the opinion that numbers are of great assistance.

I was thinking of courts, for instance. The larger part of my official life I have been in a court where three sit together, and that seems to me of immense advantage; indeed, I know it is, an immense advantage. The joint judgment of three is worth much more than three times the judgment of one, unless he is a genius.

Senator Aiken. But is the feeling of responsibility as keen in a commission of seven as compared to one?

Judge Hand. Perhaps not; it is more collective. But if you are willing to listen to the others, the collective wisdom, in my opinion, is enormously improved. That was the point you had in mind?

Senator Aiken. That is the point. I know in state government, and I think most of the states have had the experience, we will go along for a term of years with a commission, and then the legislature decides to change it to an administrator, and after a few years they go back to a commission; evidently neither system is perfect.

Judge Hand. Nothing is perfect.

Senator Aiken. Nothing is perfect, fortunately; otherwise we would not have anything to strive for. But in the RFC, which Senator Douglas and Senator Fulbright have been interested in, we have done away with the board now and set up an administrator.

Senator Fulbright. If the Senator will yield, do you not think, Judge, that you cannot generalize with regard to what the function is that board is to play? You were speaking of the function of judging.

Judge Hand. That is all I know about.

Senator Fulbright. But it is an executive function. For example, in private life, running a business or in governmental life, not in either policy making or in legislation, but in carrying out a policy determined by other people, it might be a different result, and a single executive might be more effective. In fact, the Hoover Commission in a general way said just that, that in the executive, that multiple executives are not nearly as efficient as single executives. But if the function is what you said, Judge, which is a different thing from carrying out a law, I think in the executive sense—

Judge Hand. I do not really know enough to have an opinion on that. I should have to speculate and I do not think I could give an opinion. I concede it might well be necessary in certain kinds of activities; as for instance, when you must have prompt and decisive action. It is then not so critical whether you are exactly right or whether you are in part wrong.

Senator Fulbright. It is not so difficult in those cases. It is the action rather than the judgment. No one that I know of has ever proposed, for example, that we abolish the Supreme Court, and have a single judge. It is only in these agencies, and the RFC. Our theory was that the board of directors is the committee, and what we want is to have someone carry out the duties efficiently, and we can put the responsibility on them.

Judge Hand. When you speak of carrying out, there is not anything quite so definite that you can speak of, as it was almost automatic. We have to deal with words, and there is nothing more fluid than words. I think we sometimes can deceive ourselves into supposing that administration is just a question of getting a man and having him learn the facts and following a perfectly definite rule. You do not find that, do you, in anything.

Senator Aiken. I think the Senator from Arkansas has made a very strong argument for a single administrator as far as operation goes. I will accept that. At least I am perfectly willing to give it a good fair trial. But we had another discussion this morning in regard to the quasi-judicial agencies of government who are constantly in contact with the people that they are supposed to regulate.

Judge Hand. You mean like the commissions?

Senator Aiken. Yes. The quasi-judicial commissions. They are constantly in contact with the people they are supposed to regulate, and not much with anyone else. After so long, depending upon the members of the commission, they begin to see things in the light as presented by the people that they are supposed to regulate, and I would say get farther away from the public which they are supposed to represent.

Judge Hand. Well, I do not know. Are they really in substance distinguishable from courts? Do not the same rules apply to them as to courts? The Supreme Court has been very severe with us if we do not give them almost complete autonomy. They are not quite as severe as they used to be four or five years ago, while we were held on a very close rein. There was attributed to them a specialized acquaintance with the subject matter which gave them—to put it in logical form—major premises that we did not possess; and in deference to which we ought to yield.

Senator Aiken. I think it is almost superhuman to avoid gradually becoming very sympathetic, if not prejudiced to favor the industry which they are set up to regulate. They are in contact with them all the time. They hear their problems all the time. They hear their troubles all the time. They would not be human if they did not become sympathetic to that side of it. And yet it is perhaps the greatest cause of complaints in government or against government. I am not asking you for a solution, Judge.

Judge Hand. Of course, that is a very, very vital question for the next 50 years, and I am sure I do not know how to answer it.

Senator Douglas. I was going to follow up the

question of Senator Aiken. Senator Aiken is saying that since quasi-judicial bodies deal with the same set of people over and over again, and do not have the variety of cases which the judiciary has, that the habit develops a sort of bias in favor of the people who customarily appear before them. It seems to me that you in the courts have built up a series of protections in which you are able to insulate yourselves from the pressures which beat in upon these quasi-judicial bodies.

For instance, if anyone were to try to talk to you in chambers or at dinner about a case which you had under consideration, in the first place I do not believe he would dare to talk to you, but if he did, we all know you would walk away.

Judge Hand. That happens more than you think.

Senator Douglas. Oh, does it, really? That is very interesting.

Judge Hand. I did not mean personally. I have got so old that they do not do it.

Senator Douglas. You mean that lawyers actually do sidle up to judges at dinner parties?

Judge Hand. Sidling up is not perhaps the best word, but they communicate, yes, they do.

Senator Douglas. In other words, the insulation is only relative?

Judge Hand. It is not absolute. There will be a leakage of current at times.

Senator Douglas. Presumably.

Judge Hand. I really do not want you to suppose that it has any effect. I think it is like the man in a case which I recall, which will be nameless—a very important case. Someone said if you would like to know about the character of that industry, I know a man who will tell you a great deal more than you will get out of the record about this industry. I said, "I am awfully sorry, but you see we are very much confined as courts." He did not mean anything wrong about it, but I guess he read some of my opinions and thought I needed enlightenment, and thought he knew where I could get it.

Senator Douglas. But the person who does that is more the exception than the rule?

Judge Hand. Yes.

Senator Douglas. And a majority refrain from doing it?

Judge Hand. Yes.

Senator Douglas. You know I have been approached to intercede with judges, which I always refused to do except in one case which I will not mention now.

Judge Hand. I do not think the commissions become disposed to favor those industries which come before them; it is apt to be the other way. True, the whole relation of the expert specialized commission to the courts, and its relation to society as a whole, is one of the problems that you gentlemen will always have to face; it is one of the most difficult that you do have to face. But I believe that the history of commissions is very largely this: when they start, they are filled with enthusiasts, and they are flexible and adaptive. Like all of us—and that is constantly the fault charged, and properly charged, against courts—after they have proceeded a while they get their own sets of precedents, and precedents save "the intolerable labor of thought," and they fall into grooves, just as the judges do. When they get into grooves, then God save you to get them out of the grooves.

On the other hand, they also get an expertness from familiarity with the subject matter that judges cannot possibly have. The thing that teases me most—and I confess seems to be insoluble as far as I have been able to judge—is at what point in the procedure should courts intervene and how far should they be allowed to go. I am satisfied that somewhere along the line they must intervene; you cannot leave the last word with the administrative tribunal. But, how can the judges, who have no specialized acquaintance with the subject, know when and where to do it? I wish I had some light on it.

Mr. Willkie. Judge Hand, what would you think of the idea of having an administrative court of appeals over all the commissions which go much more into the evidence, that is, set it up by law, than the ordinary courts of appeal can now?

Judge Hand. I do not think you will do it now.

Mr. Willkie. Say have a panel of 15 or 8, 10, 12 judges sitting in different panels of three.

Judge Hand. You mean a floating one?

Mr. Willkie. Yes.

Judge Hand. Let us suppose just for the sake of illustration that you have a court which would be recruited by selections from the ordinary courts, or did you mean made up or staffed by people who would have no other duty than in this administrative court?

Mr. Willkie. No, I had the idea staffed with people who had no other duties. In other words, create an administrative court of appeals with a number of judges

242

whose task was to hear appeals from the quasi-judicial body.

Judge Hand. Was it your idea that would be final?

Mr. Willkie. Final with respect to the findings of fact. We would have the Supreme Court decide on the question of law.

Judge Hand. It is awfully hard to determine what is a question of fact and law.

Mr. Willkie. Let us say they would be final.

Judge Hand. All right. I do not think one court could possibly do it. You would have to have an enormous court.

Mr. Willkie. Here is what I was trying to drive at. Create a court of appeals from the commissions whose task it would be to specialize in those subjects and not concern itself with other subjects.

Judge Hand. This would have a jurisdiction, as I understood you, from all the different commissions. It would be the SEC and the ICC, and it would be the Tax Court, too.

Mr. Willkie. Not the Tax Court, because there is Tax Court of Appeals.

Judge Hand. One, but it is not the final one.

Mr. Willkie. Let us not say final, but a court of appeals which would break it up into sections.

Judge Hand. I would have to think about that suggestion more. At first blush, as you put it to me, I should not think that would be the way, but I have not any substitute. I am only sure that one way or another that is the great problem and it gets more and more so,

243

of course, because the tribunals are growing all the time in number, and new ones are being created all the time.

Mr. Willkie. Here was my notion, to have two or three judges whose duty it was to devote their time to hearing aeronautics cases from the CAB, and three men for another commission.

Judge Hand. Then you have a series of specialized appeal boards. I think that somewhere in order to avoid the almost inevitable—I call it sclerosis—falling back on your own set of principles and precedents, you have got to introduce a review by people who do not know as much about the subject.

Let me put it as vaguely as that; I cannot say any more.

Mr. Willkie. You feel that the regular Court of Appeals ought to have more opportunity to inquire into the evidence behind the decisions than they do now under the present rules?

Judge Hand. No, I know that is thought to be one of the great disadvantages. Take Labor Board cases—because I have sat on a great many Labor Board cases; you get a cold record of witnesses in absolute conflict. If you do not start with some bias, it is almost impossible, at least for me, to tell which one is lying and which one is not. I used to try cases; and God knows, I was very unsure about it, even then, though I have known judges who thought they could tell just as soon as a man comes into the room whether he is going to lie or not.

When you come to the documents, it is quite different, because there they are, and you are in just as good position to decide as the lower court or the Board. But even as to them your system will break down if you de-

mand too much review of facts, because of the very bulk of the work; so that there has to be a very large measure of finality even aside from that part of the evidence which the printed word does not preserve. I chance now to be going over an admiralty case, as to what happened to a cargo on the inside of a ship; and on such cases I do not feel, and never did feel that I know much after I am done.

Senator Aiken. I would like to point out what I consider to be one of the major ailments of government and see if you have any suggestion on that. Congress passes legislation and necessarily cannot legislate in detail, so they authorize the agency concerned with the legislation to promulgate rules and regulations for putting it into effect, and it frequently happens that the agency concerned will promulgate such rules and regulations that completely controvert or contravene—I do not know the legal word for that—the Act of Congress. And then we sometimes pass legislation and the agencies have not got away from the practice which was originally set up of asking the Attorney General for an interpretation when the meaning of the law is in doubt. Each has its own solicitor's department, and the solicitor hired by the department head is supposed to bring to the department head such interpretation of the law as he wants.

In some cases that has happened. Sometimes the solicitor's interpretation is directly contrary to the intent of the Congress. Have you any suggestion as to how we can get away from that, because it is pretty common practice.

Judge Hand. No, that is the great issue of interpretation—that fascinating issue which has made 40

245

years of doing it still to me not altogether dull. What are the meanings of words?

Senator Douglas. We have attempted to cope with it by diminishing the number of government lawyers. Do you regard that as an accomplishment in that regard?

Judge Hand. In general.

Senator Aiken. I tried setting up an agency of Congress to follow through the Acts of Congress, just as the Comptroller General's office follows through the expenditures of the appropriations of Congress, but I ran into some constitutional difficulties there.

Judge Hand. You mean too much delegation?

Senator Aiken. No, I mean the suggestion was made to me that Congress should set up an agency to follow through and pass on the rules and regulations which the agencies used to implement an Act of Congress or the agencies should clear those interpretations or rules just as the Comptroller General follows through the appropriations of the Congress, and approves or disapproves the manner in which they are expended.

Judge Hand. Do you find that very often the regulations in your judgment or the judgment of any of you conflict with the Act?

Senator Aiken. Yes.

Judge Hand. That has not been much my experience.

Senator Aiken. I think the classic on that is the claim of those who eventually were opposed to it that the regulations set up to implement the Wagner Act were contrary to the intent of Congress. That was the claim. I am not passing on the validity of the claim.

246

Judge Hand. I do not remember that that has very often come up. Of course, you do have the difficulty which is inherent in the situation, because of the increasing infiltration of government into private life. The result of statutes and regulations is a wilderness of words, although indeed that is inevitable, since it is the only protection of the individual against the unlimited discretion of small officials. But it is a hideous job to find one's way through, and people cannot possibly get on without expert help; i.e., without lawyers.

Senator Aiken. We have the Congress spending considerable time trying to legislate and find words which the executive agencies cannot misinterpret.

Judge Hand. No, they are trying to do that in the American Law Institute. A most interesting group is now trying it in the case of taxes, quite with the accord of both Houses of Congress.

Senator Douglas. I wonder if I can come back very briefly to the question of safeguards to judicial integrity which has been built up, and whether it is possible to extend them to the so-called quasi-judicial bodies and high administrative officials.

As I understand, you are supposed to judge on the record or the evidence produced in the court room, and not on anything which is extraneous. You are not expected to take favors or undue entertainment from litigants. People closely connected with you are not expected to appear as attorneys, and so on. I do not think you have yet built up the employment that a judge should take, if and when he retires. We had a case in Chicago where a judge retired and went into practice on cases which he had previously heard when he was a judge, which I thought was a violation. Certainly relatives, law associates are not expected to practice before a judge.

Now in the quasi-judicial bodies and top administrators in the government, we have not yet developed parallel safeguards. We know as a matter of fact that members of the regulatory commissions and top administrators will accept entertainment, frequently quite copious entertainment, from people with whom they are dealing. Lawyers will be hired to appear before them who we suspect have been hired because of their intimacy or connections with the commission or with the administrators. Men will resign from high governmental bodies and very quickly appear before those same bodies as attorneys.

I feel that there is such an interlocking and lack of safeguards that the integrity of a great deal of our regulatory processes and the integrity of our top administrative action is seriously threatened.

I wonder if you would express yourself on the possibility of building up parallel safeguards.

Judge Hand. I do not see that there is any difference between a tribunal and a court; each is there to administer a law impartially, whatever the intent means, in the case of an individual or group. What can the difference be whether it happens to be a judge or administrator? The poor wretch who loses is in an equally bad case anyway.

Senator Douglas. What you are saying, then, is that you believe that the regulatory bodies, the administrators who make decisions on rate subsidies should take over a larger degree of the ethics of administration?

Judge Hand. I do.

Senator Douglas. That is my feeling very deeply.

Judge Hand. May I say something that perhaps I should not say? I hope this will not offend you. Take immigration cases. I have seen this in a good many records: "Congressman Jones or Senator McGill is interested in this case." Now, frankly, when I see that, I do not like it. I hope it does not influence me in the result, but it makes me pretty mad.

Senator Douglas. We undoubtedly sin, but there are other sinners besides ourselves.

Senator Fulbright. I just wonder, too, do you think that a commission such as has been suggested could make any contribution?

Judge Hand. You mean the one Mr. Willkie suggested?

Senator Fulbright. Like a commission to consider the overall problems would make any contribution. Is it a useful device or not?

Judge Hand. Frankly, Senator, I doubt if it will.

Senator Fulbright. Do you think there is anything that could be done to improve the situation?

Judge Hand. You mean by way of law or body?

Senator Fulbright. No, not by way of law.

Judge Hand. Yes, of course. If we could all change our spots a bit, if we realized that most of these things that seem so new have been tried over and over again, I do not know that it is quite true to say that the only teaching of history is that history does not teach anything, for history does give us education in this sense: it teaches us skepticism about any easy explanations. That was really the purport of my song when I started, which I am aware I said very, very hazily. But, if we are going to get along, it can only be by the growth of skepticism; and skepticism comes best from acquaintance with the past. You are speaking of whether there was degradation in our morals. Take the violence of much of the controversy of the eighteenth century—take the letters of Freneau, for instance. Again the violence in Andrew Jackson's day. It is doubtful that we have retrograded; I incline to a slightly opposite view.

Senator Fulbright. Do you have a wish that you should have gone into politics instead of the judiciary?

Judge Hand. I would not have been any good, Senator.

Senator Fulbright. Why not?

Judge Hand. I could not tell you that.

Senator Fulbright. I thought that is what would have been your answer. I think maybe that is one of the points that is bothering me—wherever I go and we see really intelligent and honest men, I have yet to see one that wished he had gone into politics.

Judge Hand. If you asked me whether I should like to be a United States Senator, if I did not have to deal with my constituents, there is nothing I should like so much in the world. But I want it for life so I will not have to answer letters, and I will not have to see people. I would just sit there and make speeches, and have a wonderful time.

Senator Fulbright. Have you ever thought of any way in which we could have a Senate without constituents?

Judge Hand. They have a House of Lords in England. The hereditary House of Lords does not count for anything. They do not let them do anything. They pick them out. They make them lords, and do not give them much power except to talk. But I am told they are very important.

Senator Douglas. You remember the passage from Milton that the immortal garland is not to be won without sweat and heat.

Judge Hand. Oh, yes, I know.

Senator Fulbright. You do not believe that any more than you believe what we just said?

Judge Hand. Yes, I do. You asked if I liked politics. I wanted the glory without the dust and heat, and that is not a very democratic way of thinking.

Senator Fulbright. One thing that prompted that when in a poll that we were discussing the other day that question was asked, and 70 per cent of the people—I take it parents—were asked, if they had a son would they like him to go into politics, 70 per cent said no. That seems rather odd to me. In a supposedly self-governing public, 70 per cent said they want no part of it. Only 16 per cent said yes. I wonder if in the earlier days that was also true? It seems to me that the profession of politics has suffered a considerable decline in the esteem of the people. It may not be so, but it looks that way.

Judge Hand. I do not know. It may be; I do not know.

Senator Fulbright. In the days of Jefferson, do you not think that there was some respect for the members of the House of Burgesses in Virginia?

Judge Hand. I just do not know. I do not know enough about the history. We believe, and I think properly, that when the men who met in 1787 to make a

Constitution made the best political document ever made, they did it very largely because they were great compromisers. Do not forget that. They did put in the Bill of Rights afterwards; but the thing that made it stick was that they were great compromisers as to the immediate issues which were before them.

Senator Douglas. Thank you very much, Judge Hand. It has been a great honor to have you here.

Judge Hand. Thank you.

34

AT FOURSCORE

[1952]

Learned Hand reached the age of eighty on January 27, 1952. In anticipation of that occasion, the Harvard Club of New York invited him to be the speaker at its annual dinner, on January 18. Of this address, Judge Hand wrote to the collector of these papers:

There is only this to be said about this speech. It does more completely represent my views about ultimate values than anything else I have written—at least I think so—and it is probably the last time I shall put them out with the same detail. I should be the last to think that important, were it not that apparently you have seen fit to think it worthwhile to take all the trouble you have to publish my earlier stuff.

This address, with its memories of that other great Harvard law graduate, O. W. Holmes, Jr., appeared in the Harvard Alumni Bulletin, February 23, 1952 (Vol. LIV, No. 10, pp. 424–6).

It was nearly forty years ago that in this building Justice Holmes ended a long-remembered speech with these words:

"If I am right it will be a slow business for our people to reach rational views, assuming that we are allowed to work peaceably to that end. But as I grow older I grow calm. If I feel what are perhaps an old man's apprehensions, that competition from new races will cut deeper than working men's disputes and will test whether we can hang together and can fight; if I fear that we are running through the world's resources at a pace that we cannot keep, I do not lose my hopes. I do not pin my dreams for the future to my country or even to my race. I think it probable that civilization somehow will last as long as I care to look ahead—perhaps with smaller numbers, but perhaps also bred to greatness and splendor by science. I think it not improbable that man, like the grub that prepares a chamber for the winged thing it never has seen but is to be—that man may have cosmic destinies that he does not understand. And so beyond the vision of battling races and an impoverished earth I catch a dreaming glimpse of peace.

"The other day my dream was pictured to my mind. It was evening. I was walking homeward on Pennsylvania Avenue near the Treasury, and as I looked beyond Sherman's Statue to the west the sky was aflame with scarlet and crimson from the setting sun. But, like the note of downfall in Wagner's opera, below the sky line there came from little globes the pallid discord of the electric lights. And I thought to myself the Götterdämmerung will end, and from those globes clustered like evil eggs will come the new masters of the sky. It is like the time in which we live. But then I remembered the faith that I partly have expressed, faith in a universe not measured by our fears, a universe that has thought and more than thought inside of it, and as I gazed, after the sunset and above the electric lights there shone the stars."

That was in February 1913, and we must all be struck with the premonitions which time has shown to have been so prophetic. In those days we were not "bound in to saucy doubts and fears"; few of you can now realize

the sense of security we had. It is true that there had indeed been plenty of "scares" and sabre rattlings; nor had
we forgotten that only fifty years before we had ourselves
been through a bloody war. But as the years passed, we
had somehow managed to slip by each international
crisis as it came up; and our Civil War, unlike most wars,
did "settle" something. France had been overwhelmed
in 1870, but it had been a short job; she soon recovered
and the indemnity was perhaps a benefit; at any rate, as
you remember, Bismarck is reported to have said that the
next time he would make it a condition of peace that
France should accept an indemnity from Germany.
When we looked within, there were plenty of drastic
economic adjustments in sight, but nobody thought that
they would entangle us with other nations; and Holmes's
fears that they might weaken us in any "competition
from new races" would have appeared far-fetched to
most of us. Had we not set up a World Court at The
Hague, and were we not developing an International
Law for it to administer? Confirming all this was the increasing habit of resort to arbitration and diplomatic
compromise. It was common belief that war was becoming an obsolete way of settling disputes, and that mankind might have already abandoned it. As an example,
however fatuous, I can remember that a not altogether
inconsiderable member of the bar assured me even in
July 1914, that there could be no war because the "bank-
ers" would not allow it. (Shades of Andrew Jackson!)
Nor did the First War disabuse us of these illusions.
Whatever the cost, Good had emerged triumphant,
Evil had been utterly overwhelmed; and there had at
length been set up a permanent institution, charged with

the duty of composing all disputes between nations in accordance with Right and Justice. It is true that we would not join it, but that was principally because we did not wish to limit our freedom of choice; in any event it presupposed that we did not think that we stood in vital need of protection. It seemed even more possible than in 1913 that Holmes's hopes might be coming true; we might be catching "a dreaming glimpse of peace." It took the decades after 1918 to bring down upon us the full measure of our latent savagery, and to show us that, ingenious and cunning as we might be, we were still at bottom the same sanguinary animals we had been for many millennia; and, further, that we were subject—indeed, because of our vastly improved apparatus for propaganda, more subject—to those mass manipulations which can infect whole nations with the panics, the infatuations and the bestialities of the herd. Today we stand at bay, with all those conventions challenged that have for so long saved us from "the intolerable labor of thought." The slogans we live by: "Democracy," "the Common Man," "Natural Law," "Inherent Rights of Man," "the Bill of Rights," "the Constitution"—the whole paraphernalia of our eighteenth-century inheritance—all must now make good their claims against the furious repudiation of powerful and relentless enemies.

We are in the distressing position of all who find their axioms doubted: axioms which, like all axioms, are so self-evident that any show of dissidence outrages our morals, and paralyzes our minds. And we have responded as men generally do respond to such provocation: for the most part we seem able to think of nothing better than repression; we seek to extirpate the heresies and wreak vengeance on the heretics. We have authentically reproduced the same kind of hysteria that swept over England in the time of Titus Oates and during the French Revolution, and over us ourselves after the Civil War and the First War, except that in our own case we have outdone our precedents. Happily there are a substantial number who see that, not only when they were first announced, but as they still persist, the doctrines that so frighten us constitute a faith, which we must match with a faith, held with equal ardor and conviction. So we are repeatedly assured, and rightly assured; but what we much less often observe is that, in making use of our faith as a defence, we may be in danger of destroying its foundations and abandoning its postulates. What are its foundations and its postulates? On what have we staked our hopes? Is it less than the thesis, as yet quite unverified, that the path towards the Good Life is to assure unimpeded utterance to every opinion, to be fearful of all orthodoxies and to face the discords of the Tower of Babel; all with the hope that in the end the dross will somehow be automatically strained out, and we shall be left with the golden nuggets of truth? That, I submit, is a faith that you cannot teach by precept; it has never carried, and will never carry, its credentials on its face; we can learn it only by experience, only by the elimination of other faiths which have proved themselves false; long trial and infinite patience are required for that. Moreover, to acquire such habits we must succeed in repressing much of our deeply rooted animal inheritance. Nature is miserly in her endowments; although she may give her creatures responses whose results on the average will see them through, she gives no more. As William James says somewhere: if a frog jumps at a piece of red flannel on a hook, that is hard on that particular frog, but red patches do often announce the presence of edibles, and frogs who jump at red are more likely to be fed than to be hooked. Life is made up of constant calls to action, and we seldom have time for more than hastily contrived answers; to follow one's hunch is usually better than lying doggo, and rough generalizations that have worked well in the past easily take on the authority of universals. It does violence to our inner being to be obliged to give a hearing to opinions widely at variance with those we are accustomed to, and to come to a conclusion unweighted by desire. We can put up with the wrench only after the severest and longest discipline. Yet, only in so far as we have learned to do so have we come up from those arboreal ancestors of ours, whose great-grandnephews fascinate and appal us in their cages by the indubitable evidence of their cosinage. Yes, just in measure as we have trained ourselves to pause, to refrain, to scrutinize, to test and test again and to venture upon the unknown: in short, as James Harvey Robinson used to say, "to monkey around"—have we learned to understand ourselves and to exploit our environment. Is it not true that our hope, and so our faith, the faith in the eventual success of the democracy we boast, lies here and here alone?

Many years ago, like you, I sat in the halls of Harvard and brought out of them whatever I did bring out. One man carries away one thing; another, another; some, perhaps, nothing. For myself I learned and took away the creed that I have just tried to describe, a creed which has endured and whose conviction has grown upon me as the years have passed. You were not taught it in words; you gathered it unwittingly from uncorrupted and incorruptible masters. It was in the air; you did not affirm or proclaim it; you would have felt ashamed to demonstrate the obvious. You came to know that you could hold no certain title to beliefs that you had not won; and indeed you did not win many. But that did not so much matter, for you had come into possession of a touchstone; you had learned how to judge a good title; and, although tomorrow might turn up a flaw in it, you believed that you could detect the flaw. And chiefly and best of all, you were in a company of those who thought that the noblest of man's works was the pursuit of truth; who valued the goal so highly that they were never quite content that the goal they had reached was the goal they were after; who believed that man's highest courage was to bet his all on what was no more than the best guess he could make; who asked no warranties and distrusted all such; who faced the puzzle of life without any kit of ready-made answers, yet trusting that, if they persevered long enough, they would find—in the words of John Dewey—that they might safely "lean back on things."

That creed still lives in the halls of Harvard; surely it can have no more unwavering disciple than he who now presides there; and never in the history of our college has the need for it been greater than now. For, make no mistake: these are the days of testing. It is just in such times of stress that wide horizons and a suspended judgment become least bearable; that men, not content to follow the lights they have, will reach out for other lights— warmer, rosier, more comforting. Indeed, such other lights there are, whose consolations we may indeed envy

259

their possessors: lights to which many are turning. Let us meet the issue squarely: ours is a stern creed, and we do not prophesy the outcome; we carry no passports to paradise; we accept the chance that it may prove a creed too Spartan for men to live by. Time's womb may be full of monsters; the salvation of mankind from complete liquefaction may turn out to demand infallible rulers, having absolute power, choosing their own successors and exempt from all control. Plato has not been alone in that belief. Granted that "all power corrupts, and absolute power corrupts absolutely"; absolute power must in the end be lodged somewhere. Although nobody any longer believes that Heaven will be at hand when the last king shall be strangled, it is surely no more probable that we should attain the New Jerusalem, if the last member of the Politburo were to meet the same untidy fate.

Suppose then that in the end the chance we take—the chance which we deliberately make implicit in our creed —suppose that that chance goes against us; suppose that in democracies the conflicts between the constituent groups turn out so often to submerge the common weal, that societies so organized cannot "hang together and . . . fight," as Holmes wondered. What then? Shall we have failed? I will venture to say no, not even then. For consider. Win or lose, the day will come when "the great globe itself, yea, all which it inherit, shall dissolve and . . . leave not a rack behind"; and on that day it can be said of each of us: "Thou thy worldly task hast done, home art gone, and ta'en thy wages." That is the nature of all things; though, little as we may like to acknowledge it, it is irrelevant to their value and their significance; for permanence as such has neither value nor significance. All that will then matter will be all that matters now; and what matters now is what are the wages we do take home. Those are what we choose to make them; we can fix our pay; the splendor and the tragedy of life lie just in that. Values are ultimate, they admit of no reduction below themselves; you may prefer Dante to Shakespeare, or claret to champagne; but that ends it. Nevertheless, I believe you will agree to put among the most precious and dependable of our satisfactions the joy of craftsmanship. In that I include all efforts to impose upon the outside world an invention of our own: to embody an idea in what I shall ask your leave to call an artifact. It is not important what form that may take; it may be in clay, in bronze, in paint or pencil, in a musical score or in words; it may even be in a sport; it may be in the mastery or exercise of a profession; it may be in a well-balanced nature, like Aristotle's "Great-Souled" man; or it may be in redeeming the world. It is enough that we set out to mould the motley stuff of life into some form of our own choosing; when we do, the performance is itself the wage. "The play's the thing." Never mind that we are bound to fail, for the artifact will never quite embody the image; and besides, the image changes as the work goes on. A friend recently sent me this quotation from Lord Acton: "There is no error so monstrous that it fails to find defenders among the ablest men. Imagine a congress of eminent celebrities such as More, Bacon, Pascal, Cromwell, Bossuet, Montesquieu, Jefferson, Napoleon. . . . The result would be an encyclopedia of error." Therefore let us not fear failure: " 'Tis not in mortals to command success but we'll do more, Sempronius,—we'll deserve it." And deserve it we can; not necessarily in our harvest, but in the resolution with which we till the soil. In the work, moreover, we shall find our reward, and reward enough—on the whole the best of rewards—let performance fall as far behind conception as it may.

And so as I close, I shall dare accept Holmes's foreboding of 1913, and yet claim to share his vision. Perhaps man is not preparing "a chamber for the winged thing" he "has never seen but is to be"; perhaps he has no "cosmic destinies that he does not understand"; perhaps "beyond the vision of battling races and an impoverished earth" we should be wrong to "catch a dreaming glimpse of peace"; perhaps "the Götterdämmerung" will last longer than we "care to look ahead"; perhaps no "new masters of the sky" will ever come. So be it. I answer, like Carlyle: the Present is our Indubitable Own; we can shape it, for we can shape ourselves; we can shape them as near to the Heart's Desire as we have constancy and courage. We can live without dishonor, and to live without dishonor is to live with a high heart, and in such fashion that we shall not wince when we look back upon our past. We are indeed the masters of our fate; for us this can be "a universe not measured by our fears, a universe that has thought and more than thought inside of it." And, if only we shall prove steadfast and unperturbed, above the "globes clustered like evil eggs" we too shall see the stars.

35

ROBERT P. PATTERSON
[1952]

ROBERT PORTER PATTERSON (1891–1952) was one of Learned Hand's younger colleagues on the "C.A.2." Born at Glens Falls, New York, Patterson was graduated from Union College in 1912 and from the Harvard Law School three years later. He was admitted to the New York bar in 1915 and, aside from the years of his distinguished military service, practiced law in New York City until 1930, when President Herbert Hoover appointed him to a federal district judgeship.

On the bench Robert Patterson served in the British tradition of a third man at the trial who seeks for facts not brought out by counsel on either side. In 1939 President Franklin D. Roosevelt advanced him to the Federal Court of Appeals to sit with the Hands and their associates. But the very next year the same President recalled him from the bench to be Assistant Secretary of War under Henry L. Stimson. Patterson was soon made undersecretary in charge of the Army's vast procurement program for World War II. He succeeded Henry Stimson in the secretaryship in 1945, and worked vigorously for the administrative merger of the armed services under the Department of Defense.

Patterson's military service began when he was a New York National Guard private on the Mexican border. In World War I he trained at Plattsburg, New York, and in 1918, as a company commander in the 306th Infantry of the 77th Division, went to France, where he was twice wounded in action. He was awarded the Distinguished

Service Cross, the Silver Star, and the Purple Heart for gallantry. On two occasions he declined the deanship of the Harvard Law School. His reason was that the office of dean required "genuine scholarship," which he felt he did not have. He also declined an offer from President Harry S. Truman of the judgeship on the New York Federal Court of Appeals from which Learned Hand retired in 1951. His non-legal posts included the presidencies of the Council on Foreign Relations and of Freedom House.

An airliner crash at Elizabeth, New Jersey, on January 22, 1952, ended Robert Patterson's life much too soon. Among his many friends and associates who were profoundly shocked was Learned Hand, who contributed to a group of tributes on the editorial page of the New York Times, January 27, 1952. Then, on March 11, Learned Hand presented one of three memorials at a meeting of the Association of the Bar of the City of New York. The text is reprinted from a pamphlet published by the sponsoring organization (pp. 10–17).

I had no acquaintance, so far as I can remember, with Robert Patterson's work as a lawyer before he became a district judge in 1930, and much of the service of a district judge, perhaps the most important part, does not reach an appellate court at all. We did of course see a good many printed records of his during the ten years that he was on that court, and they revealed what you would expect from the quality of what followed in later years. His opinions were clear, penetrating, short, crisp, thorough, unostentatious, and unobtrusive, without a trace of vanity or of any desire to shine. They never avoided the troublesome issues or left any doubt as to what he decided; they were supported by adequate authority, but never encumbered by too much or by needless side excursions. Moreover, they disclosed his underlying attitude to his duties, his understanding of the position of a judge, as interpreter. Although he never availed himself of the tempting but evasive refuge of construing a precedent or a text by resorting to the literal meaning of the words, he recognized that he was the mouthpiece of a purpose, which he was bound to treat as authoritative, and to which he must therefore conform; that he had no mission to set right what he might not approve; and that it was not the function of courts to resolve the major conflicts of interest in a democratic society. He had a well-settled and an unconcealed scorn for that temper, then and still orthodox in many quarters, which transfigures a judge into a crusader for righteousness as righteousness may appear to his incandescent conscience. His conclusions at times of course collided with ours; and nothing was to me more engaging, or more endearing, than the vigor with which he tore to pieces the fragile fabric with which we had tried to obscure his light. I can think of more than one instance in which I was not sorry that I could not be called into the open lists to defend my difference from him, but could resort to the seclusion of my position in the hierarchy. Indeed I can remember one important decision in which we reversed him, where I have at times asked myself whether I did not do exactly what I have just disclaimed: brought about the desirable results at the expense of the rules, however flexibly one might interpret them.

But, as I have already intimated, it is open to doubt whether the work of a judge of first instance is to be best appraised by that part which is recorded; and at any rate the other part must be reckoned a close second, if not an equal: I mean that which takes place in the courtroom and either slips away into anonymity or remains only in the transient recollections of those who may be present. It so happens that I had the benefit of the testimony of an exceptionally competent witness—a friend of his and a near friend of mine—who once spent a morning in his courtroom. This man was not indeed a lawyer, but he was intelligent, sensitive, keen, and critical as few men of my acquaintance have been. I wish I could remember in fuller detail how he described the impression that he carried away. The personality of the judge pervaded the whole occasion throughout: he was always the dominant figure. That is not indeed surprising in this instance; and it happens often enough in a form that is highly regrettable. But this was quite otherwise; for this judge betrayed a constant, almost anxious, solicitude, not only that both sides should get a hearing, but that everything should be brought out which might be relevant, so that in the end all should be laid bare. This he did in no passive spirit, content to await whatever parties might disclose; it was a spirit determined to make sure that all *should* be disclosed. Do not, I pray you, mistake this last. You know and I know, for we have both suffered from them, the kind of pragmatic judges, who deem it their duty to take over the conduct of the trial, who assume an advocacy of both sides, and impose upon each their view of the proper position for it to take. That was the exact opposite of the impression that my friend got; this judge did not try to substitute what he thought the parties should maintain; but he was forever trying to help them bring out what he saw that they were trying to maintain. This he could not have done as a neutral observer, but as one possessed of that steadfast and enduring will to award to each his own, which in the immortal words of Ulpian, is the very being of Justice. "There can be few callings in the world," said my friend, "which give greater opportunity for satisfaction to oneself, or which are of more benefit to one's fellows."

This I have ever since taken as a veracious sample of his ten years of service in the district court, and, although I do not put it forward as approaching those other public services which he rendered later in very different causes and of which General Greenbaum has told you, yet it is easy to underrate the significance and the value of these ephemeral duties. It seems to me, and perhaps you will agree, that all societies, including our own, may be moving towards a pattern in which some central authority will interpose with increasing detail in the life of the individual. Personally, I look upon this with much reserve, though I am not sure that it is not the inevitable consequence of the fabulous increase in communication and ease in movement, coupled with the mounting numbers and concentration of modern societies. Success in this will of course demand the utmost skill in structure and plan, as well as high competence and character in the upper levels. But these will not be enough; no plan, however adequate, no top leaders however gifted, can make such a government work if the lower strata are not staffed by men of understanding, sympathy, and courage, who will not seek safety from criticism in the strictest adherence to the written word. Human affairs teem with variants, each presenting a new occasion; it is idle to try to provide for these in advance; they must be left to those who deal with them at first hand, and if they be either petty autocrats or timid routineers, in the end the system will collapse. The man in whose memory we have met showed, in other positions of vastly greater consequence, a capacity, courage, and devotion which made him a national figure; but in the minor positions of the judge of first instance, and, for a short time, of intermediate appeal, he set an example which, were it to become the standard, would put an end to much of our troubles.

However, it is not as a judge that I wish principally to speak of him; rather as the man and the friend who was near to me. We repeat to ourselves often enough that we live overarched by impending catastrophe; but we scarcely act as though that belief had sunk in. If we really believed that we are in such mortal danger as we profess, it is strange, is it not, that we do not more nearly lay aside our personal conflicts and merge our energies in the common defense. I see no evidence of a willingness to submit to a regime of severe austerity: we continue to take Saturdays off, and we keep on crying about the high cost of meat. Look about you any day in the subways and buses at the provender on which the "common man" feeds; consider how he is flattered, coaxed, and cajoled, how his prejudices are tickled and his resentments and cupidity are worked upon. Do you not at times ask yourself whether in the end a society can continue, based on the assumption that truth and restraint will emerge from such continual appeals to our primitive emotions? The

268

end is not yet, nor do we know what it will be. But I submit to you that, if at long last we are to come through, it must be through the leadership of the few who, like him, believe that this is a world not to be won by coddling or soft assurances that all will somehow come right, provided only one is not inexorable and has a tender heart. Perhaps at times he was too uncompromising, though never more so than with himself; but it was because he always kept in sight the overall purpose: "First things, first." You may answer that it is not possible so to deal with human beings, when you must have their co-operation. Maybe; yet I suggest that one of the most effective ways of securing that co-operation is by your own inflexible example. That example he gave, it was largely by it that he succeeded, and the depth and breadth of the feelings revealed when he died attest the measure of that success. Not only those who knew him by direct acquaintance, but those who had only read or heard of him, came spontaneously to realize that here was one who was incorruptible in a sense that few men are. I have always liked a story which Norman Hapgood used to tell of Theodore Roosevelt. They were talking of some public man of whom Hapgood asked: "Colonel, is he an honest man?" Roosevelt answered: "After the manner of you and me, yes; after the manner of John Hampden, no." Patterson was an honest man after the manner of John Hampden. His mind had a pellucid quality that one perceived almost at once; looking into it was like looking into a spring. Corollary to this was a considerable naïveté in his judgment of people, which was by no means unerring, but which was an authentic result of his rectitude.

269

One recalls the epigram of Justice Holmes: "We can forgive a man the defects of his qualities, if only he has the qualities of his defects."

He was guileless, indifferent—indeed too indifferent—to money, careless of the impression he made on others, fearless, generous, without envy or jealousy, merciful and even tender with the weak, and neither deferential nor assertive with the strong; and he was too apt to ascribe these qualities to others. Once in his good books, you remained there indefinitely. On the other hand, if you had disclosed some unworthy or dishonorable weakness—cowardice, cruelty, sham, or pretentiousness—you fell into the company of the lost, from which, so far as I know, you never emerged. I do not mean that he so divided all mankind; indeed he had a sane and temperate estimate of the great majority of those with whom he dealt. I am thinking, on the one hand, of those whom he had accepted as his friends and, on the other, of those in whom he had discovered what he thought to be some deep moral flaw. This disposition had its somewhat disturbing side, for if you were among the elect it was difficult to avoid a sense of duplicity. At least so I found it in my own case. I had the good fortune to be among his intimates, and he endowed me with some of his own qualities in which I was sadly lacking. I used at times to try to undeceive him, but always without success; and it usually followed when we parted, that I had a desperate feeling that we could never come to a common footing because he so obstinately refused to listen to the truth about myself which I knew and he would not believe. Out of this there generally came the compulsive conclusion that, as he insisted that I had been made in the heroic mold, I ought to try to make good his faith. The sense of duplicity came from the fact that long experience had taught me that, however elevated I might feel at the moment, the effect would not last. In short, I never parted from him without deciding to be more loyal to my better self, watered down by the subconscious awareness that I should almost certainly in fact go along as before.

He was an intensive reader on subjects which interested him, especially on our Civil War, of which he had a detailed and accurate knowledge whose equal I have personally never encountered. It seemed to me, and I think rightly, that there was no campaign and no major engagement that he did not know throughout, even to the disposition of the different regiments and the share they had in the fighting. He was an admirer of Cromwell, and knew much about him as a soldier, though not, I think, with the same intimacy. I have also heard from a friend that he went through Thucydides's account of the Sicilian Expedition in 413 B.C. with the same care, and could recite on it with accuracy. I am not in a good position to speak of the breadth of his reading, for our talk did not turn a great deal upon books; but I surmise that he did not go much into poetry or *belles-lettres*, and very largely confined himself to history. Indeed, the appearance of things seemed not to have much importance to him. I think that I never heard him speak of pictures, and, for that matter, very seldom of music, which is curious, as he had an accurate ear.

He had a very alert and engaging sense of the comic, though at times this seemed to me strangely spotty, as for example, his dislike of the magazine, *The New Yorker,* in which he could not see anything funny. On

271

the other hand nothing was more delightful than to hear him repeat parts of *Huckleberry Finn*: especially the account of the "Royal Nonesuch" as produced by the King and the Duke. He delighted in yarns of Abraham Lincoln; and some of the anecdotes of his experiences in the first war I would demand over and over again, always with renewed relish. He always retained a strong sense of fellowship with the members of his former company and went to their dinners, from which he would bring back tales, which, if, like mine, your taste was not fastidious or prudish, could be, and were, the occasion of unrestrained Homeric merriment.

I am quite aware that I have not succeeded in giving you an adequate picture of this man in whose death we have all lost so much, and especially those of us whom he took into his amity. Twice I had to swear him in as a public official, once when he became a circuit judge, next when he became Secretary of War. Each time I feared that I might not get through without some unseasonable show of emotion. As I looked into the steady blue eyes and at the small lithe frame, as I saw the uplifted hand and called to mind with what dedication he was accepting the post, there came over me with more force than I was certain I should manage to conceal, what was the measure of the man, and how he stood out among those whom I had known. In one sense his death was not a frustration, for he had accomplished that which all of us wish to accomplish, or at any rate ought to. He had done what he had set out to do, though it is doubtful that he ever was fully conscious of how well he had done it. He had conceived what was the character that he aspired to build, and he had built it more nearly in accordance with the plan than all but a meager few of us succeed in doing. That conception was of one who should be strong and true and brave and generous, of one who asked no quarter of a world which he knew would give none, of one to whom baseness should be impossible, of one who should prize most of all an untarnished soul, of one who should live in the world, but not ask its approval or flinch at its detraction, of one who should set and live by his own values. That conception he realized and manifested to us in an enduring memory, which will serve to strengthen us when we need help and shame us when we have been unworthy. We cannot indeed ignore the years which were cut off—they might, alas, have been a score: years of increasing service to us and to this nation. There is no consolation for that loss; but it pales before the luster of what he has left. And as we, who have shared the bounty of his fellowship, gather here today to note our loss, shall we not stand in grateful awe that such a world as ours does on occasion bring forth such men? Shall we not take heart, so far as may lie in us, to pattern ourselves after his pure spirit and make its image our heritage: our possession for all time?

36

A PLEA FOR THE OPEN MIND
AND FREE DISCUSSION
[1952]

THE MOST promptly quoted of all Learned Hand's addresses was that which he delivered before six hundred
education officials at the eighty-sixth convocation of the
University of the State of New York, in the State Education Building in his native Albany on October 24, 1952.
This address, delivered just after the speaker received the
degree of Doctor of Laws, weighed the risk of "refusing
to act till the facts are all in" against the potentially
"greater risk in abandoning the conditions of all rational
inquiry." Learned Hand made his own choice in words
that were quickly sent out over the country by the news
press associations. He said: "Risk for risk, for myself I
had rather take my chance that some traitors will escape
detection than spread abroad a spirit of general suspicion
and distrust, which accepts rumor and gossip in place of
undismayed and unintimidated inquiry. I believe that
that community is already in process of dissolution where
each man begins to eye his neighbor as a possible enemy,
where non-conformity with the accepted creed, political
as well as religious, is a mark of disaffection; where denunciation, without specification or backing, takes the
place of evidence; where orthodoxy chokes freedom of dissent; where faith in the eventual supremacy of reason
has become so timid that we dare not enter our convictions in the open lists, to win or lose. Such fears as these
are a solvent which can eat out the cement that binds
the stones together; they may in the end subject us to a

despotism as evil as any that we dread; and they can be allayed only in so far as we refuse to proceed on suspicion, and trust one another until we have tangible ground for misgiving. The mutual confidence on which all else depends can be maintained only by an open mind and a brave reliance upon free discussion." The text of this clarion call to reason and fairness is from a pamphlet of the occasion (pp. 1–7). Many Americans found in this address the answer to McCarthyism. The Saturday Review, believing that the "words deserve as wide an audience as possible," reprinted most of the address as its leading article, in the issue of November 22, 1952, under the heading, "The Future of Wisdom in America" (Vol. XXXV, No. 47, pp. 9–10, 55–6).

The honor which the University of the State confers upon me today is doubly grateful: it is one that all would crave, and in my own case it has an especial personal value; for I was born in a house only a few rods from the building in which we now are, and I lived there for over thirty years. I can remember how, as a little boy, in the early morning I used to hear all the chisels begin together to chip the stones that were to be used in building the Capitol; and how it seemed to me that that sound and the construction of that building were part of the permanent order of things and would always go on. Now, will you forgive me, if toward the close of a long life I lapse into a sentimental mood, as I reflect that an old man has been called back to the same spot where he took his first breath to be told that he has deserved well of his state during the intervening years. My father was born in New

York, my grandfather lived in it all his professional life; they were loyal citizens of their state, and I like to fancy that their shades would join in my satisfaction at this evidence of your approval.

The theme today is education, as to which you, the Regents of the University, have an overarching superintendence. What I have to say will be directed toward one aspect of your responsibility: the preparation of citizens for their political duties. I shall argue that the "humanities," instead of being regarded only as a solace, a refuge, and an enrichment of the individual—as indeed they are—are also an essential factor in training him to perform his duties in a democratic society, as important even as acquaintance with the persons and the current events on which he is called upon to pass. The gifted men who contrived that great compromise, the Constitution of the United States, and secured its ratification by a society which might very probably have repudiated it upon a referendum, were well aware of the dangers which surrounded a totalitarian government, as well when power was lodged in the people at large as when it rested in one man or in an aristocracy. Indeed, some of the ablest of them, Hamilton for example, did not believe that any society could endure in which the voters had uncontrolled authority, even though the suffrage was as limited as it then was; and the experience of France in the next ten years seemed to them a demonstration that they had been right. The compunctions that all felt, including the people at large, were the reason why so many of the states made the first ten amendments practically a condition upon ratification, and they were added all at once, as you know. It is not important here whether it was from the outset inevitable that the word of the Supreme Court should be final as to what the Amendments meant; but it is important that they, and in particular the First and Fifth, contained hallowed phrases which thoughtful people at the end of the eighteenth century usually believed to embody mandates that either were of divine origin or could be deduced from the inherent nature of man in society. Against these mandates no statute should prevail, and the Amendments, so far as they embodied them, were, strictly speaking, redundant. Moreover, it would not be true to say that this belief is not still widely held; indeed, one of the striking political agitations of the present is the recrudescence of the notion of "natural law" after its general repudiation by English-speaking lawyers in the nineteenth century. We are even assured that those who do not share it are "materialists" and amoral upholders of the doctrine that might makes right.

Most parts of the Constitution are specific enough to be treated like other legal commands; when we have to decide their meaning, we can proceed just as in the case of a dispute over the meaning of a statute; we look to their history and their setting with confidence that these will disclose their purpose. And that also applies to a large part of the Amendments themselves. For instance, no general cultural background is needed to reach a right opinion as to whether a statute has infringed the provision that the accused must be tried in the district where the crime was committed, or that he must be "confronted" by "the witnesses against him." But the situation is quite different when we are dealing with the broad clauses on which the conduct of a free society must in the end depend. What is "freedom of speech and of the press"; what is the "establishment of religion and the free exercise thereof"; what are "unreasonable searches," "due process of law," and "equal protection of the law": all these are left wholly undefined and cannot be effectively determined without some acquaintance with what men in the past have thought and felt to be their most precious interests. Indeed, these fundamental canons are not jural concepts at all, in the ordinary sense; and in application they turn out to be no more than admonitions of moderation, as appears from the varying and contradictory interpretations that the judges themselves find it necessary to put upon them. Nor can we leave to courts the responsibility of construing and so of enforcing them, for the powers of courts are too limited to reach the more controversial questions that arise under them. As you know, courts will not intervene—or at least they constantly avow that they should not—unless the action challenged infringes the Constitution beyond any fair dispute. While there are any plausible arguments in support of a measure, they must abstain; and so it results that in much the larger part of such controversies it is the voters, speaking through their delegates, who have the final word and the final responsibility; and that in the end it is they and they alone who can and will preserve our liberties, if preserved they are to be. For their guidance there are no vade mecums, no handbooks, no manuals; they must depend upon such enlightenment as they can muster from within, and upon their conscience, so far as they have one. That enlightenment and that conscience they may indeed find in divine revelation; but when they do, they tap sources that I am not qualified to discuss; not any better qualified than I am to discuss what doctrines are inherent in the nature of man in society. I know of none of either sort, nor can I find direction from those who profess to know. It is because I am shorn of such resort that, to me at any rate, there appears to be no escape in each situation from balancing the conflicting interests at stake with as detached a temper as we can achieve.

A constitution, a statute, a regulation, a rule—in short, a "law" of any kind—is at once a prophecy and a choice. It is a prophecy because it attempts to forecast what will be its effects: whom it will benefit and in what ways; on whom its impact will prove a burden; how much friction and discontent will arise from the adjustments that conformity to it will require; how completely it can be enforced; what enforcement will cost; how far it will interfere with other projects or existing activities; and in general, the whole manifold of its indirect consequences. A thoroughgoing and dependable knowledge of these is obviously impossible. For example, although we can anticipate with some degree of assurance who will pay a steeply graded income tax and in what amounts, there is no way to tell what its indirect effects will be: what activities of the taxpayers in the higher brackets it will depress; if they do not work so hard, in what way they will occupy their newly acquired leisure; how any new activities they may substitute will affect others; whether this will be offset by a loss of the mellowed maturity and the wisdom of those who withdraw. Such prophecies infest law of every sort, the more deeply as it is far-reaching; and it is an illusion to suppose that there are formulas or statistics that will help in making them. They can rest upon no more than enlightened guesses; but these are likely to be successful as they are made by those whose horizons have been widened, and whose outlook has been clarified, by knowledge of what men have striven to do, and how far their hopes and fears have been realized. There is no substitute for an open mind enriched by reading and the arts.

So much for what I have called the element of prophecy; refractory as it is, at least it depends only upon facts, however inaccessible. There remains the much more difficult element of choice. In such inquiries, as I have said, I see no escape from a calculus of, and balance between, the group interests—that is, the desires and values—whose conflict the measure under consideration is an attempt to adjust. But desires and values are not quantitatively measurable, for they seldom have any common constituents, and without these they cannot be objectively compared. On the other hand, an individual has the necessary means in his own case, for, although his personal desires and values are absolute, irreducible, and undeducible, and have just that authority which he feels them to have, he has as authoritative a competence to compare them and to prefer one to another as he has to appraise them separately. Thus, although such preferences are themselves as final as the desires and values, it would be easy to choose between the desires and values of conflicting social groups if we could safely impute to them our own preferences. But by what right can we do so; and, if we cannot, what other means of vicarious choice have we? I submit that we have none except in so far as we can imaginatively project ourselves into the position of the groups between which we must choose. Surely I need not dilate upon how hard it is to do that. Even in our own affairs how often have we tried to anticipate how we shall feel on a future occasion, only to be surprised by the unexpected difference when it comes to pass. And if it is hard to foreshadow our own feelings, how much harder is it to do so for others? It is not enough to be personally detached, although that is of course a condition; we must also acquire a capacity for an informed sympathy with, and understanding of, the desires and the values of others; and that, I submit, only those have any chance of attaining whose experience is supplemented by some acquaintance, the wider the better, with what others have thought and felt in circumstances as near as possible to those of the groups in question.

I dare hope that it may now begin to be clearer why I am arguing that an education which includes the "humanities" is essential to political wisdom. By "humanities" I especially mean history; but close beside history and of almost, if not quite, equal importance are letters, poetry, philosophy, the plastic arts, and music. Most of the issues that mankind sets out to settle, it never does settle. They are not solved, because, as I have just tried to say, they are incapable of solution properly speaking, being concerned with incommensurables. At any rate, even if that be not always true, the opposing parties seldom do agree upon a solution; and the dispute fades into the past unsolved, though perhaps it may be renewed as history, and fought over again. It disappears because it is replaced by some compromise that, although not wholly acceptable to either side, offers a tolerable substitute for victory; and he who would find the substitute needs an endowment as rich as possible in experience, an experience which makes the heart generous and provides his mind with an understanding of the hearts of others. The great moderates of history were more often than not men of that sort, steeped, like Montaigne and Erasmus, in knowledge of the past. Let me quote from one of these, our own Franklin. After long, and at times bitter, controversy, the final draft of the Constitution was accepted on Saturday, September 12, and was sent to be engrossed over the weekend. Nevertheless, there was still doubt about what might happen on Monday when the delegates were to sign. On Sunday, Franklin wrote out a statement which Wilson read for him the next day. It is too long to quote *in extenso*, but I cannot forbear a sentence or two, so appropriate is it to what I am trying to say. "I agree to this constitution with all its faults, if they are such, because I think a general Government necessary for us and there is no form of Government but what may be a blessing to the people if well administered, and believe further that this is likely to be well administered for a course of years, and can only end in Despotism, as other forms have done before it, when the people shall have become so corrupted as to need despotic Government, being incapable of any other. I doubt too whether any other convention we can obtain may be able to make a better constitution. For when you assemble a number of men to have the advantage of their joint wisdom, you inevitably assemble with those men all their prejudices, their passions, their errors of opinion, their local interests and their selfish views. From such an Assembly can a perfect production be expected? . . . Thus I consent, Sir, to this constitution because I expect no better, and because I am not sure it is not the best."

Out of such a temper alone can come any political success which will not leave behind rancor and vindictiveness that are likely so deeply to infect its benefits as to make victory not worth while; and it is a temper best bred in those who have at least what I like to call a bowing acquaintance with the "humanities." For these are fitted to admonish us how tentative and provisional are our attainments, intellectual and moral; and how often the deepest convictions of one generation are the rejects of the next. That does not indeed deny the possibility that, as time goes on, we shall accumulate some body of valid conclusions; but it does mean that these we can achieve only by accumulation; that wisdom is to be gained only as we stand upon the shoulders of those who have gone before. Just as in science we cannot advance except as we take over what we inherit, so in statecraft no generation can safely start at scratch. The subject matter of science is recorded observation of the external world; the subject matter of the statecraft is the soul of man, and of that too there are records—the records I am talking about today. The imagination can be purged and the judgment ripened only by an awareness of the slow, hesitant, wayward course of human life, its failures, its successes, but its indomitable will to endure.

I cannot but think that we of this generation are politically in especial need of such education. Our nation is embarked upon a venture as yet unproved; we have set our hopes upon a community in which men shall be given unchecked control of their own lives. That community is in peril; it is invaded from within, it is threatened from without; it faces a test which it may fail to pass. The choice is ours whether, if we hear the pipes of Pan, we shall stampede like a frightened flock, forgetting all those professions on which we have claimed to rest our polity. God knows, there is risk in refusing to act till the facts are all in; but is there not greater risk in abandoning the conditions of all rational inquiry? Risk for risk, for myself I had rather take my chance that some traitors will escape detection than spread abroad a spirit of general suspicion and distrust, which accepts rumor and gossip in place of undismayed and unintimidated inquiry. I believe that that community is already in process of dissolution where each man begins to eye his neighbor as a possible enemy, where non-conformity with the accepted creed, political as well as religious, is a mark of disaffection; where denunciation, without specification or backing, takes the place of evidence; where orthodoxy chokes freedom of dissent; where faith in the eventual supremacy of reason has become so timid that we dare not enter our convictions in the open lists, to win or lose. Such fears as these are a solvent which can eat out the cement that binds the stones together; they may in the end subject us to a despotism as evil as any that we dread; and they can be allayed only in so far as we refuse to proceed on suspicion, and trust one another until we have tangible ground for misgiving. The mutual confidence on which all else depends can be maintained only by an open mind and a brave reliance upon free discussion. I do not say that these will suffice; who knows but we may be on a slope which leads down to aboriginal savagery. But of this I am sure: if we are to escape, we must not yield a foot upon demanding a fair field and an honest race to all ideas. "Blame not before thou hast examined; understand first and then rebuke. Answer not before thou hast heard; interrupt not in the midst of speech." Those words were written nearly two thousand years ago; they came out of an experience already long, and refined in the fires of passion and conflict; they are the product of a wisdom bought by ages of bitter trial; and by that wisdom alone shall we be saved, we, who boast ourselves to be the apostles of a faith in the eventual triumph of wisdom. Listen also to these as ancient words that tell of the excellence of wisdom: "There is in her a spirit quick of understanding, holy, alone in kind, manifold, subtil, freely moving, clear in utterance, unpolluted, distinct, unharmed, loving what is good, keen, unhindered, beneficent, loving toward man, steadfast, sure, free from care, all-powerful, all-surveying, and penetrating through all spirits that are quick of understanding, pure, most subtil. . . . And if a man longeth even for much experience, she knoweth the things of old, and divineth the things to come; she understandeth subtilties of speeches and interpretations of dark sayings; she foreseeth signs and wonders, and the issues of seasons and times. I determined therefore to take her unto me to live with me, knowing that she is one who would give me good thoughts for counsel, and encourage me in cares and griefs. . . . For she knoweth all things and hath understanding thereof; and in my doings she shall guide me in the ways of soberness, and she shall guard me in her glory. And so shall my works be acceptable, and I shall judge the people righteously, and shall be worthy of my Father's throne."

A NOTE ON THE TYPE

This book was set on the Linotype in ELECTRA, *designed by W. A. Dwiggins. The face is a simple and readable type suitable for printing books by present-day processes. It is not based on any historical model, and hence does not echo any particular time or fashion. It is without eccentricities to catch the eye and interfere with reading—in general, its aim is to perform the function of a good book printing-type: to be read, and not seen.*

Typographic and binding designs are by W. A. Dwiggins. The book was composed, printed, and bound by The Plimpton Press, Norwood, Massachusetts.